Hazardous Devices

Hazardous Devices

Memoir of an FBI Bomb Technician, Accountant and Sniper

Barry T. Black

Jefferson, North Carolina

Aside from people widely covered in national media,
names have been changed for reasons of privacy.

ISBN (print) 978-1-4766-9992-9
ISBN (ebook) 979-8-3686-0045-1

Library of Congress Cataloging-in-Publication Data

Front cover images: Federal Bureau of Investigation (FBI)/Shutterstock

Printed in the United States of America

Exposit is an imprint of McFarland & Company, Inc., Publishers

Exposit

Box 611, Jefferson, North Carolina 28640
www.expositbooks.com

Table of Contents

Acknowledgments

There are too many people to thank at the end of a project like this, but I'll begin with my family. Sadly, my parents didn't live to see the book's publication, but the opportunities they provided made it possible. As is true for all law enforcement and military families, my wife Kelly and son Tyler were basically on the job with me. I was often gone for extended periods of time and missed important family events. But they were always there for me, even through some very difficult times. Thanks for your love and support.

This book had its genesis when I told my closest childhood friends I was going to be in the FBI one day. Years later when I opened my orders to Quantico, Mary Ann Renna insisted I start taking notes, certain it was the beginning of something exciting. She was right.

George Mauldin, a good friend, sniper, and bomb technician, reviewed the manuscript numerous times, as did Jim Sellers and Ashley Norman. These three were incredibly insightful and I appreciate all their time, advice, and friendship.

Then there's the FBI family. I met Jack Owens when I was 10, and throughout my high school and college years he patiently answered all my questions about the Bureau. Roy Forman, my Training Agent, taught me how the real world differed from Quantico. He was a devout Christian man and deadly accurate with a bolt-action rifle. Jim Norman was a mentor and was responsible for my becoming a bomb technician. He was a good friend with a great sense of humor who was taken from us too soon. Then there's that cowboy from Nevada, Bill Jonkey. Bill's a quiet, unassuming man with a quick wit and a glimmer in his eye that says he knows something you don't. I traveled the world with Bret Hood. He went on to write several books and was extremely helpful and very generous with advice and encouragement.

For 31 years I was honored to work alongside highly dedicated law enforcement, military, and intelligence professionals. Day or night, I could count on them anywhere in the world and we had some amazing adventures.

Finally, I'd like to acknowledge Lisa Camp and Susan Kilby at McFarland. We met to discuss a forensic science textbook and ended up with this. Thanks for your patience and guidance.

Abbreviations

ANFO—An explosive made from ammonium nitrate and fuel oil
ATA—U.S. State Department's Antiterrorism Assistance Program
AUSA—Assistant United States Attorney
CIRG—FBI Critical Incident Response Group
CP—Command post
DOE—Department of Energy
EOD—Military Explosive Ordnance Disposal unit
ERT—FBI Evidence Response Team
FOB—Forward operating base
FTX—Field training exercise
HDS—FBI Hazardous Devices School
HME—Homemade explosive
HMTD—An explosive compound, hexamethylene triperoxide diamine
HRT—FBI Hostage Rescue Team
ICS—Incident Command System
IED—Improvised explosive device
ITOS—FBI International Terrorism Operation Section
JTTF—FBI Joint Terrorism Task Force
MLAT—Mutual Legal Assistant Treaty
MWD—Military working dog
NCIC—National Crime Information Center
NSSE—National Special Security Event
OHP—Oklahoma Highway Patrol
OIO—FBI Office of International Operations
RIB—Rigid-hull inflatable boats
RSO—Embassy Regional Security Officer
SABT—FBI Special Agent Bomb Technician
SAR—Search and rescue

SCIF—Sensitive Compartmentalized Information Facility
SME—Subject matter expert
SNM—Special nuclear material
TATP—An explosive compound, triacetone triperoxide
TDY—Temporary duty assignment
TEDAC—FBI Terrorist Explosives Devices Analytical Center
TPU—Time and power unit
TTP—Tactics, techniques, and procedures
VBIED—Vehicle-borne improvised explosive device
VPO—Victim's protection order
WMD—Weapon of mass destruction

Preface

I grew up in a suburb of Birmingham, Alabama, in the 1960s and '70s. As a boy, I recall seeing the Ku Klux Klan in their long white robes collecting money on street corners. When I asked my mother who they were, she said, "Don't even look at them."

Birmingham had become known as "Bombingham" because of horrific events such as the bombing of the 16th Street Baptist Church and egregious civil rights abuses. I realized at a young age that people hiding behind pointed hoods and oppressing the helpless was unacceptable. Things in Birmingham changed over time, but that sense of justice and injustice stayed with me.

Real-world events merged with my favorite TV reruns of *The FBI* with Efren Zimbalist, Jr., Jimmy Stewart's *The FBI Story*, and Eliot Ness's autobiography *The Untouchables*. The allure of being an "untouchable" merchant of justice, bringing objectivity and cutting-edge techniques to catch the bad guys, captured my young imagination. When I learned my Little League coach was a real live FBI Agent, I was hooked and my career path was set. What that 10-year-old boy couldn't have known was the world of intrigue and opportunity that would be opened by those FBI credentials.

Getting accepted into the Bureau was going to be a long shot. But as with any aspiration, tenacity and hard work were rewarded. I was sworn in as a 24-year-old accountant, the youngest Agent in my academy class, and at its conclusion, the FBI sent me to Oklahoma City amid the "oil bust" of the 1980s, which exposed outlandishly risky banking practices. Institutions failed and financial fraud was rampant. Working bankruptcy fraud and stock manipulation cases wasn't quite as exciting as the TV shows of my youth, although one of my fugitives was featured on *Unsolved Mysteries*.

I was finally part of that elite, untouchable Bureau, meting out justice and solving crimes. Financial investigations were satisfying, but more dynamic opportunities soon became available. I landed a spot on the SWAT team and was later selected for sniper school. We hunted dangerous fugitives and, as part of a national strategic response, spent 51 days at the Branch Davidian standoff in Waco, Texas, in 1993. Most Agents have one major case in their career and I presumed that was mine. But in Waco I learned that the FBI has a small, highly specialized cadre of bomb technicians. The new challenge was to become part of that world, far removed from bank records and spreadsheets.

I was accepted into the FBI's extremely competitive Hazardous Devices School and returned to Oklahoma City as a newly minted bomb technician, just 53 weeks before a man named Timothy McVeigh blew up the Alfred P. Murrah Federal Building. That was my first bombing investigation. As one of only two FBI bomb technicians in the state, I was intimately involved in that case for years.

As a break from the long hours and stress of OKBOMB, the Bureau's Critical Incident Response Group asked me to lead a counter–IED team at the 1996 Atlanta Olympics. Eric Rudolph was later convicted of that bombing. Domestic terrorism was now a major concern, and my workload shifted from white-collar crime to the FBI's counterterrorism mission.

Upon returning from New York City's Ground Zero after the 9/11 attacks, I was assigned to the FBI's Joint Terrorism Task Force, the Worldwide Rapid Deployment Team, and became an international counterterrorism instructor. My unique skill set of incident command, tactical and counter–IED operations, and the ability to connect with specialized military and law enforcement personnel provided opportunities to serve around the globe.

I taught booby-trap schools for the DEA, underwater post-blast for the Australian Navy, weapons intelligence for NATO, and major case management in far-flung places like Nepal and Trinidad. From the Middle East, the former Soviet Union, Africa, and Ukraine, I trained war fighters and counterterrorism commandos on every continent but Antarctica. After 30 years, my final case was an undercover operation resulting in the conviction of a domestic terrorist bent on detonating another McVeigh–style truck bomb in downtown Oklahoma City.

The dreams of that little boy were stripped away by the reality of a long career in the finest law enforcement agency in the world. The Bureau has periodically endured its share of wounds inflicted by a reckless few who overstepped their authority. But as a whole, the FBI is made up of highly qualified, exceptional men and women who work long hours to stop things most people will never know about. It was my honor to be counted among them.

One

Six Percent

Over half my adult life was spent as an FBI Agent with a front row seat to history. I was a counter-sniper at the Branch Davidian standoff in Waco, I was on scene moments after the bombing of Oklahoma City's federal building, I stood at Ground Zero as smoke billowed from the World Trade Center, and I built a 1000-pound truck bomb used by a would-be terrorist. The job took me around the world from major city centers to remote places like Tashkent, Kathmandu, and Mogadishu. I essentially had two careers spanning more than three decades: an accountant investigating financial crimes and a bomb technician fighting the Global War on Terrorism.

Pursuing a childhood dream of becoming a G-Man, I contacted an FBI recruiter in Birmingham when I was 18. She patiently explained, "You have to be at least 23 years old with a four-year degree, three years of practical work experience, a clean background, and be willing to relocate anywhere in the U.S. It's not easy; less than 6 percent of applicants are accepted."

It was the mid-1980s. At that time, Special Agent applicants were divided into five entry categories based on academic and work experience. The four most desirable applicant categories were lawyers, accountants, scientists, and linguists.

The recruiter continued, "I see you're an engineering major. Is that really what you want to do? Because engineers fall into our fifth and largest group of 'diversified applicants.' However, there's a shortcut for accountants. If you have an accounting degree and can pass the FBI's accounting exam, we waive the requirement of three years' work experience. You could get in much sooner."

Intrigued, I transferred from the University of Alabama at Birmingham to the main campus in Tuscaloosa, changed majors, and joined the university's Accounting Society. It was good to see the

FBI recruiter regularly attending campus job fairs; maybe she would remember me. I cornered her at a Society banquet one evening and pressed for more information.

"Yes, I remember you. But you can't even start the initial application until you're 22 and a half. Concentrate on getting your degree, then call me."

Exactly six months before my 23rd birthday, I pecked out the lengthy application on a typewriter and submitted it via U.S. Mail (there were no personal computers then). Like everything in the government, the process was slow and often stalled by hiring freezes and budget cuts. Recalling that less than 6 percent of applicants were accepted, I reluctantly took an accounting position upon graduation. It was a fine job with a good firm, but not how I wanted to spend the next 40 years. The company sent me to Norfolk, Virginia, where I made a point of meeting the local FBI recruiter. After 18 months of silence, Norfolk's recruiter finally called. "We have a date for your accounting exam."

The "accounting specialty" program was terminated in the 1990s. But passing that test allowed me to take the Special Agent's exam just 30 days later. Successfully completing the Agent's exam led to another extensive background and security application. Once it was accepted, a formal interview was scheduled.

The recruiter cautioned, "OK, there'll be three Agents on the panel with over 75 years of combined experience. They'll pepper you with questions; just be yourself."

I arrived at the FBI office early on the day of the interview. After what seemed like hours, the recruiter led me down a long hallway and pushed open the door to a nondescript conference room where three stern-looking men were waiting, purposefully intimidating for a 24-year-old accountant. One asked questions, one took notes, and the third Agent just stared at me. The interview seemed to go on forever with awkward lulls between questions until finally the third, heretofore silent Agent spoke up.

"Your application says you've never used drugs. Does that include marijuana?"

"Yes, sir, that's correct." Marijuana was illegal then and even casual use could disqualify an applicant.

"What if I told you we couldn't hire someone that hadn't at least experimented with marijuana as a part of the college experience?"

"Well … if that's the criteria I guess I don't qualify."

He jotted something down and didn't say another word for the rest of the interview. The other two men continued their tag-team questioning before abruptly dismissing me with absolutely no indication of how I'd done. It was disconcerting and I began to worry I might have to spend the rest of my life as an accountant in the public sector.

Weeks passed before a one-paragraph letter arrived, instructing me to report for an extensive medical evaluation. A clear medical history and minimum standards for uncorrected sight, hearing, weight, and blood pressure were all strictly enforced. Next came a physical fitness test consisting of pull-ups, push-ups, sit-ups, and a timed 1.5-mile run conducted under the watchful eye of an Agent assigned to Norfolk's physical fitness program.

The summer wore on with no further contact until the recruiter called one Friday evening. "Congratulations, you have a slot at Quantico. But it opens in two weeks. Is that going to be a problem?"

"No, ma'am, that's not a problem at all."

I was elated. Maybe it was actually going to happen. I arrived at the accounting office early Monday morning, drafted a resignation letter, and scheduled a meeting with the boss for that afternoon. But my excitement was dampened when the phone rang as I left for lunch; it was the recruiter.

"You haven't quit your job yet, have you?"

My heart sank. "No, ma'am. Not yet."

"There's been a budget snag and your academy class got canceled. They could find funding somewhere, but there's no way to know if it'll be rescheduled. The problem is your medical exams are only good for a few more weeks. If we don't get you a slot in time, they'll have to be redone and you might run into another hiring freeze."

Dejected, I slid the resignation letter into my desk drawer and canceled that meeting with the boss. I heard nothing for two weeks, but then finally the recruiter called again.

"Congress reallocated some money; your class will start in 12 days. Can you make it to Quantico by then?"

I drove from Norfolk to the FBI Academy located on the sprawling 59,000-acre Marine Corps base at Quantico, Virginia. The first meeting of New Agents Class (NAC) 8812 occurred at 7:00 p.m. when a Bureau legend, Ed Mireles, introduced himself as our class counselor and recounted a harrowing story.

Two years earlier, on April 11, 1986, Mireles and a team of FBI Agents were tracking two violent bank robbers who had murdered several people over the last few months. Their paths collided in Miami when the felons' stolen car was spotted by the team. As one of the robbers took aim at a trailing Bureau vehicle, another Agent rammed the stolen Monte Carlo, pushing it off the road. Gunfire erupted, and within minutes, 145 rounds were exchanged. Two Agents, Benjamin Grogan and Jerry Dove, were shot at close range as the criminals tried to commandeer their vehicle. Mireles's left arm had been shattered by a rifle bullet; though barely conscious he managed to fire five rounds from his shotgun using his only good hand. The shotgun now empty, he advanced toward the heavily armed subjects, killing both with his revolver. When it was over, Grogan and Dove lay dead and five other Agents were wounded in one of the most violent shootouts in FBI history (Mireles, Edmundo, and Elizabeth 2017). His chilling personal account brought a sobering reality to the first day of class.

The next four hours were spent completing personnel forms, security documentation, and an orientation of the Academy, which was designed much like a college campus. We were assigned a roommate and a room in one of two dorms, Washington or Madison. Each room had two single beds, two desks, two four-drawer dressers, and a common bathroom shared with Agents in the adjoining room. Forty-five strangers with extremely diverse backgrounds were suddenly immersed in a curriculum of firearms, defensive tactics, and academics. The long hours and close quarters produced lasting relationships; many of us remain close friends to this day.

Across Hoover Road from the academic campus was Hogan's Alley, a training village for arrest scenarios. Actors role-played as criminals in loosely scripted plots set in the mock city's bars, businesses, and the Bank of Hogan, the only bank in America that's robbed almost every day. For an even more realistic experience, some covert surveillance exercises occurred in the surrounding towns outside the Academy gates.

Every hour was strictly scheduled, and the pace accelerated throughout the 14 weeks of training. The days were filled with timed 10K runs through Quantico's wooded tank trails, defensive tactics, weapons training, and written exams covering everything from bankruptcy fraud and foreign counterintelligence to wiretaps. It wasn't unusual to execute a search warrant in Hogan's Alley at 11:00 p.m. and be on the firearms range eight hours later.

At the time, firearms training consisted of a revolver qualification course that began at the 60-yard line and various shotgun courses. As threats and weapons evolved, our Model 13 Smith & Wesson revolvers were replaced with semiautomatic pistols and newer shoulder weapons like the MP-5 submachine gun. At Quantico's high-tech indoor gun range, known as the Thunderdome, new Agents now fire about 4,000 pistol rounds and hundreds of rounds through shotguns and AR-15–style carbines.

Since the FBI investigates public corruption and police civil rights violations, new Agents were rarely assigned to an office near their hometowns. It avoided the possibility that they might have to investigate a childhood friend or family acquaintance. That meant the Bureau could send you anywhere in the country, often with very little personal input. We were told assignments were based on "the needs of the Bureau," but scuttlebutt likened it more to a monkey throwing darts at a map.

Most often "first office Agents" were assigned to smaller offices for about three years before being reassigned to major cities like New York, Chicago, or LA. But as relocation expenses soared and applicants became less willing to blindly move around the country, our class was given a choice of sorts. We could choose a random assignment to one of the largest cities in America, known as the "Top 12," or be sent literally anywhere else in the country. I chose the latter and crossed my fingers.

The financial crisis of the 1980s saw banks fail in record numbers. The banking and energy sectors of America's southwest had exploded until the price of oil dropped precipitously. Risky loans and creative accounting merged with market forces to cripple both sectors, and fraud was rampant. Most of the accountants in my class presumed we'd be sent to oil towns like Houston or Dallas where bank and bankruptcy fraud were endemic. But our assignments wouldn't be divulged until the last few weeks of the Academy.

That day finally came. With great fanfare, Mireles drew names from a hat. Each Agent opened a sealed envelope and marked their new home with a pin on a large U.S. map. My name was the last one called. I trepidatiously pulled out the card and read aloud, "Oklahoma City." As I pushed a pin in the Sooner state, the class began singing the theme from *Bonanza*.

We were given some time to compare assignments before classes resumed with late-night surveillance in the surrounding towns of Woodbridge and Dumfries. The next morning, we were back on the firearms range and in the gym for physical fitness training (PT). The PT instructors came up with creative challenges such as the Red Line

Express, which consisted of running two miles around the red perimeter lines of a basketball court, sporadically interrupted by push-ups and sit-ups. Another favorite was called the Belly of the Beast. Our lead instructor, a former Marine who loved to run, shouted, "Form up on the road in a column of two; we're doing a little Ranger run."

In the early morning light, he explained what that meant to a group of lawyers and accountants. "The last two in line will outrun the column. When they get to the front, the next two move up. Don't worry. We have 6.5 miles, so everyone will get a chance."

Halfway through we saw that the "belly" of the beast was a depression with an impossibly steep incline on the other side. The instructor yelled, "Pick it up, ladies, I'm running a marathon with my daughter after this!"

That night brought a "gas familiarization" exercise. The FBI was getting away from standard military tear gas in favor of another incapacitating agent known as Cap-Stun, derived from pulverized capsicum peppers. We filed onto a bus and took our seats wearing gas masks. Once aboard, several aerosol cans of Cap-Stun were tossed in, filling the bus with a heavy mist. As the instructors, wearing gas masks, pointed to each Agent, we were to remove our mask, state our name and hometown, then walk off the bus. As soon as I lifted the mask, a hot, burning sensation ran down my throat and into my lungs, my eyes watered uncontrollably, and mucus poured from my nose. After uttering the required information, I groped my way to the bus door and joined the class at a garden hose to wash off the irritant still burning our eyes and skin.

Fall arrived and the end was finally in sight. Classes shifted to mock trials and testifying skills while firearms took on more practical applications like room clearing and close quarters combat. But PT didn't change; we ran, then ran some more. On the final Friday afternoon, we boarded the familiar white government bus for a trip to the Marine Officer Candidate School. Unsure of what to expect, we lined up on a football field, were given boxing gloves, and were told to pick a partner. A half hour of pummeling each other was followed by grappling, basically wrestling inside a circle. I found myself at the mercy of a huge former Marine who had obviously grappled before. The boxing and grappling were naturally followed by running through the forest to a remote installation called Radar Hill. We had never seen this trail before. An undulating dirt path meandered through thick woods and was studded with obstacles: a three-rope bridge over a dry creek, overhead traverse (monkey) bars, wooden walls, and vertical cargo nets. The rough ground eventually turned into a gravel road so service vehicles could navigate the steep grade, which terminated at a radar installation. Not quite exhausted, we sprinted to the hilltop for a few sets of push-ups, a process repeated three times before running back to the bus, a mere four miles away.

Sunday night brought a welcome respite, some time to unwind in the Academy's bar, the Boardroom. Most of the instructors joined the class for a beer and tall tales. But it was an early night because sunrise would find us on the Marine Corps' confidence course known as the Yellow Brick Road. Named for yellow bricks that mark the wooded trail, it covers 6.1 miles of various obstacles and terminates in a large mud pit. Completing it is a rite of passage for new Agents and police commanders attending the FBI National Academy leadership course. After slogging through the mud and crossing the finish line, someone suggested we run the 2.5 miles back to the Academy for old times' sake. The next morning NAC-8812 assembled in the main auditorium to receive our credentials. It was official: I was now a Special Agent of the FBI.

Two

Brother Derrell

I arrived in Oklahoma City to meet my new supervisor, Willie Jernigan. He was a laid-back, silver-haired native Oklahoman who was literally a cowboy. He raised horses, dressed in western-cut suits with cowboy boots, and called everyone "son." He invited me into his office and motioned to a chair in the corner. "Welcome to Oklahoma, son. Take the next few days to acclimate yourself and find a place to live. Roy here will be your Training Agent. He'll show you what you need to know."

Roy Foreman was an old-school G-man actually hired by J. Edgar Hoover. He was a former Naval officer with a degree in electrical engineering, pilot, firearms instructor, defensive tactics instructor, and sniper. I learned a great deal from him and we became good friends. At the end of that first day, Roy delivered a little unsettling news.

"Listen, I've got to go out of town for a few days. Find your way around town and we'll get started next Monday. Nothing should happen, but just in case, your radio call sign is Seven Bravo."

As suggested, I spent the next two days with a realtor, found a house, and began moving in. Late Friday afternoon a nameless secretary called on my new home phone. "You've got weekend duty. Come get the pager." Much like the military, the Bureau has Duty Agents assigned on weekends and holidays to handle problems that arise when the office is closed. Cell phones weren't commonplace yet, so she handed over a device the size of a deck of cards. "Sign here. Keep this with you." I'd never had a pager, but it seemed simple enough.

That evening at a Christmas play, the pager sounded. From a lobby pay phone I called the office switchboard and spoke with the operator, who nonchalantly advised, "The airport police are reporting a bomb aboard an aircraft. What do you want me to do?"

"Well, umm. Can you put me through to the supervisor of whatever squad works this kind of thing?"

A gruff man answered and after hearing the scenario barked, "So is there a bomb on the plane?"

"I don't know."

"Call me when you do know." The line went dead. I put another quarter in the pay phone and called the office. The switchboard routed me to the airport police, who ultimately determined the threat was a hoax.

It was Saturday afternoon when the pager went off again. From another pay phone, I dialed the unfamiliar number on the LCD; a man answered saying he was the other Duty Agent. Why hadn't they called *him* about the bomb? Surely he'd have more experience than I did. "Do you have your gun and body armor?" he asked.

"Well, I'm buying some furniture right now, but I am armed. My body armor is at the office."

"Meet me there right away, in the secure Bureau parking garage beneath the office."

An older man I'd never seen before was waiting for me; he was dressed completely in black and seemed to have Velcro everywhere. Pointing to a Caprice Classic, he mumbled, "Get in."

After a very cursory introduction he explained we were going to meet a small element of the SWAT team to arrest an armed and dangerous bank robber, a three-time felon. Seeking a little more information, I asked, "What's this guy's name?"

Without taking his eyes off the road he blurted out, "Name's 'Halt, motherfucker.'" That ended our conversation and we arrived at the rendezvous point in silence. Fortunately, the SWAT team leader had a much more detailed plan. Velcro and I were told to secure the back of the house. As the three-man SWAT team entered through the front, the back door flew open and the fugitive ran out. We confronted him in the yard and ordered him to the ground; two 12-gauge shotguns hastened his compliance.

A bomb threat Friday night and a felony arrest Saturday; what would a regular work week bring? Unsurprisingly, the pager sounded again Sunday night. Perhaps it was a kidnapping or hijacking; this was incredible. The switchboard operator answered on the first ring. "Come down to the office right away. The freezing temperatures burst some pipes and an Agent has to babysit the plumbers." By comparison this was a pretty disappointing call-out, hardly the stuff of movies.

Monday morning Roy asked, "Well, how was your weekend? Did you get moved in?" He was dumbfounded to hear what had happened;

new Agents weren't supposed to have weekend duty for at least six months.

Roy remained my Training Agent for the requisite one-year probationary period; he reviewed my investigative work and exposed me to the various aspects and opportunities within the Bureau. As a champion competitive marksman, Roy was also the SWAT sniper team leader. One evening he suggested we go to the rifle range.

After firing his SWAT-issued, fully automatic M-16, we switched to his custom-built bolt-action .308 sniper rifle. As the sun set he said, "Let's make this a regular thing. We'll come out every Wednesday."

That fall, after months on the range, Roy asked, "Ever thought about trying out for the SWAT team? I'll introduce you to Hank. I think you'd be a good fit."

Hank was the SWAT team leader, a hulking man who'd earned two purple hearts as a Green Beret. With their support, I was selected for the basic SWAT course, which included night maneuvers, old-school land navigation, rappelling, dynamic room entries, and various live-fire exercises.

After completing that training, Roy put me in for sniper school. The course occurred in January during a severe winter storm. We crawled through freezing mud to discreet firing positions in the woodline to engage targets hundreds of yards away under the merciless hands of a stopwatch. The cold made it difficult to focus on the crosshairs; my fingers lost their flexibility and feeling. One phase of fire required us to manually load and fire single rounds of ammunition in a timed course; repeated contact with the rifle's cold metal receiver caused my fingers to split and bleed. Upon completion of that course, Roy and I formed one of three sniper teams assigned to the Oklahoma City Division. Training in those adverse conditions made actual operations seem easy.

Being on the SWAT team was a collateral duty; there was no extra pay and I still had a regular caseload. But the training was great, and the high-profile deployments were exciting. One of my first operations pertained to a dangerous fugitive wanted for drug trafficking. An informant indicated Juan Lopez, a former Colombian soldier, was in town at his old girlfriend's house. He was usually armed, had a propensity for violence, and boasted that he'd never be taken alive. Five other SWAT operators and I met near the girlfriend's house. A surveillance team told us the fugitive had been there earlier, but several people fitting his description had recently left. We could see three men closely matching Juan's description still sitting on the porch.

On Hank's command, Agents with shotguns and submachine guns scaled the back fence to cover the rear. Simultaneously our two Suburbans jumped the curb and slid to a stop in the front yard. Eager to avoid arrest, one of the men uttered in broken English, "No, no, wait! You're looking for Juan. He just took Luis to work." Under further interrogation, we learned Luis worked at a Holiday Inn near the airport and Juan was driving an old red Trans Am. That information was relayed to the surveillance plane circling overhead.

With only a couple of logical routes to that Holiday Inn, the plane quickly spotted the Trans Am westbound on I-40. Our team regrouped and radioed ahead, instructing the undercover surveillance team to begin backing up traffic on the off-ramp to the hotel. By the time we caught up, the Trans Am was stuck in traffic. Once surveillance confirmed Juan was in the driver's seat, we surrounded the car and made the arrest without incident. As soon as he was in handcuffs, the fabricated traffic jam magically cleared and we were on our way.

Another deployment began when a violent escaped convict stole a car. Running low on fuel, he pulled into a convenience store in the small town of El Reno, Oklahoma, demanding gas and all the cash in the register. The lone female attendant refused to comply, sounded the alarm, and chased the fugitive back to his car. She jumped into her pickup truck and followed him, calling out mile markers to the sheriff over a CB radio, "He just crashed in a bar ditch and he's runnin' into the woods by the river!"

Familiar with the terrain, the sheriff knew he'd need more resources and requested assistance from the FBI and Oklahoma Highway Patrol (OHP). It was about 10:30 p.m. when I pulled into that same gas station for fuel en route to the rally point. Noting my woodland camouflage and the pistol strapped to my leg, the attendant nonchalantly said, "I reckon you must be goin' to the manhunt. Several of y'all stopped by here already. Good luck and be careful out there, honey. He's nasty."

The command post (CP) was established along a section line road; a helicopter equipped with FLIR (forward-looking infrared) cameras flew low overhead, and the baying of bloodhounds could be heard. A fresh German Shepherd leapt from his truck-mounted kennel and immediately headed for a hedgerow separating two fields, about 40 yards from us. The handler admonished the dog, thinking he was just responding to nature's call, and led him into the darkness.

Our team walked 12 abreast through the wooded river bottom

looking for any signs of the fugitive as OHP's team searched the far bank. Another group relieved us about 6:30 a.m. and continued the search. It was time for breakfast, so, being highly trained investigators, we located a diner called Biscuit Hill which was already awash with law enforcement.

The telephone by the register rang and the cashier shouted, "Hey, this lady wants to talk to a cop." Ironically, the caller knew to call Biscuit Hill instead of the police station. Hank took the call and listened intently as the panicked woman cried, "Some guy just ran up to my kitchen window. He threw down a gun and he's just sittin' in my garden with his hands in the air!"

We radioed the woman's address to a deputy in the area and the fugitive surrendered to a single officer. During an interview he told the deputies, "Yeah, I been out there all night. At one point I was hidin' in some bushes and this huge German Shepherd headed straight for me, but the cop pulled him away. I guess I should've given up then, but I's afraid I'd get shot in all the confusion."

Hunting for fugitives in rural, sparsely populated areas poses unique problems. Late one December, a sheriff in a remote southern county requested assistance in locating and arresting Jamie Bridger. While awaiting extradition for a series of brutal murders across several states, Bridger had escaped from the county jail and was now armed and on the run. The sheriff believed Bridger would hole up in an area known as Little Dixie, a heavily wooded, isolated area in southeastern Oklahoma.

Local police developed an informant who confirmed Bridger was moving between several farms owned by friends and relatives. The informant was adamant: "If any of his people see a car or somebody they don't know, Jamie'll be gone. They don't much like the police 'round here."

After weeks of discreet surveillance, we finally determined Bridger spent most of his time at the farm of his brother, Derrell. Harboring a fugitive is a felony, so a federal arrest warrant was issued for Derrell Bridger.

Christmas was only two days away and our surveillance noted a lot of people visiting the Bridger farm. We instructed the informant, a family acquaintance, to stop by and make sure Jamie was there.

"Yep, he's there, all right. But he ain't stayin' long. He's got a cousin with a place a few miles east of here. He'll be leavin' in a day or so."

It was time to move in. This was going to be a big operation, so we called upon OHP's SWAT team and brought up another FBI team from Dallas.

It was a cold, rainy night as we assembled across the county line and developed a raid plan. Snipers would go in first to gather intelligence. Roy and I, along with an OHP sniper team, were to make our way to Derrell's house; snipers from Dallas would take the cousin's farm. Under the cover of darkness, each team loaded into the beds of old pickup trucks driven by other Agents. Taking circuitous routes, the trucks navigated a maze of muddy dirt roads dotted with the homes of Bridger's relatives. Aerial maps identified ruts and washes in the narrow roads that would require any vehicle to slow down. As our truck slowed to clear these natural barriers, we rolled off the tailgate and made our way into the woods and fields.

Technology like GPS and night vision weren't readily available then, so we navigated the rural terrain using compasses and spotty moonlight, careful to avoid the farmhouses. After slowly traversing about 1.5 miles of farmland, we assumed a position in some high grass beneath a barbed wire fence roughly 100 yards from Derrell's home. We didn't venture too close because aerial photos showed dozens of pit bulls staked out in a field west of the house. From our vantage we could cover the front, relying on OHP to cover the rear. A specialized Bureau plane called Nightstalker began relaying our intel and infrared images back to the CP.

In the weeks leading up to the operation, analysts had obtained as much information as possible about the entire Bridger family. Things like physical descriptions, personal habits, unique traits or mannerisms, and the types of cars they drove. The informant cautioned that Derrell's wife and son were in the house, which was important to know in case we had to make a tactical entry.

The wind and rain finally stopped and the night grew quiet. We could barely hear Nightstalker circling high overhead. Shortly after 10:00 p.m., several people began hanging Christmas lights along the porch; their voices carried on the still night air. About 11:30, a man fitting Derrell's build stepped off the porch, backlit by the house. I could only see a silhouette through my scope, but he got into an old Pontiac like Derrell was known to drive. Just before the engine started, a boy of about 10 ran onto the porch and shouted with a noticeable stutter, "Dad, Mom said don't forget the milk."

Our background on Derrell's family indicated his 10-year-old son had a speech impediment. The boy's age, description, and speech pattern fit the intel, so I radioed Nightstalker, "Darrell Bridger is alone in the vehicle that's pulling through the gate now."

They tracked the car using thermal imagery and vectored in an arrest team once he was a safe distance from the house. Under interrogation he admitted, "Yeah, Jamie's there. But you boys should know he's always got his rifle handy."

Based on that information, the house was surrounded just after midnight; our SWAT team covered the front and OHP's team approached from the rear. Over a bullhorn, Jamie was ordered to come out. A woman opened the front door and shouted, "Jamie ain't here. Leave us alone."

About that time our radios crackled. Troopers at the back reported Jamie had just knocked out a second floor window and was stepping onto the roof. "I think he's seen us. He ducked back inside. Second floor, northwest corner of the house."

Our team immediately entered the first floor and secured each occupant, quickly confirming Jamie was upstairs. When called by name, he cracked open the door of a small bedroom, brandishing an assault rifle and daring Agents, "Come on up and get me!"

The standoff ended when Hank tossed a flashbang into the room. Often called a "stun grenade," its deafening report and intense, seven-million-candela flash had the desired effect. Jamie dropped his rifle and staggered to the landing, saying, "Don't bomb me no more." It was a successful operation with two arrests and no injuries.

Three

The Real Condia

SWAT operations were relatively infrequent, which meant most of my days were spent unraveling financial crimes. Though requiring less adrenaline and much more time, piecing these puzzles together brought its own satisfaction. Take the case of Richard Condia and FirstCare Medical Supply.

Condia blew into town and posted newspaper ads seeking entrepreneurs. That's how it was done before the internet. The ads captured the attention of a struggling college student named Adam Byrd, who was lured by the promise of easy money. Adam agreed to meet Condia for a job interview at a questionable hotel near the airport.

"I own and operate an international firm called FirstCare Medical Supply. We manufacture specialized medical devices overseas and sell them through distributorships throughout the country. The entire venture is funded through the sale of regional distributorships. Before investing as much as $54,000, some investors want to see the company's physical location. We don't currently have a U.S. footprint, so I'm opening a small distribution center in Oklahoma City and need a manager to oversee operations. You'll be in on the ground floor of our domestic operation. I think you'll be a great fit, Adam; you're hired."

As soon as Adam accepted the position, Condia made a hasty departure, citing pressing international business. "I'm usually overseas so my associate, Phil Swanson, will be your point of contact."

Swanson began calling Adam every day with specific, detailed instructions. "I know this is a lot of responsibility, but Mr. Condia feels you can handle it. Find an office with warehouse space and hire three or four assistants. Some of your college buddies will be fine; they'll be well paid. Just get it all set up and I'll wire any money you need."

Once the office was operational, a wall-sized map of the world was delivered. It had flashing lights in various countries where FirstCare factories were located. Forklifts, warehouse shelving, and giant empty crates were delivered. Adam grew uneasy and began asking questions, especially about the empty crates which were marked "medical supplies." But Swanson reassured him with every phone call.

"No need to worry, everything is fine. Just sign for the deliveries and file the invoices. I'll have accounting handle it all. Our clients will start flying in soon; a limo will bring them over to meet you. Just make sure they see the map and give them a quick peek into the warehouse. Don't let them go back there, though—it's an OSHA violation."

As predicted, people soon began arriving in stretch limousines. The chauffeur never came inside, preferring instead to stay in the car. As instructed, Adam touted FirstCare's global operation—evidenced by the blinking map—and allowed the would-be investors to peer into the warehouse through a tiny window where forklifts were busy shuttling crates around. Had they been allowed inside the warehouse, they would've seen two college kids moving the same empty boxes back and forth. Adam didn't like lying, but the money was too good. In a matter of weeks, he'd accepted more than $1.3 million from investors and was supposed to get a cut for himself. Per Swanson's instructions, Adam deposited the money at a local bank. He had no way of knowing that the funds were immediately transferred to other accounts around the country.

Adam and his employees soon began to wonder why they never saw any actual medical supplies. Despite their huge paychecks, the staff became uneasy and demanded reassurance from Adam, who confronted Swanson on the next call.

"Look, Adam, it may seem a little strange but this is how an international business operates. Your local operation is just getting started, so tell your people not to worry. We're working with Customs to physically store our products stateside; it just takes time. Besides, things are a little slow due to some labor problems in Asia. Just keep up the good work, you're doing fine. Don't worry."

But soon investors began to complain. They weren't seeing any return on their investment, and Adam was their only point of contact. Their concerns were relayed to Swanson, who always had a plausible answer. At first he cited a 30- to 60-day processing period, then a textile shortage in Mexico, union problems in Malaysia, and so on. Succumbing to the investors' visceral complaints, Adam finally insisted Swanson do something.

"All right, I'll send out Alan Orr. He's my VP of Operations."

Within 48 hours a man arrived in Oklahoma City and introduced himself in a private meeting with Adam. "I'm Alan Orr. Swanson and Mr. Condia sent me to reassure you. Things are fine; you're doing a great job. In fact, Mr. Condia authorized me to give you and your staff a raise, plus a bonus if you'll all stay on. FirstCare is growing and loyalty will be rewarded; convince your team to keep working."

To prove the point, Orr rented even more office space for corporate expansion. He met with a couple of contractors, but left town as soon as the new office was up and running.

Tired of Adam's excuses, disgruntled investors from around the country began filing complaints with the FBI. Since FirstCare was physically in Oklahoma City, the case was opened and assigned to me. A compilation of all the complaints readily identified 147 victims nationwide. Subpoenas provided bank records, allowing me to trace the funds as FirstCare moved money through various accounts until finally landing at a brokerage house in Texas. Records showed a man named Richard Condia paid $253,000 in cash for gold Krugerrands during the time FirstCare was in operation.

Of course there were no medical supplies or overseas operations; it was all a sham. Financial analysis and victim statements provided enough probable cause to get a search warrant for FirstCare's office and warehouse. As the search was underway, we simultaneously interviewed every current and former employee of the Oklahoma City office. It became apparent that Adam was the only executive known to the staff. A few of them saw Alan Orr once when he came to meet Adam, but they didn't know anything else about him. Adam had only met Condia one time and no one had ever seen Swanson.

Except for a telephone installation order, very few documents were recovered in the search. Fortunately, the work order had been personally signed by Alan Orr. I sent the document to the FBI Lab, where a single latent thumbprint was recovered on the bottom left corner next to Orr's signature. They ran the print through AFIS, the FBI's fingerprint database, and matched it to a known con man named Russell Bates.

Subpoenaed phone records revealed hundreds of calls tied to an out-of-state number that traced back to a fictitious company in North Carolina; its sole proprietor was another known con man named Shane McLemore. McLemore and Bates had lengthy criminal histories, including convictions for a nearly identical scam in Florida called Dixie Medical.

Based on all the information collected so far, a federal grand jury indicted Bates and McLemore on 16 counts of conspiracy, mail fraud, wire fraud, and money laundering. A judge then issued arrest warrants for both men, but their whereabouts were unknown. Meanwhile, Condia remained a complete mystery. In an effort to identify him, Adam gave Condia's description to a sketch artist.

The sketch looked a lot like McLemore's mugshot to me, but no positive ID could be made. I began to believe McLemore was both Condia and the voice of Phil Swanson. These alter egos would give him a degree of separation he didn't have in the Dixie Medical scam; he had learned from his mistakes.

Prior to the internet, television was the best way to solicit public assistance. Capitalizing on its huge audience, I arranged for the case to be featured on the popular TV show *Unsolved Mysteries.* Calls poured in as soon as the segment was over. From the Burbank studios I evaluated the incoming data and sent leads to Agents across the country. Based on tips from San Antonio, Bates was arrested two days later with gold Krugerrands in his pocket. It took four months to locate McLemore in Atlanta. Records revealed he'd sold 26 Krugerrands to a precious metals dealer in Atlanta just prior to his arrest.

However, not one tip pertained to Condia, and neither Bates nor McLemore would discuss him. After reviewing all the evidence and talking with every witness, I was certain Bates and McLemore had simply recreated the Dixie Medical scam. But this time they played different roles and assumed various aliases to further confuse witnesses. At trial, the entire case hung on that theory.

One of the first witnesses to testify was an angry investor who pointed at Bates seated at the defense table. "That's the man I know as Cloyce, the chauffeur that picked me up at the airport." But under withering cross-examination the witness recanted: "Well, I guess I can't be completely sure."

The next witness was the telephone repairman who'd picked Bates out of two different photo lineups during the investigation. He testified that Bates was Alan Orr, the man who authorized the new office's phone installation. However, during a raucous cross-examination, the defense attorney pointed to Bates, still at the defense table. Incredulous, he asked the repairman, "Are you absolutely certain this is the man you know as Alan Orr?"

The repairman answered emphatically, "Yes, that's him."

With spellbinding drama, the attorney spun on his heels and

pointed to the crowded gallery of spectators. "Are you sure it wasn't … this man?" The lawyer motioned to a gentleman who began to stand up in the back of the courtroom. I hadn't noticed him before, but he could've been Bates's twin. All eyes focused on the stranger and the courtroom fell silent. For what seemed like an eternity the witness just stared before whispering, "Oh, well. I didn't see him back there."

"What? Please speak up so the jury can hear you."

"Yeah, I guess that could be the guy. Maybe…. I don't know anymore." The repairman's eyewitness identification lost all credibility.

But the defense couldn't overcome the testimony of the FBI latent fingerprint examiner. He showed the jury that telephone work order with Alan Orr's signature and highlighted the latent fingerprint next to it. He then explained how that print unequivocally matched the left thumbprint of Russell Bates taken when he was arrested for the Dixie Medical scam. Bates was convicted and sentenced to 115 months in federal prison.

McLemore had successfully argued for a separate trial, as he didn't want to be seated next to Bates in the courtroom. His trial was delayed for several months, which allowed me to shore up my theory that McLemore was the voice of Phil Swanson, the man who provided Adam with daily operating instructions over the phone.

Just as handwriting exemplars can tie a person to a document, a voice exemplar might be able to link McLemore to Swanson. Adam recalled that Swanson often repeated unique phrases and financial instructions during their daily conversations. While McLemore was in jail awaiting trial, a judge signed a court order compelling him to provide voice exemplars reciting those unique phrases. McLemore refused because he had nothing to lose; even if the judge found him in contempt of court, he was already in jail.

At trial the defense tried to suppress the fact that McLemore had refused to comply with the court order. But the judge allowed me to testify that he refused to submit to the voice exemplars, which carried a lot of weight with the jurors. That, coupled with other testimony and overwhelming documentary evidence, led to McLemore's conviction on all 16 counts.

Since this was a white-collar crime, he was sentenced to a minimum security prison and allowed to participate in work details "outside the wire." But prison life didn't sit well with him. Late one afternoon he failed to report back from a work detail. After a quick search, guards found his orange prison jumpsuit in a heap by the roadside. In his cell they found several letters from his daughter and books on how to speak Spanish.

The U.S. Marshals Service is responsible for hunting escaped federal prisoners. The chase was on. Based on those letters, Deputy Marshals interviewed McLemore's daughter in Asheville, North Carolina. She swore she hadn't seen him, but made a reference to his penchant for fine cigars. There were only two local smoke shops that sold his preferred brand, so Marshals showed his photograph to the proprietors. The first merchant didn't recognize him, but the second knew McLemore as a regular customer. "As a matter of fact, that's him pulling in across the street."

Approaching the car, they shouted, "U.S. Marshals! Turn off the ignition and slowly exit the vehicle!" Instead, McLemore slumped below the dashboard, threw the car in gear, and sped across the sidewalk toward them. Shots were fired as he drove away with Marshals and local police in hot pursuit. After a brief chase he was captured and sent to a more secure facility to serve the remainder of his 10-year sentence, plus a few extra months for escape.

Condia has never been located and remains the subject of podcasts and amateur sleuths. But I believe McLemore, Swanson, and Condia were one and the same.

As with FirstCare, most white-collar investigations begin with complaints directly from victims or financial institutions. So I was surprised when a conversation over Thanksgiving dinner led to a joint operation with the Internal Revenue Service (IRS).

I'd only been in Oklahoma for a year. Not wanting me to be alone for the holidays, the neighbors invited me over for a big Thanksgiving meal. Their children, Lori and Lauren, were home from college and joined us. Lori, the oldest daughter, was only a couple of years younger than I was. As the evening concluded, she asked, "Mind if I walk out with you?"

Once outside she whispered, "I know you're with the FBI and, well, … please don't tell my parents, but I'm afraid Lauren is messed up in something bad."

"Really? Like what?"

"Her roommate up at OSU is Tristen Nelson. Her dad is always up there and asked Lauren to hide a bunch of money for him. Supposedly his wife is leaving him and if he doesn't hide some money from her Tristen won't be able to finish school."

"All right, that's odd. But why are you telling me?"

"Well, I've heard he's in some kind of trouble with the IRS and I don't want Lauren mixed up in it. Tristen hasn't mentioned anything about her folks splitting up and it just doesn't sound right to me. I'm worried and don't know what to do. But nobody can know I told you, not Lauren, my parents, nobody, OK? Promise you won't tell."

"It's all right, I won't say anything. What do you know about the money?"

"Lauren told me Mr. Nelson waited until Tristen was gone one night and brought two backpacks full of cash to their apartment in Stillwater. He said Tristen didn't know anything about the divorce, so Lauren couldn't mention that or the money. He told her to rent a safe deposit box and put the money there but insisted she rent the box in her own name and never mention him. Lauren didn't want Tristen to drop out of school, so she rented the biggest box the bank had. But all the money wouldn't fit; there was too much. She hid the rest in her closet. Is she gonna be in trouble?"

"That's quite a story. I'll look into it but won't be able to tell you anything even if something's going on. Don't worry, nobody will know we've talked."

I called a friend with the IRS and learned that Tristen's dad, Duane Nelson, was the subject of an ongoing gambling and money-laundering investigation. There were only a few banks in Stillwater, so we checked each one to see if a safe deposit box had recently been rented in Lauren's name. We were surprised and a little dismayed when we got confirmation at the third bank. "Yes, here it is. She rented Box 211 on November 9 and hasn't accessed it since."

If there was money in the box, then the rest of the story must be true. Armed with a search warrant, we drilled out the lock and found the box was literally stuffed with hundred-dollar bills. The IRS Agents now wondered if Lauren was involved; what college kid would "store" tens of thousands of dollars for some stranger? "You've met this girl, right? Would you take a run at her and see if she'll talk?"

"I only met her once at her parents' house. I can't say I know her. Let's go talk to her, but you guys get a search warrant for the apartment in case she doesn't cooperate."

It was 6:30 p.m. when Lauren opened the apartment door. "Hi, Lauren. We met at your parents' house at Thanksgiving. You may not remember, but I'm with the FBI and this lady's an IRS Agent."

Lauren nodded. "Oh, umm, yeah. Hang on."

She quickly turned and headed upstairs. We believed the backpack was in her bedroom closet and worried she might try to dispose of the cash or even escape through a window. Of course other IRS Agents were watching the apartment from across the street.

I shouted up the stairs, "Hey, we really need to talk. Can we come up?"

"Sure … I'm just … putting on some shoes."

We located her in the bedroom. "Look, Lauren, this is a little unusual. But we're here on official business and you need to be honest with us."

"OK, what's up?"

"Did Duane Nelson ask you to keep anything for him?"

I was disappointed by her answer. "No, why?"

"Do you expect us to believe the $117,000 we just seized from your safe deposit box belongs to you?"

She hung her head and admitted the money belonged to Mr. Nelson. "He just asked me to hold it for him. I wasn't supposed to tell anybody. Sorry for lying to you."

"Did he give you any more money?"

Once again her answer was disappointing. I pulled a document from my coat pocket and laid it on the bed. "This is a search warrant. We don't want to go through all your stuff, so if he gave you any more money it'd be better if you just show us where it is."

After a few seconds of silence, she walked to her closet and retrieved an orange and black backpack containing $225,000 in cash. She never asked how we knew.

The cash was proven to be proceeds from a gambling operation Nelson had been laundering for some time. With Lauren's testimony, he was convicted and sentenced to a lengthy prison term.

After the trial the IRS agents informed me of a little-known incentive program. "We wouldn't have convicted him or recovered that $342,000 without your information. Whoever tipped you off is eligible for a sizable reward. They're entitled to a percentage of the seizure." Lori ultimately got the reward, but my neighbors never mentioned it. Maybe the girls never told their parents; I sure didn't.

Time moved on and an endless stream of complex financial cases landed on my desk. In several instances I arrested the same person two or even three times for fraud. They went to prison after every conviction, but the lure of easy money was too strong.

Four

Major Case: WACMUR

I met my wife, Kelly, through work. She was a federal Probation Officer assigned to supervise many of the people I'd convicted. We got married in Oklahoma City and were unpacking after a long Caribbean honeymoon when one of her bridesmaids called in a panic.

"Are you guys all right? CNN says some federal agents were killed." We flipped on the TV to see live coverage from Waco, Texas. It was February 28, 1993, and early reports indicated that ATF, the Bureau of Alcohol, Tobacco, Firearms, and Explosives, which was then part of the Treasury Department, had attempted to execute a search warrant at the compound of a purported religious group known as the Branch Davidians. Outgunned from superior positions, four ATF Agents were killed and 15 wounded in a two-and-a-half-hour firefight. Following a negotiated cease-fire, Attorney General Janet Reno called upon the FBI to resolve the situation. This was similar to the way the Bureau had become embroiled in another standoff just one year earlier.

In 1992, U.S. Marshals attempted to arrest Randy Weaver at a remote cabin near Ruby Ridge, Idaho. On initial contact, a Deputy Marshal and Weaver's son were both killed. As a result, additional resources, including the FBI's elite Hostage Rescue Team (HRT), were requested. Under imprecise rules of engagement, an errant HRT sniper bullet killed Weaver's wife, who was concealed behind a door. That 11-day standoff ended with Weaver's surrender, but controversy surrounded the entire operation. Ruby Ridge galvanized anti-government groups and foreshadowed the tragedies of Waco and Oklahoma City (Department of Justice 2002).

As the CNN reporter continued his coverage from Waco, my pager warbled with the SWAT callout notification; our team would leave for Texas within the hour. Kelly asked, "So exactly how does this work?"

"It'll probably be over before we cross the Red River, but I'll pack for three days. I'll call you once we get there."

By the time we arrived, the FBI had already set up a CP and assumed tactical control of the situation. There was no way to know then that this operation would last 51 days and evolve into one of the nation's biggest controversies.

Our SWAT team met the Bureau's command element in a large hangar, miles from the compound. As additional resources including FBI negotiators and HRT poured into Texas, we were briefed on ATF's failed raid and advised of the type of firepower we could expect. It was staggering: explosives, assorted assault weapons, and .50 caliber rifles with an effective range of over a mile. We rallied closer to the compound and met with a senior member of ATF's Special Response Team, who detailed the sources and ferocity of fire he'd encountered during the initial raid. His goggles were cracked like a windshield, the cloth cover of his Kevlar helmet was torn, and there was a hole in the inside collar of his body armor from a shotgun blast fired through an upper-story window.

Known as the Mount Carmel Center, the large complex had a multistory tower that provided a commanding view of the dirt access roads and surrounding open prairie. There was no way to safely approach it with standard vehicles. Bullets from a .50 caliber weapon are powerful enough to knock down an airplane; the SWAT team's Suburbans would be shredded before reaching the compound. In the early '90s, most law enforcement agencies didn't have armored vehicles like BearCats or MRAPs (Mine-Resistant, Ambush Protected), so we borrowed Bradley Fighting Vehicles from the U.S. Army at nearby Fort Hood. The Bradley's heavy weapons wouldn't be used—there wasn't even any ammo for them—we just needed the armor for protection. My team advanced on foot down Elk Road on the safe side of the tracked vehicle, well within range of the Davidians' rifles. The Bradley stopped at the intersection of Elk Road and Double EE Ranch Road. Just beyond lay the long dirt driveway leading to Mount Carmel.

We waited for instructions from the CP and were initially told the Davidians intended to surrender. They were instructed to walk down the driveway in small groups. We would search them for weapons and escort them back up Elk Road to be formally arrested by ATF. We waited, but nothing happened. Time passed until finally, one afternoon,

My initial sniper position near the Branch Davidian compound at the intersection of Elk Road and Double EE Ranch Road, Waco, Texas (March 1993).

a voice crackled over our radios. "Stand by, surrender is imminent." We checked our gear and steeled ourselves to receive groups of potentially armed and dangerous individuals. But again, nothing happened. Hank, the SWAT team leader, eventually contacted the CP, only to learn that negotiations had fallen apart hours before. Negotiations continued to ebb and flow for weeks with only occasional progress. About two dozen children were released in the early days of the standoff.

One morning a Bradley approached my position. The back ramp opened and an HRT operator emerged holding a little girl who was about 10 years old with sandy hair and light-colored eyes. I took her from his arms, speaking softly to reassure her, and carried her to one of the child welfare workers assisting us. Sadly, she was one of the last children released by the group's leader, David Koresh.

As time wore on, incident commanders made contingency plans in case negotiations failed. Additional resources began to arrive; helicopters provided aerial surveillance and light towers flooded the compound, turning night into day. At one point Koresh bragged he had weapons that could defeat the Bradley's armor, threatening the Agents inside. Erring on the side of caution, we borrowed Abrams tanks from the Army to take advantage of their extraordinarily heavy armor. We also brought in combat engineer vehicles (CEVs), a type of tank designed for breaching and removing obstacles.

What's strange about these protracted events is that life goes on for the rest of the world. Fully aware of my deployment, our wedding photographer began hounding Kelly to return the 35mm proofs even though I hadn't seen any of the pictures. With no end in sight for the standoff, Roy's wife drove Kelly to Waco so we could order our wedding photos between my shifts at the compound.

It was also business as usual for the hotel in Waco. I returned one morning after a 14-hour shift and was met in the lobby by the manager. "Hey, good morning. Look, we really appreciate everything y'all are doing out there. But a basketball team is coming in to play Baylor and we're going to need your rooms." We'd been there for weeks and the hotel wanted their money.

Direct deposit and electronic transfers didn't exist back then, so we were each personally responsible for our meals, hotel, and other expenses; no one had a corporate-style government credit card. Customarily we'd submit a voucher after an operation, which usually only lasted a couple of days. But this was an unprecedented siege and little thought had been given to logistics. Eventually a pay trailer was set up within the perimeter, just outside the effective range of the Davidians' rifles. Each Thursday we lined up and signed for enough cash to pay our bills.

Outside that inner perimeter, concentric rings of security were manned by local police and ATF to keep the sea of onlookers and protesters at bay. One morning a college journalism student noticed a protester selling bumper stickers that read, "Ban Guns—Make the Streets Safe for a Government Takeover" and "A Man with a Gun Is a Citizen, A Man Without a Gun Is a Subject." During her interview, the man stated this standoff was only the beginning and people needed to prepare to defend themselves against government control. The reporter had no way to know that 24 months later this man would commit the deadliest act of domestic terrorism in American history. She was interviewing Timothy McVeigh.

The media was allowed to set up a little closer than the general public; close enough to get a sense of the situation, but far enough so as not to broadcast tactical movements. However, that didn't prevent wild speculation. At each shift change, or whenever more heavy equipment arrived, the media would breathlessly report there had been a major breakthrough.

One cold night, SWAT sentries were on watch as the rest of our team played cards in the Bradley. All the unsecure electronic transmissions in the area were being monitored and everything was quiet until a generator backfired inside the compound. We didn't think much of it, but the communications gear instantly came to life. One reporter on an open walkie-talkie began to report anxiously, "There's been an explosion in the compound. Agents are springing into position." I finally told Kelly to quit watching the news unless it came from a Bureau spokesman.

Attempts to encourage the Davidians to surrender increased as tactical positions were moved closer to the compound. Regional SWAT snipers were eventually integrated with HRT snipers to staff the closest positions. I was assigned to Sierra Two, a cinder-block garage located behind the main compound which we'd reinforced with steel plates and sandbags. An armored vehicle dropped me off and resupplied the position every few days. We ate prepackaged military food known as MREs (Meals, Ready-to-Eat) and slept on foam mats, huddled around a space heater for warmth. The doors at the rear of the garage were always guarded and seismic sensors arrayed to the rear warned if anyone, usually cattle, approached from the open ground outside.

My view of the Davidian compound from sniper position Sierra Two (April 1993).

The high-powered optics utilized at Sierra Two provided vital information to the command post (April 1993).

My HRT sniper partner happened to have fired the ill-fated shot at Ruby Ridge that killed Randy Weaver's wife. Weaver's trial was ongoing in Boise, so when my partner wasn't manning his rifle, he was on a satellite phone discussing a split-second decision he'd made more than a year before. That was a lot to ponder as I stared through the powerful Leupold scope of my own sniper rifle. The State of Idaho later unsuccessfully tried to file criminal charges against him for the death of Vicki Weaver.

On the morning of April 19, TVs across the nation showed footage of a CEV introducing non-lethal tear gas into the compound. Announcements made over loudspeakers told the occupants what was happening and urged them to evacuate, but with little effect. Shortly after noon, the complex erupted into an inferno as gunfire could be heard coming from within. In what seemed like seconds, the entire structure was engulfed in flames fanned by strong winds; only nine Davidians fled the blaze. Our team was assigned to secure the scene as firefighters doused the flames.

The carnage was a horrific, unforgettable sight. I recall one charred body with bandoliers of ammunition slung across his torso; gas masks, weapons, and thousands of rounds of ammo lay all around. In the

As firefighters battled the flames, our SWAT team went in to secure the compound (April 19, 1993).

center of the complex stood a cinder-block bunker where the remains of many of the women and children were located. I remember seeing dozens of gun barrels lining the walls, protruding from the rubble that filled the room.

After the inferno, the only intact structure was a concrete block room in the compound's interior (April 19, 1995).

All of the subsequent mindless babble insinuating the FBI started the fire as part of some master plan was utterly ridiculous. In fact, to ensure objectivity, the renowned Texas Rangers were immediately given primary responsibility for combing through the crime scene. They recovered nearly 400,000 rounds of ammunition; 305 firearms, including 32 fully automatic rifles and two .50 caliber rifles; anti-tank armor-piercing ammo; and a live hand grenade. They also recovered 75 bodies. A third of them were children, many of whom had been shot or stabbed to death (Office of Justice Programs 1993). The adults could have simply walked out, but these children were helpless and had no choice. Koresh controlled his own fate; Rangers found him with a single gunshot wound to the head, leaving his followers to die of smoke inhalation, burns, and suffocation (Department of Justice 2019).

Electronic listening devices and thermal imagery utilized that day proved that three fires were intentionally set in separate locations within the building. A team of independent arson experts confirmed that all three fires had been deliberately set from inside the compound using flammable liquid accelerants. Beyond the forensic evidence, Rangers interviewed surviving Davidians, who stated lantern fuel had been poured throughout the complex.

The events at Mount Carmel spawned congressional hearings, TV movies, books, and endless speculation of misdeeds and conspiracy. Lawsuits were filed decrying the way the situation was handled, blaming the FBI for the loss of life. Years after the fire, I was contacted by a congressional investigator still reviewing details. Finally, in July 2000, a report was issued by Special Counsel and former Senator John Danforth. After interviewing 849 witnesses, reviewing over two million documents, and examining thousands of pounds of evidence, he unequivocally concluded the government was not responsible for the fire (Danforth 2000).

Jim Norman was a Special Agent Bomb Technician (SABT) assigned to the Oklahoma City office. He deployed to Waco immediately after the fire to address any improvised explosive devices (IEDs) discovered in the rubble. Until then, I was unaware the FBI had bomb technicians. Jim explained that during the social unrest of the '60s and '70s, Congress had tasked the FBI to establish and train civilian public safety bomb squads. As a result, the FBI's Hazardous Devices School (HDS) was established in 1971 at Redstone Arsenal in Huntsville, Alabama. Initially it was a partnership with the Army, but the FBI assumed full operational control in 2017.

The six-week "Basic School" teaches demolition procedures, X-ray interpretation, safe handling of explosives, and advanced techniques to defeat IEDs. The majority of HDS students are state and local police officers. The Bureau pays for all the training, certifies the individual bomb techs, and accredits each local bomb squad in their respective jurisdictions. In return, those local officers serve as force multipliers for a cadre of about 200 FBI SABTs scattered across the country. The SABTs work closely with police and military bomb techs, provide national and international training, and support National Special Security Events (NSSE) such as presidential inaugurations, the Olympics, Super Bowls, or other major events requiring unique security protocols. FBI bomb techs return to HDS annually for specialized training and are recertified every three years with our state and local partners. Intrigued, I put my name in for one of the scarce HDS slots reserved for FBI Agents. I was accepted in 1994, one year after Waco.

At that time HDS consisted of two Quonset huts located at the center of Redstone Arsenal. The explosives ranges were nothing more than roughly mown fields on the installation's outskirts. Live-fire scenarios consisted of IEDs, which we had to imagine were placed on trains or in make-believe office buildings. Our X-ray systems used wet film from Polaroid, and homemade disrupters were common. A disrupter is a tool designed to remotely separate the components of an IED. It can fire a variety of solid projectiles or water at very high velocities. However,

My final bomb technician recertification at the FBI's Hazardous Devices School (2016).

commercial disrupters are expensive. So in the early days, many bomb squads fabricated their own using steel water pipes and modified shotgun shells.

As terror attacks and IEDs became more prevalent, Congress authorized a $26 million upgrade to HDS. In 2009, the campus was transformed into a state-of-the-art training facility with actual trains, planes, and entire villages for live-fire exercises. Leaps in technology produced digital X-ray systems and highly advanced precision disrupters designed to counter the emerging threats of the 21st century. Years later I received a patent as the coinventor of a tool specifically designed to defeat IEDs like those encountered at the Boston Marathon bombing. But other unthinkable events would unfold in the not-too-distant future. Until then, the more mundane world of financial crimes awaited me back in Oklahoma.

FIVE

The Mounties and Big Wayne

For years I'd been working on a money-laundering case targeting a Canadian company called Dragon Coding. It was in the business of illegally altering satellite encryption software and shipping it to American dealers. Under a Mutual Legal Assistance Treaty (MLAT), the embassy in Ottawa enlisted the assistance of the Royal Canadian Mounted Police (RCMP). Since the FBI has no authority outside the U.S., the Mounties adopted my probable cause in order to obtain a search warrant for the company's headquarters in Vancouver. Being unfamiliar with the intricacies of the investigation, they invited me to participate in the raid as an advisor.

I met Sergeant Paul Magoin and members of his Commercial Crimes Section at a little diner in Vancouver's warehouse district. Over breakfast we discussed the details of the case and planned the raid. As soon as RCMP surveillance teams confirmed the subjects were at the office, we executed the warrant and seized a significant amount of critical evidence. Once the Mounties inventoried all the computers, software, and mountains of documents, they would deliver the material to the U.S. embassy for shipment to FBI headquarters.

After the raid, Paul extended a gracious invitation. "If you don't have any plans this evening, why don't you join me at our training academy? We're wrapping up our national conference with a little banquet, plus hockey is on."

The prestigious halls of the old Tudor building were covered with pictures and plaques recounting the Mounties' colorful history. We made our way to the bar where everyone was watching the Canucks in the final game of the Stanley Cup. Outside on the parade grounds, steaks and lobsters were on the grill and ice-cold kegs bobbed in the horse troughs. When it became apparent the Canucks couldn't win, the festivities began to wind down. Paul finished his beer and offered to take me back Vancouver. "I can take you as far as Gastown, if you'd like. It's just a few blocks from your hotel, an easy walk." There was no Uber back then.

He dropped me off just as the cobblestone streets began to fill with boisterous crowds. The party atmosphere changed quickly and people started throwing fireworks, fighting, and breaking into stores. As the looting and violence worsened, uniformed police arrived and the drone of low-flying helicopters could be heard. Being just a tourist with no law enforcement authority, I pulled out my state-of-the-art 8mm videotape camera and asked a nearby group, "What's happening?" Several drunken revelers confirmed the Canucks had lost the Stanley Cup.

The mob grew angry as police tried to make arrests. I was watching from a street corner when the crowd suddenly turned; running, coughing, and covering their faces. That's when the first whiff of tear gas wafted by. I proceeded upstream toward the hotel until a chevron of riot police blocked the road. In the distance was the familiar sound of a 40mm grenade launcher like we used on the SWAT team. It's basically a big shotgun that can fire tear gas grenades.

Foolishly the throng began taunting police, throwing bottles and stones. When the looting and belligerence intensified, the riot squad advanced in lockstep, pounding riot batons on their Lexan shields with each step. About 20 men began to fight within arm's length of me; a RCMP grenadier noticed the melee and landed a 40mm tear gas grenade right in the middle of the brawl. It was time to find an alternate route to the hotel.

Paul and his Commercial Crimes squad came in a little late the next morning; many had been out all night on the riot squads. "You boys throw quite a party," I joked over coffee. "I took some pretty good video of the looting; nobody back home will believe Canadians act like this."

As he watched the tape, Paul became quite interested. "This is pretty good. I think we can identify some of these chuckleheads. Mind if we get a copy?"

"Just take the original. It'll be better quality."

Within two days the squad completed the Dragon Coding evidence inventory and provided a list to the court. The company's lawyers immediately filed an injunction barring transmission of any evidence to the United States, arguing the MLAT process was illegal and violated

Canadian sovereignty. A Canadian court would have to rule on what, if any, evidence could be released. Until then there was nothing more to do.

The Commercial Crimes squad gathered in Paul's office before he took me to the airport. "Well, I guess we'll see you again for the evidentiary hearing, eh? It's been a pleasure working with you. Thanks to your tape, we were able to identify several of the looters. Here's a little token of our appreciation." With that the squad presented me with a RCMP lithograph and one of their iconic Biltmore campaign hats.

About six months later I was summoned to testify in Canadian court about my probable cause, which the Mounties adopted for the search warrant. Paul emerged from the courtroom Friday afternoon following nearly two days of testimony. "Well, that's it for today; the judge wants to reconvene Monday. It's senseless for you to fly back tonight and return Sunday. Ever been to Vancouver Island?"

I bought a ticket at Coal Harbor's seaplane terminal for a 35-minute flight to Victoria. Despite the posted warnings of aggressive bears and cougars, I spent the weekend hiking the China Beach trails. After an opulent Sunday brunch at the Empress Hotel, I took the last floatplane back to Vancouver.

Paul completed his testimony at noon that Monday and emerged from the courtroom with a big smile. "I have some good news and some bad news. You won't need to testify as the judge is happy with our probable cause; the search was legal. But the defense filed an immediate appeal, so this will probably go to our Supreme Court."

It took six years for the Canadian courts to determine the search was legal and all the evidence could be released. Unfortunately, the key U.S. witness had died in the interim. The Assistant U.S. Attorney (AUSA) felt the witness's death substantially weakened the case and dismissed the indictment against the Canadians. However, 11 U.S. citizens were convicted and Dragon Coding was forced out of business.

Juggling complex multiyear investigations was common. In addition to Dragon Coding, I'd been investigating a large oil field equipment company headquartered in Pawhuska, Oklahoma. Spartan Industries was an old, family-owned business that prospered during the oil boom. But the ripples of the oil bust took a toll on the company and its elderly founder. In an attempt to save his business, the owner hired a man named C.W. "Big Wayne" McEachern. Big Wayne was a charismatic man who stood about 6'5". He often carried a Bible and was known to step off the corporate jet and lead his entourage in frenetic prayers while standing in the 100°F runway heat. His bona fides as a corporate turnaround king were impressive and appeared to be well deserved.

With Big Wayne at the helm, Spartan began experiencing unprecedented growth while the rest of the oil industry collapsed. Spartan stock was publicly traded on the Nasdaq and all the activity pushed its price up. But its meteoric performance raised suspicions at the Securities and Exchange Commission (SEC).

No fewer than two dozen companies across the country had been acquired by Spartan, each secured through stock swaps. In this type of transaction, all shares of the target company are exchanged for shares in the acquiring company, so no cash changes hands. Of course it's crucial that each company's shares are accurately and fairly valued to determine a fair swap ratio. Spartan's stock, which historically traded at about 25 cents per share, had exploded to over $8.00 per share, and Big Wayne boldly predicted a future value of over $13.00 per share.

As a former auditor, I knew the key to proving any illicit activity would be Jeb Holmes, the company's comptroller. As the company's senior accounting executive, his signature was on all the corporate financial documents, so if something was amiss, he'd have the most to lose. In response to a purposely vague voicemail, Jeb met me at an IHOP one morning on the outskirts of Pawhuska.

"Mr. Holmes, this is a spreadsheet charting Spartan's financials and holdings. It begins three years prior to Mr. McEachern being hired and runs through last month. This incredible uptick coincides with his hiring and is pretty hard to explain. So where should we begin?"

There was an awkward silence as Jeb stared into his coffee cup. Looking up, he sighed. "You're right. I wondered when somebody'd show up. It's really not hard to explain. The whole thing's a fraud."

He admitted Spartan was completely strapped for cash; sometimes they couldn't even make payroll. The company only appeared viable due to Big Wayne's ability to influence its stock value. The inflated value was then used to acquire other companies through stock swaps so Spartan could siphon their cash. He explained that Spartan's falsified net worth was based on grossly inflated values assigned to their technological assets and a vast inventory of very expensive equipment that didn't exist. That nonexistent inventory turned out to be Big Wayne's Achilles heel.

Publicly traded companies must be audited. When external auditors couldn't locate the valuable inventory shown on Spartan's books, they started asking questions. To explain the missing inventory, Jeb had the bookkeepers create false sales receipts. But if inventory had actually been sold, the Accounts Receivable should reflect the sales. Of course there were no actual sales because the inventory never existed, so the Accounts Receivable records had to be falsified. All that false data flowed into the company's financial statements, which were filed with the SEC. Spartan then used the SEC filings as the basis for lines of credit at several banks, which provided Spartan with another source of desperately needed cash. Every false statement provided to a bank or the SEC was a federal felony, as was manipulating the stock market.

The public relied on the SEC filings, which served as the basis for market makers' decisions to buy and sell Spartan stock. The falsified filings coupled with the rapid acquisition of so many diversified companies made Spartan a very attractive investment. As investors bought, the stock price rose, which had a snowball effect and perpetuated Spartan's market growth.

Big Wayne's scheme to acquire capital was ingenious. He would target a small company with plenty of cash reserves, personally fly out to meet the owners, and review Spartan's financials with them. Wayne would share his grand corporate vision and offer a takeover deal on the spot, but he wouldn't offer mere cash. Instead he offered a stock package whereby Spartan would acquire 100 percent of the new company's assets in exchange for Spartan stock plus future stock options. It seemed like a great opportunity.

But the scheme wouldn't work if each new subsidiary sold its Spartan stock immediately; flooding the market would drive down the stock price. So the lure of future stock options was the key. Wayne was quick to point out the fantastic growth potential under his management. Any prudent businessman would certainly want to hold the newly acquired shares since this latest merger would drive the stock even higher, plus they could eventually exercise their options to acquire even more shares at a discount. In the end, these people lost their companies in return for worthless stock certificates. One man actually borrowed money to buy his company back from Spartan before the business collapsed completely.

Big Wayne couldn't pull off such an elaborate scheme alone. He handpicked David Stroud to serve as his right hand and chief executive officer (CEO). Stroud was a CPA who made sure Jeb Holmes and his bookkeepers kept cranking out the false numbers. In return, they were very well paid, at least as long as their paychecks cleared.

Stroud reassured the staff: "These are just temporary measures until Mr. McEachern can turn things around. Besides, you're already implicated and will certainly go to prison if this gets out. We're all in it together, sink or swim."

Jeb knew he was in too deep, but he couldn't afford to lose his job. He'd been Spartan's comptroller for years and needed his lucrative retirement package, so he agreed to perpetuate the fraud. But as a CPA, Jeb also knew he was playing with fire.

Over that tepid cup of IHOP coffee he finally blurted out nervously, "I want a deal. I knew this day would come so I kept a second set of books. I can show you all the falsified records, who prepared them, and even give you the actual figures. I just can't go to prison."

With Jeb's information, I discreetly began interviewing everyone in Sparton's accounting department. When confronted with the ledgers, each insider folded and agreed to testify. Like Jeb, they seemed relieved to finally tell the truth. Some even produced additional documents like handwritten instructions from Big Wayne and Stroud; it was a gold mine.

These cases are the reason the FBI hires accountants; there were hundreds of financial transactions and bank accounts to analyze. At a meeting in D.C., the SEC provided every suspicious Spartan filing as well as the stock's trading volume and pricing history. All that data, coupled with Jeb's secret accounting ledgers, provided a clear picture of the magnitude of the market manipulation.

Tio Ramos was a good friend and aggressive AUSA. Outraged by the scale of this brazen scheme, he agreed to accept my method of determining its impact on the stock market. The difference between the false entries and the actual value was only about $5.3 million, but the effect on the market was much greater. By calculating the stock's average closing value and the volume traded during the time alleged in the indictment, the loss totaled over $24 million.

This type of securities fraud had never been charged in the Western District of Oklahoma, but Tio wasn't deterred. The grand jury named Big Wayne and Stroud in a 15-count indictment for filing false financial information and stock manipulation. Naturally the loss calculation was fiercely contested by the defense, but the court found my calculations to be reasonable and even conservative. Tio was subsequently contacted by other AUSAs who adopted our loss formula for use in other high-profile securities fraud cases.

I located Stroud at his large estate outside town. "Mr. Stroud, the grand jury has indicted you and Mr. McEachern on a litany of fraud charges. The AUSA is willing to offer a deal if you'll cooperate, but the clock is ticking. Why don't you discuss your options with a lawyer?"

After consulting his attorney, Stroud quickly agreed to plead guilty and testify against Big Wayne. To ensure his testimony was truthful, he wouldn't be sentenced until Wayne's case was adjudicated.

Wayne proved to be more elusive, so an arrest warrant was issued for him. An anonymous tip indicated he was staying at a home owned by his son in a town ironically named Waynesboro. Another Agent accompanied me on the 90-minute trip and we found Big Wayne's truck in the driveway. The front door was ajar and we could hear the television, but no one answered when we announced ourselves. As we knocked again, the door drifted open to reveal a giant man in suit trousers and an old stained T-shirt. As he stumbled toward us I shouted, "FBI! Wayne McEachern, you're under arrest. We're taking you to Oklahoma City."

"What? No, I'm too sick. That ride'll kill me."

Staggering back inside, his trousers fell to his ankles and he tripped, falling backward. It was only 10:00 a.m., but this man was drunk. Cases of beer were stacked all around the room. A rolling oxygen cylinder and empty prescription bottles were strewn about what was obviously Wayne's favorite recliner.

He combatively slurred, "I'm not going; I can't travel without my oxygen and meds. Besides, I want my lawyer."

This was going to require some thought. Nobody wants to go to jail and people have faked medical conditions to avoid it. But we were almost 100 miles from the office and couldn't risk a medical crisis in transit.

"All right, Mr. McEachern. Why don't you give your attorney a call? Have him contact the AUSA and we'll see what they can work out."

I called Tio and relayed the situation. In this instance he agreed it was best to allow Wayne to surrender himself to the U.S. Marshals, which was where I would take him anyway. Wayne was still talking to his attorney when the front door flew open. An irate Wayne, Jr., stormed in demanding to know who we were.

"You have no right to be here! You're lucky I wasn't here when you showed up; one of you might have got shot!"

That was enough from Junior. After a quick discussion about his dad's outstanding arrest warrant and the ramifications of shooting at the FBI, he settled down and we got back to business. It was decided that Big Wayne would surrender to the Marshals within 48 hours. If he failed to appear, he'd be arrested regardless of his situation.

Two days later Wayne's lawyer called Tio. "I'm obligated to inform you that my client checked himself into the hospital. His doctors don't feel he can handle any stress right now."

Tio had no choice but to extend the deadline. In fact, several other deadlines expired until we learned Wayne had been discharged from the hospital; at that point he was a fugitive and subject to arrest. Surveillance revealed the house in Waynesboro was vacant, and neither the neighbors nor Junior would admit to his whereabouts.

We located and interviewed Wayne's estranged wife who was working near downtown Oklahoma City. "Nope, I haven't seen him but I'll be glad to call you if I do." There was no love lost between them.

My partner and I were sitting in the car debating our next move when a thunderous explosion shattered the still morning air. It was 9:02 a.m., April 19, 1995.

Six

Major Case: OKBOMB

I looked west toward Oklahoma City and saw a cloud of thick black smoke drifting over downtown. My pager went off as the Bureau's encrypted radio began directing assets to the Alfred P. Murrah Federal Building. Something terrible had happened. Initial reports speculated a plane might have crashed or a gas main exploded. Whatever the cause, it was obvious that hundreds of people must have been killed or injured. As I raced downtown, my thoughts were of my wife; she parked her car in the Murrah garage and was often in the building. I didn't have a cell phone then, so there was no way to contact her.

I arrived about 28 minutes after the explosion to an apocalyptic scene. Trying to process the devastation, I recalled the vehicle-borne IED (VBIED) that detonated beneath the World Trade Center in 1993, but this was vastly different. Debris littered the street, so I jumped the curb and parked on the sidewalk just west of the building, or what was left of it. One-third of the nine-story structure was gone and a 30-foot crater in the street marked the seat of the blast. Cars had burst into flames, windows were blown out for several blocks, and more than 300 buildings were damaged. Walking wounded mingled with first responders as trapped survivors desperately sought any kind of help. The blast was heard in Stillwater, 55 miles away, and a seismograph registered the ground shock as a 3.2 magnitude earthquake. I'd never seen anything like this (FBI 2018c).

Frantic people arrived searching for their loved ones as others loaded victims into personal vehicles for transport to the hospital. One nurse self-deployed from home and was tragically killed by falling debris. In another horrific case, a surgeon could only free a woman from the rubble by amputating her leg; there was no anesthesia and the

An image of the bombed Murrah Building on display in the Oklahoma City National Memorial and Museum (April 2015).

procedure was completed with a pocket knife. To make matters worse, that woman's mother and two children had been killed in the blast. These tragic individual stories recurred time and again.

I'd been a bomb technician for exactly 53 weeks and was now staring at the deadliest domestic terrorist attack in American history. My immediate responsibility was to conduct a post-blast assessment, but as I surveyed the perimeter of the building I was also looking for Kelly. I wasn't certain she was safe for over an hour. Since there were no cell phones, she paged me and input my office voicemail as the callback number. Her message indicated she'd left the Murrah Building at 9:00 a.m., two minutes before detonation. She and the other U.S. Probation Officers were now safe at their emergency relocation site.

Mayhem and confusion reign in any disaster of this magnitude. But first responders must manage the chaos because critical, yet disparate activities have to occur simultaneously. Firefighting and rescue efforts can't be impeded by evidence collection, but crucial transient evidence must be rapidly located and properly secured. I requested the newly formed FBI Evidence Response Team (ERT) to document the entire scene as quickly and thoroughly as possible. Photographs are especially important so a jury can see the scene in its earliest stages. Aerial photography would be useful to cover such a large area, but drones didn't exist then and there was no way to know when a plane would be available. So I turned to a fire captain who agreed to let us use one of his aerial ladder trucks, which would give our photographer a bird's-eye view of the destruction.

Over the chaos I shouted, "OK, Jannetta. Climb up and they'll maneuver you over the crater for the best vantage."

She shook her head. "I have vertigo! I can't go way up there, hold on, and try to take pictures by myself. You'll have to go with me." As I held her by her belt, we ascended the ladder and were swung into position. Dangling 100 feet above the carnage, she took crucial images documenting the early phases of the catastrophe. Many of her photos were later used at trial.

The YMCA, diagonally across the street from the Murrah Building, had been heavily damaged by the blast. I joined a small team in a quick search for victims, survivors, and evidence. On the third floor, the indoor running track had been flooded by ruptured pipes. As we slogged through ankle-deep water, a fuse box burst into flames. I was wrong to assume the building's power had been shut off. Stepping through a blown-out window onto the portico's roof, I could see utility workers moving in our direction to cut the power.

About 10:15 a.m., I walked across buckled sidewalks to the south side of the federal building and onto a small playground. America's Kids Daycare was in the Murrah Building, and 15 innocent children had been killed there. The playground's northern elevation was two stories above Fifth Street and offered an overview of the crater. While I surveyed the blast pattern with a State Trooper, the roar of a helicopter echoed among the tall buildings behind us. As we turned toward the noise, first responders began fleeing the Murrah Building; they seemed to be shouting something. At first I thought it was crashing, but as the low-flying police helicopter passed we could hear the firemen's warning: "There's another bomb!"

The FBI trains first responders to be alert for secondary devices, especially in bombing cases. It's a common terrorist tactic; if bomb techs and rescue workers are killed by a second blast, there's no one left to carry on the appropriate response. Standard operating procedures (SOPs) dictate that when a second device is discovered, first responders evacuate the danger zone until a proper response can be brought to bear.

While processing the firemen's warning about a second bomb, I looked back at the building and saw two women standing in a window several stories above me. It was a hopeless feeling, but in that instant there was no way to help them. Following SOP, the Trooper and I began looking for a way down from our second story perch. A row of trees lined the east side of the building, so we jumped to the closest limb and clambered down to street level. From there we regrouped with members of a local bomb squad on the safe side of a heavy bomb truck. "What happened? What caused the evacuation?" I asked.

The alarm was raised when rescue workers discovered a long, rectangular wooden crate with orange labels reading Explosives. Once the exact location of the crate was ascertained, bomb techs carefully made entry, recovered the crate, and lowered it into a specialized trailer for transportation to a nearby bomb range. With the item safely removed, rescue and recovery efforts resumed.

Examining the device at the range, I was shocked to see what appeared to be a TOW missile. Why would a tube-launched, optically tracked, wire-guided (TOW) anti-tank missile be in the federal building? It appeared to be fully functional and in its original packing crate. Since this was military ordnance, it fell under the purview of military Explosive Ordnance Disposal (EOD) technicians, who are experts on military ordnance. I contacted the commander of the nearest Army EOD unit located at Fort Sill, Oklahoma.

Captain Bradley's team met me at the range and examined the missile. Their examination determined it was actually inert, but modified and weighted to appear fully functional. A serial number on the launch tube was used to trace the device back to Redstone Arsenal. After a thorough investigation, we determined this particular system had been repurposed and reconfigured as part of an undercover sting operation for another federal agency that was housed in the Murrah Building.

The provenance and inert condition of the missile were indisputable. However, conspiracy theorists insisted it was part of some grand scheme to cover up the fact that explosives that were illicitly stored in the Murrah Building contributed to the devastation. Another conspiracy theory stated that multiple IEDs must have been placed within the building, because a single VBIED couldn't produce that kind of damage.

Three years after the bombing, I testified as an expert before a county grand jury to dispel misinformation about the TOW missile and discuss the type of damage VBIEDs can cause. To drive the point home, I showed the jurors a video of an unrelated test conducted by the British government in which a 5,000-pound VBIED, similar in size and composition to McVeigh's device, was detonated. After hearing my testimony and seeing that video, they were convinced a single VBIED could certainly produce the type of damage seen in Oklahoma City (Baldwin and Kuhmlan 1998).

As the morning of April 19 wore on, mangled pieces of a cargo truck were recovered. Part of the frame was embedded in a van across the street from the crater, a wheel was found half a block north, and part of the front end was lodged in a wall more than a block away to the east. A five-pound rear door latch was found inside an eighth-floor apartment one block to the west, and 1,100 feet further was a differential gear. The distribution of these pieces indicated the bomb-laden vehicle was facing east when it detonated, a fact later confirmed by a nearby surveillance camera.

The most critical piece of evidence was part of the truck's rear axle. This 300-pound twisted piece of steel had flown 600 feet to the west before hitting a parked car. A sheriff's deputy called me and my mentor, Jim Norman, over to take a closer look. He wiped away a thick layer of grease to reveal a confidential vehicle identification number (CVIN) stamped into the metal. As the deputy called out the unique alphanumeric string, Jim and I both jotted it down. We read it back to one another to ensure there were no errors and sent Jim's note to the CP

The rear axle of the Ryder truck bearing the critical CVIN on display in the Oklahoma City National Memorial and Museum (April 2015).

so they could trace the CVIN. My hastily scribbled note is now in the Oklahoma City National Memorial and Museum with other artifacts provided by the FBI.

The rest of April 19 is a blur. I recall standing in a cold rain that night, but when I went to my car to retrieve some Gore-Tex, it was gone. I'd parked on the sidewalk shortly after the blast, but my car had been towed to make room for a triage station.

The rain made recovery of chemical residue difficult. One small piece of fiberboard, later determined to have come from the interior of the truck's cargo area, was recovered and proven to have a minute amount of explosive residue embedded within. That particular piece of evidence, identified as Q507, had come to rest upside down, which protected it from the rain. The unique chemical signature of that residue was later matched to materials seized in the home of Terry Nichols, McVeigh's coconspirator.

I don't even remember going home that night; in fact, the subsequent days and weeks remain indistinguishable. I can recall specific events in great detail, but we were working very long hours, seven days a week, so the exact chronology of some events is lost.

The rear axle's CVIN proved to be the biggest break in the case. The CP traced it to Ford Motor Company. Ford confirmed the truck had been built for Ryder Truck Rental. Contacts at Ryder advised that particular vehicle was assigned to a rental facility called Elliott's Body Shop in Junction City, Kansas. Agents were on the ground in Junction City within hours of the CVIN's discovery.

Rental records at Elliott's Body Shop revealed a man named Robert Kling paid cash for the rental on April 15 and came back to pick up the truck on the 17th. The body shop manager thought another man might have been with Kling at that time, so physical descriptions of both men were given to a sketch artist who produced composite sketches. The man using the name "Kling" was referred to as "John Doe No. 1" and the second man as "John Doe No. 2."

Armed with the sketches, law enforcement descended on the small town of Junction City. On April 20, the owner of the Dreamland Motel, located about five miles from Elliott's Body Shop, recognized John Doe No. 1. "That man rented Room 25 on April 14 under the name Tim McVeigh. Here's his registration." It indicated he was alone, identified his vehicle as a Mercury with an Arizona license plate, and gave an address in Decker, Michigan. In addition to what she described as his old yellow Mercury, McVeigh was also seen in a Ryder truck a few days later.

A canvass of all the restaurants in Junction City revealed that on April 15 an order of Chinese food had been delivered to a man named Kling in Room 25 at the Dreamland Motel. It now appeared Kling and McVeigh were the same man, though both names might be aliases. All the information gleaned in Junction City was immediately passed to the CP in Oklahoma City.

As events in Kansas unfolded, Agents in Decker, Michigan, investigated the address McVeigh had used on the Dreamland registration. It was a farm belonging to James and Terry Nichols, who, according to neighbors, had no love for the federal government. A look into Terry Nichols's background revealed he had served in the same Army unit as McVeigh, and witnesses recalled seeing them together at the farm. Terry Nichols was now a person of interest.

During the overnight hours of April 20, we conducted an offline NCIC (National Crime Information Center) search for the name Tim McVeigh based on the Junction City information. NCIC is a database maintained by the FBI that serves as a clearinghouse for law enforcement agencies across the country. This type of search could tell us if any police officers had recent contact with McVeigh. The result was amazing: Timothy McVeigh was sitting in a county jail.

About 75 minutes after the bombing, OHP Trooper Charlie Hanger noticed a car driving northbound on I-35 that didn't have a license plate. He fell in behind the old yellow Mercury and pulled it over near Perry, Oklahoma. As the driver exited the vehicle, Hanger noticed a bulge under his jacket. Aware the Trooper was suspicious, the man volunteered, "I have a weapon … my weapon's loaded." Hanger placed his pistol to the driver's head and assured him, "So is mine." Hanger was unaware he'd just arrested the most wanted man in America.

Charged with failure to display a license plate and carrying a concealed weapon, which was illegal in Oklahoma at the time, McVeigh was booked into the Noble County jail. Through a series of fortuitous delays, he was still in custody when our inquiry was made. We placed a federal hold on him to ensure he wouldn't be released.

I called ahead and had a helicopter readied to fly us up to Perry. It was 12:20 p.m. when we landed on I-35 at mile marker 202.6, where Trooper Hanger was waiting at McVeigh's car. I seized the vehicle and awaited a search warrant while Jim Norman and the rest of the team flew to the county jail and took custody of McVeigh. Crowds converged on the little county courthouse chanting "baby killer" as he was led out in orange prison garb.

My seizure of Timothy McVeigh's car along I-35 (April 21, 1995).

McVeigh's clothes and personal property were inventoried before being sent to the FBI Lab for testing. Trace chemical residue from the high explosive PETN, EDGN, and nitroglycerine were found on his earplugs, pants, and shirts. His T-shirt had the words "Sic Semper Tyrannis" on the front, a line spoken by Brutus as he assassinated Julius Caesar and shouted by John Wilkes Booth after assassinating President Lincoln. The phrase is Latin for "thus always to tyrants." The back of the shirt bore the words "The tree of liberty must be refreshed from time to time with the blood of patriots and tyrants."

A search of Trooper Hanger's vehicle where McVeigh had been seated revealed a crumpled business card from a military surplus store. McVeigh's fingerprints were on the card with a handwritten note reading in part, "TNT @ $5 a stick. Need more."

Documents found inside his yellow Mercury included a hand-printed sign reading, "Don't tow; need battery & jumper cables." This was the sign McVeigh left in the getaway car when he and Nichols dropped it off a few blocks from the Murrah Building on April 16. A large sealed envelope contained notes and copies of various magazine and newspaper articles. One document referenced a quote often attributed to Thomas Jefferson that read, "When the government fears the people, there is liberty." In the margin, written in McVeigh's own hand, were the words "Maybe now there will be liberty."

The envelope also included clippings from *The Turner Diaries*, an anti-government screed popular with rightwing extremists; it was preferred reading for McVeigh and he recommended it to friends. In the novel, a VBIED made of ANFO is detonated at 9:15 a.m. beneath FBI headquarters, killing hundreds of people. One passage from the book had been highlighted. It read, "The real value of our attacks today lies in the psychological impact, not in the immediate casualties."

At 7:00 p.m., I joined the SWAT team to take McVeigh into a makeshift courtroom at Tinker Air Force Base. Ordinarily a defendant's initial appearance would be held at the federal courthouse, but it had been damaged by the bombing. Tinker was selected as an alternate site as its physical security features would help ensure McVeigh's safety. As at the jail in Perry County, angry crowds had already gathered outside the fences. U.S. Magistrate Ronald Howland determined there was sufficient evidence to hold McVeigh, and at 9:25 p.m., Jim and I joined the convoy escorting him to the federal prison in El Reno.

Terry Nichols, who was already under surveillance in Kansas, saw the news coverage of McVeigh's arrest and surrendered to local authorities at 3:00 p.m. The two men responsible for this cowardly, heinous act were in FBI custody within 54 hours of detonation. But their arrests were just the beginning.

As the scope of the investigation became international, teams continued to sift through debris at the blast site where small but important bits of evidence were recovered. Chemical residue and blast analysis indicated the bomb was made from ANFO, the same type of explosive used in *The Turner Diaries*. Tiny, twisted shreds of thick blue and white plastic were found, which appeared to be from barrels that contained the ANFO.

After Nichols surrendered, a search warrant was executed at his home in Herrington, Kansas. ERT recovered four blue and white barrels that matched the plastic pieces found at the scene. They also recovered blasting caps, a cordless drill, drill bits, and other incriminating evidence like ammonium nitrate (AN) fertilizer prills and a receipt for 2,000 pounds of AN. The receipt was in the name of Mike Havens, an alias Nichols was known to use, and bore the fingerprint of Timothy McVeigh.

ANFO is a powerful, but insensitive explosive. It's manufactured commercially or can be improvised by mixing AN with fuel oil (FO) or some other fuel; McVeigh selected nitromethane. ANFO, known as a blasting agent, requires the energy of an explosive booster and blasting cap to make it detonate. Realizing boosters are often stolen, I began poring over stolen explosives reports until one caught my eye. Just months before the bombing, hundreds of pounds of boosters and blasting caps were stolen from a quarry near Terry Nichols's home. I interviewed quarry personnel and obtained an inventory of the stolen materials; the blasting caps recovered in Nichols's home were the same type as those stolen from the quarry.

Even more damning forensic evidence centered on Nichols's cordless drill and drill bits. When the quarry theft was initially investigated, one of the storage bunker's padlocks was found; it had been inadvertently left by the thieves. Realizing the lock had been drilled to gain access to the explosives, it was retained by local police as evidence. We sent that lock to the FBI Lab for comparison to the drill and drill bits seized at Nichols's home. Microscopic tool marks and metallurgical analysis proved those tools were used to drill out the lock, tying Nichols to the theft.

The receipt for the 2,000 pounds of AN recovered in Nichols's home came from a nearby farm supply store called Mid–Kansas Co-Op. Agents pored over records there and discovered a second 2,000-pound purchase, also in the name of Mike Havens. Co-Op workers' description of Havens and the pickup he drove matched that of Nichols and his truck. Even more telling was the unusual chemical signature of the Co-Op's AN. The coating used on their fertilizer prills was unique and had the same specific elemental profile as the AN prills recovered from Nichols's home and the residue embedded in Q507.

A deep dive into McVeigh's and Nichols's associates led to Michael Fortier. All three served in the same unit at Fort Riley, Kansas, and McVeigh kept in touch once they left the Army. In fact, McVeigh often stayed with Michael and his wife Lori in their Kingman, Arizona, home.

What's troubling is that both Michael and Lori were well aware of McVeigh's plan, but chose to say nothing. It was Lori who laminated the fake Robert Kling ID McVeigh used to rent the Ryder truck. While at their house, McVeigh used soup cans to demonstrate how the explosive laden barrels would be arrayed in the truck. He discussed how he and Nichols purchased AN from a farm supply store and stole explosives from a quarry. While in Oklahoma City, he even showed Michael the Murrah Building and the alley behind the YMCA. He described where he would park the VBIED and the alleyway escape route leading to his getaway car. Among all the debris, ERT found the Ryder truck's ignition key in that alley, dropped by McVeigh as he ran away.

The Fortiers' intimate knowledge tied all the physical evidence together: the use of barrels, the drill used in the quarry theft, purchasing the AN, McVeigh's route to the getaway car, Nichols's participation, and of course their undeniable intent. In return for their testimony, a plea agreement was reached. Lori wasn't prosecuted and Michael pled guilty to failing to report the plot, lying to the FBI, and selling guns stolen by McVeigh and Nichols to help finance the attack. He was eventually sentenced to 12 years in prison and fined $200,000. Upon his release, he and Lori entered the witness protection program.

The magnitude of the investigation was staggering. The 1,400 people assigned to this case generated more information in 32 months than the Unabomber investigation did in 18 years. The exhaustive, global investigation consumed over 1,008,000 man-hours, recovered roughly 16,000 pieces of evidence, conducted more than 28,000 interviews, and covered 43,000 leads. No stone was left unturned.

Every lead, no matter how remote, received critical consideration. In one instance I had to prove a man who'd confessed to the bombing could *not* have done it. The U.S. was seeking his extradition for a major art theft; realizing the country holding him wouldn't extradite for a capital offense, he claimed to have bombed the building. I worked with our international partners and Legal Attachés in various embassies to track the man's movements prior to and after the attack. Of course we proved conclusively he had nothing to do with the bombing.

As the investigation played out around the world, 11 Search and Rescue (SAR) teams worked tirelessly searching for survivors, a grim task that lasted 17 days. Sadly, the last survivor had been rescued at 10:05 p.m. the night of the blast (Oklahoma Department of Civil Emergency Management 2005). With that somber realization, efforts shifted to victim recovery. It was heartbreaking every time a victim's remains were discovered, and SAR teams ensured each victim was treated with dignity. I recall everything coming to a halt when the body of a U.S. Marine was recovered; the "blood stripe" of his dress blue trousers stood out against the dusty, gray concrete.

As time wore on, three victims remained unaccounted for and weeks passed until cadaver dogs pinpointed their likely locations. They were buried in a collapsed part of the building that was too unstable for recovery teams to enter. The locations were marked, and on May 23,

Overnight operations at the Murrah Building (April 1995).

A makeshift memorial sprang up before the Murrah Building was imploded (May 23, 1995).

1995, the building was imploded. Heavy equipment then removed the debris, allowing recovery personnel to extricate the victims' remains.

As with most major investigations, conspiracy theories were rampant. One swirled around a left leg that was discovered in the rubble after the implosion. Tragically, the enormous explosive forces, flying debris, and subsequent building collapse tore some bodies asunder. Bodies and body parts were initially transferred to a temporary morgue for examination by the Medical Examiner (ME). Few ME offices are equipped to handle mass casualty events, so the FBI augmented the ME's staff with its Disaster Identification Unit along with forensic odontologists and other specialists.

On May 30, a detached left leg clad in military-style clothing and a size 7½ military boot was recovered. The ME made a unilateral public statement that the leg could not be attributed to any known victim. He went on to say it belonged to a light-skinned, dark-haired male. That statement fueled a wild theory that the leg was all that remained of John Doe No. 2, the "real bomber," or some unknown coconspirator (*New York Times* 1995).

I was tasked to definitively resolve the leg issue. Interviews with the ME's staff and a review of their files shed little light on the mysterious limb. Additional expertise was required, so I assembled a panel of experts from the Smithsonian Institution, the Armed Forces Institute of Pathology, two renowned forensic anthropologists, the FBI's Hairs and Fibers Unit, Special Photography Unit, and the relatively new DNA Unit. The group met me at the morgue on August 30 to examine the leg and provide their respective opinions; their findings were remarkable. The consensus was the leg did not belong to a man as the ME surmised, but an athletic African American woman. Their detailed report also provided an approximate height, weight, and age of the victim.

In addition to the anthropological evidence, the Special Photo Unit provided enhanced images of a handwritten, alphanumeric string located in the throat of the boot which appeared to be a letter and four numbers. I called the Army's Criminal Investigation Division and asked what the string could mean. The sergeant explained, "Sometimes soldiers use the initial of their last name and the last four of their Social to ID personal gear."

I then contacted the Social Security Administration and requested a list of all the victims' Social Security numbers. Going down the list, I found a match. The odds of the same four numbers appearing in the correct sequence were remote, so this was promising. However, the initial of the last name didn't match. Deeper examination of Social Security records indicated the number belonged to an African American woman who was employed by the U.S. Air Force. The Air Force Office of Special Investigations provided the airman's personnel file; her physical description matched the anthropologist's profile and revealed she had enlisted under her maiden name, which matched the initial in the boot.

With this new information we obtained a copy of the airman's birth certificate, which bore an inked footprint. That print was matched to the foot of the severed leg, then DNA was used to confirm the match. The leg belonged to Lakesha R. Levy, USAF. Her body had been badly damaged in the blast and was recovered prior to the implosion, but was mistakenly associated with someone else's leg.

The ME's staff had been working tirelessly under extraordinary pressure for weeks and an unfortunate series of human errors led to the confusion. Once the leg was fully identified, the ME gave a press conference, saying in part, "The reason you're here today is because we have made mistakes.... We're stressed, we're drained, and we haven't been able to grieve yet." The airman's body was exhumed and reinterred with the leg (Killackey 1996).

Author and former president Bill Clinton marking the 30th anniversary of the Oklahoma City bombing (April 18, 2025).

The entire Levy family charters a bus and drives from Louisiana to Oklahoma City on each decennial anniversary of the bombing. They place the boot, now in a Plexiglas case, on that solemn spot at the memorial which bears Lakesha's name. To mark the 30th anniversary, Governor Frank Keating and President Bill Clinton, who were both in office at the time, joined victims, families, first responders, and rescue workers from across the country to remember those we lost on that fateful day.

Some still refused to believe the findings, and controversy over John Doe No. 2 remained. The sketches of John Doe No. 1 and No. 2 generated 15,664 leads, and each had to be run to ground. Eight thousand man-hours were expended solving the John Doe No. 2 mystery. He was actually a soldier from Fort Riley who'd been in Elliot's Body Shop prior to "Kling's" rental. He had absolutely nothing to do with the bombing, but of course conspiracy theorists didn't believe that either.

OKBOMB was a massive investigation, but the FBI was still responsible for providing intelligence and tactical support for other major events. The Critical Incident Response Group (CIRG) and other FBI headquarters units were responsible ensuring assets were available for a myriad of domestic and international deployments.

Like everyone assigned to OKBOMB, I'd been working six or seven days a week since the blast. After almost 15 months, a CIRG supervisor called with what seemed like a great offer.

"I know you've been hammered out there and thought you could use a little diversion; we need SABTs to work the Olympics in Atlanta. The soccer venue is in Birmingham and I recall your folks are down there. If you can break away, we'd like you to run a counter–IED team at that venue. You know the town and it should give you a slower pace for a few weeks."

The TDY (temporary duty assignment) was a welcome relief from the stress of OKBOMB, at least until the early morning hours of July 27. I was sitting at a sidewalk café with some Olympic officials when the bartender shouted, "What's this about a bomb in Atlanta? It's all over CNN!"

Within minutes my cell phone rang, dispatching me to Centennial Olympic Park, where an IED had killed one person and injured over 100. The SABTs assigned to the venue were immersed in the post-blast investigation, so I folded into a group handling other incidents for the duration of the Olympics.

The CENTBOMB Task Force was established to investigate the bombing. Initially there was a great deal of controversy over Richard Jewel, a security guard who had located the IED hidden in a backpack. Wrongly accused and pilloried by the media, Jewel was fully exonerated and later received an apology from Attorney General Janet Reno for his name being leaked as a suspect.

In January 1997, six months after the Olympic blast, a bomb detonated at Atlanta's Northside Family Planning Services clinic in Sandy Springs, Georgia. A second device exploded an hour later, targeting first responders. In February an IED exploded at the Otherside Lounge, an alternative nightclub in northeast Atlanta. A second device was discovered in a backpack near the parking lot. Similarities in the design of the IEDs and the use of secondary devices pointed to a serial bomber.

Eleven months later, in January 1998, an off-duty police officer was killed when a bomb exploded at the New Woman, All Women Clinic in Birmingham, Alabama. That's when eyewitnesses provided a crucial tip; a suspicious 1989 Nissan pickup was seen just before the blast. That truck was traced back to a man named Eric Rudolph, and four months later Rudolph was placed on the FBI's Ten Most Wanted Fugitives list. After a five-year manhunt, he was arrested in Murphy, North Carolina, foraging for food. Upon conviction for the three Atlanta bombings and the one in Birmingham, he was sentenced to multiple life sentences at the only super-maximum security prison in the country, the U.S. Penitentiary Administrative Maximum Facility commonly known as "Supermax" in Florence, Colorado (FBI 2016d).

When the Olympics concluded, I returned to Oklahoma and resumed routine white-collar work until the next special event, San Diego's Republican National Convention. This would be the first national political convention since the Oklahoma City bombing and the midair explosion of TWA Flight 800 off the coast of New York. People were on edge, and security was a priority.

My team consisted of local bomb techs and a Navy Chief assigned to EOD Mobile Unit 5. We were killing time one evening when Chief Steele asked, "Ever heard of the mammal systems?" He explained that the Navy maintained dolphins trained to protect harbors and anchored ships from enemy swimmers. "We're having an exercise tomorrow night off Coronado if you want to come along."

"I wouldn't miss it, Chief."

After clearing security, we walked into a locker room where a group of square-jawed, serious-looking men were waiting. Steele advised, "Mr. Black will be joining us. Load up." A modified Boston Whaler was tied up at the dock alongside submerged holding pens. Once we were aboard, a dolphin leapt into the boat and was wrapped in a wet, padded tarp. A civilian named Scott boarded.

"Good evening, sir, I see you've met Charlie. Please rig for high speed."

The bow climbed as the twin outboards roared to life, speeding us into the pitch black San Diego Bay. Soon the boat settled low in the water alongside huge commercial ships at anchor. Scott put a glowing green chem stick on Charlie's rostrum (snout) as the dolphin slid over the gunnel. He asked, "Sir, can you see that orange chem stick a few hundred yards out? That's the target swimmer."

Charlie swam to the bow and began scanning left and right, attempting to echolocate the swimmer; the boat followed slowly behind. Suddenly Charlie appeared on the starboard side. Dancing on his tail, he nudged a signal bell suspended over the water to indicate he'd acquired the target. The handler fit an apparatus over Charlie's rostrum and Charlie took off like a torpedo. Within seconds, the orange chem stick violently disappeared before popping back to the surface. Like a well-trained puppy, Charlie returned to our boat and leapt aboard for some treats and praise.

Scott explained that in an actual deployment, Charlie's apparatus would've been equipped with a small harpoon that fired an illuminated buoy into the enemy swimmer to mark his position; Marines are then deployed to finish the mission. It sounded pretty effective and of course there's no harm to the dolphin (Ziezulewicz 2024).

Back at Coronado, the Chief mentioned another opportunity. "I think our next day off is Saturday. If you don't have plans, I'll take you to Miramar. TOPGUN's moving to Nevada so the Navy's having a huge final exhibition." Who could say no to a runway pass for Fightertown USA's last airshow? It was phenomenal.

In the meantime, the federal judge in Oklahoma ruled that McVeigh and Nichols would be tried separately. McVeigh's attorney successfully argued for a change of venue, so his trial was moved to Denver. A group from the OKBOMB Task Force transferred to Colorado to prepare for trial, but I stayed in Oklahoma because a trial date had finally been set for Big Wayne and Spartan Industries.

After years of delay, Judge Inga Albrecht was tired of Big Wayne claiming he was too sick to stand trial, especially when his own doctors refused to support his assertion. The judge's order was simple: "I'm setting a trial date. If Mr. McEachern elects not to appear, he'll be tried in absentia."

The judge dropped her gavel on the opening day of trial and asked the defense attorney, "Mr. Sexton, where's your client?"

The sheepish response was "We don't know, Your Honor. May we have a recess to find out?"

"No, I told him he didn't have to be here and he's made his choice. Let's begin voir dire." At that moment the huge wooden doors of the courtroom flew open; it was Junior. He stormed in and shouted, "My father won't be here today. He died of a heart attack this morning. You killed him!"

The judge immediately dismissed the jury and cleared the courtroom; in less than five minutes Tio and I sat alone and dismayed in the cavernous hall. People have been known to fake their death to avoid prison, so Tio looked at me and whispered, "You better make sure he's really dead." Junior and the family knew me, so out of respect I asked another Agent to view the body and confirm Mr. McEachern's demise. He was in fact dead, so that just left the sentencing phase for Spartan's CEO, David Stroud. At a hearing a few days later, Stroud was sentenced to 46 months in prison.

With the Spartan case fully adjudicated, I made several trips to Denver in support of the OKBOMB trial. On July 3, 1997, McVeigh was found guilty on all counts, which included the deaths of eight federal agents. They were the only victims charged in the indictment, as killing federal agents is a federal crime; murder of non-federal personnel is usually a state crime.

McVeigh was executed by lethal injection on June 11, 2001, at a federal prison in Terre Haute, Indiana. For the first time ever, Attorney General John Ashcroft arranged for an encrypted CCTV signal to be sent to a secure location in Oklahoma City where victims could witness the execution if they chose to do so. As the sun rose that morning, the SWAT team escorted Mr. Ashcroft through a back gate to meet with victims and survivors.

I joined a handful of security personnel in the Tactical Operations Center (TOC) about 6:45 a.m., where a small TV and dedicated phone line to Terre Haute were waiting. At 7:15, the TOC's phone rang and a voice on the other end confirmed McVeigh was dead. That's one terrorist who would never kill again.

On June 4, 1998, Terry Nichols's nine-week federal trial resulted in his conviction for conspiracy to use a Weapon of Mass Destruction (WMD) and eight counts of involuntary manslaughter, accounting for the eight federal Agents killed in the bombing. He was sentenced to spend the rest of his life in Supermax prison. After the federal conviction, the State of Oklahoma charged him with murdering the other 160 victims and a fetus. In 2004, he was convicted in state court and sentenced to 161 consecutive life sentences.

SEVEN

Fidelity Assurance

The FBI was evolving as the prospect of terrorism grew. There was a finite number of Agents to work both the increasing threat of domestic and international terrorism and the more traditional crimes that had been the Bureau's bread and butter. CIRG wanted SABTs to work counterterrorism, while the Financial Crimes Unit wanted accountants to work white-collar violations. I had a hand in both worlds.

After the OKBOMB trials I opened a large international money laundering case focusing on Fidelity Assurance and Casualty Company (FAC). FAC was licensed as an insurance company in the Turks and Caicos Islands, but its U.S. headquarters were in a strip mall in the small town of Enid, Oklahoma. The company raked in tens of millions of dollars in insurance premiums from clients across the country, but rarely paid any claims. Policyholders with legitimate claims became angry and filed complaints with their state's commissioner of insurance. As pressure mounted, FAC filed for Chapter 11 bankruptcy.

The rules of Chapter 11 are designed to keep creditors at bay while allowing a company an opportunity to reorganize its own affairs as a "debtor in possession." Under these rules, a judge was responsible for overseeing FAC's reorganization by approving expenses and reviewing financial data. FAC used Chapter 11 to buy time and launder its illicit cash through a labyrinth of corporate shells and elaborate accounting schemes. Any money that wasn't paid to the company principals as "expenses" was ultimately funneled to New Zealand as seed money so the scam could be reborn there.

The bankruptcy court grew suspicious and appointed an external trustee who, after a cursory financial review, immediately filed a bankruptcy fraud complaint with the FBI. I met the trustee and her forensic accountants in San Francisco and reviewed their stunning findings. Although FAC's records made it appear the company was rebounding, all its assets were gone. In fact, the company had been insolvent long before it filed for bankruptcy.

Predictably, a number of states began filing civil suits against FAC; the most vociferous was California's Department of Insurance. FAC executives reluctantly agreed to be deposed by California's insurance commissioner and provided statements under oath. They seemingly complied with document requests, but most of the information provided was useless. The commissioner's investigators pored over thousands of financial records as more funds were laundered through accounts in the Caribbean and South America.

FAC's CPA, Kerry Castle, provided a tranche of raw data to substantiate FAC's financial statements. Most of the reported assets appeared to be managed by a Caribbean stockbroker named Niles Allread. In response to a request from the California insurance commissioner, Allread provided letters summarizing FAC's offshore holdings, but failed to provide any objective documentation.

My investigation revealed Allread was actually a stockbroker with an established firm in the Netherlands Antilles. Similarly, Castle was a CPA in Arizona, but he'd been stripped of his license to practice. As with Spartan Industries, the accountant would hold the key to the case.

MLATs were required to obtain foreign financial records and conduct interviews with bankers and regulatory officials in the Turks and Caicos Islands, Bermuda, Panama, and the Netherlands Antilles. As the MLATs were being drafted, I flew to Arizona in an attempt to flip the CPA.

Agents in Phoenix who'd been surveilling Castle reported he jogged early each morning to beat the desert heat. One Tuesday as the sun was rising, he opened the door to find me on his front porch.

"Good morning, Mr. Castle, I'm with the FBI. Let's talk about your friend Randal Sulley."

His eyes grew big as I continued. "As I understand it, Mr. Sulley is a CPA, a lawyer, and serves as FAC's chief financial officer. You guys have been close friends for years, but didn't he rope you into some shady commercial deal that cost you your CPA license?" Castle just nodded.

"But all of that is just a civil matter. I'm here to discuss a series of federal crimes."

Opening a folder, I began fanning through a stack of documents. "These are all audited financial statements you prepared and signed for FAC which were then given to banks and other financial institutions. The problem is, they're completely fraudulent. Did Sulley talk you into falsifying these records or did you do that on your own?"

He swallowed hard and mulled over his options for several silent seconds. "Perhaps you'd like to come inside. I'll make some coffee."

Castle spent all day and most of the evening explaining the scheme, which confirmed FAC was a complete and total fraud. He recalled one troubling conversation is detail.

"I remember one meeting where Sulley insisted we find some way for FAC to obtain reinsurance. He kept saying if we could just get one of the big international firms to reinsure us, nobody would question our credibility. We'd be golden."

Reinsurance is basically insurance for insurance companies. Sulley knew that U.S. regulations required reinsurers to be financially solvent in order to protect policyholders. So if he could somehow convince a legitimate reinsurer to endorse FAC's operation, it would further the myth of FAC's financial solvency.

"I kept telling Sulley no reinsurer would accept us because we didn't have any real assets. That's when he said he had some Caribbean stockbroker in his pocket. I don't know what Sulley had on him, but this Niles Allread guy was willing to create a fake stock portfolio. I used those fabricated assets to produce audited financial statements which Sulley gave to a reinsurance broker in Bermuda. I never thought it would work, but the broker got us placed with a huge reinsurance company in England."

Sulley's plan was ingenious. Relying on the due diligence of the renowned English reinsurer, states across America authorized FAC to sell insurance throughout the U.S. Of course FAC never intended to pay any claims; they just stonewalled as premiums poured in and were laundered offshore. Their house of cards collapsed when the reinsurer learned of all the civil suits being filed against FAC. Citing the pending litigation, the reinsurance was canceled.

Castle explained, "We rode it as long as we could, but Sulley had an exit strategy: bankruptcy. He told me to file for Chapter 11 and drag it out as long as possible so he could get the rest of the cash offshore."

It was a remarkable story, but the records needed to prove the scheme were purposefully scattered around the world. I flew to Bermuda to question the reinsurance broker, a proper Onion wearing Bermuda shorts, knee socks, blue blazer, and tie. He made his money placing corporate clients with reinsurers for a substantial fee.

It was Friday morning when I arrived at the broker's office accompanied by a Bermuda financial crimes detective; we weren't warmly received. The broker had clearly failed to perform any due diligence before recommending FAC to the British reinsurer and was reluctant to discuss the details. The local detective took the lead and pressed the matter. "Very well, then. This is a court order for all records related to your dealings with FAC. We can expand the investigation if necessary."

In an attempt to stall the inevitable, the broker replied, "I see. Well, our attorneys will need a couple of days to review all this. Give us the weekend and I'll meet you at the hotel Monday. Hamilton Princess, right? We can discuss it then."

There was nothing to do until Monday, so I arranged a SCUBA dive on the wreck of the *Constellation* in the Bermuda Triangle. She sank in 1943 and came to rest atop the *Montana*, which went down a century before. Their commingled cargo, including ornate glass ampules of adrenaline and morphine, served as the inspiration for the novel and movie *The Deep*.

As promised, the broker delivered the documents and agreed to be interviewed Monday morning. With those pieces in place, I flew to the Turks and Caicos Islands to meet with the Commissioner of Insurance. Laws of the islands precluded me from simply interviewing the commissioner; an inquiry had to be conducted by a judge. We all stood in the sweltering courtroom as the judge entered wearing flowing black robes and a white wig in classic English tradition. The protracted proceedings and follow-up interviews took nine days, which allowed time for night dives on the steep coral walls of Providenciales.

The next stop was Kralendijk, the capital of Bonaire in the Netherlands Antilles. After a lengthy interview, Niles Allread agreed to testify to his part of the scheme in return for a guarantee that he wouldn't be prosecuted. Testimony from Allread and Castle, coupled with all the financial documentation, should be sufficient to convince any jury. I returned to Oklahoma and awaited the remaining bank records from Panama and New Zealand.

In the interim I was selected to attend a unique explosives course conducted by another three-letter agency. The training facility's existence was only discussed in hushed whispers and had historically been identified by a generic number. I met a handful of other FBI bomb techs at a small airport on the eastern seaboard, where we loaded our gear into an unmarked van. We drove for hours, winding south through the Great Dismal Swamp before finally leaving the main road about dusk. Armed guards verified our identities and escorted the van into the facility. There were no street signs, no streetlights, and the night sky was obscured by tall cypress trees draped in Spanish moss.

Daybreak offered a better sense of this place that clearly emphasized anonymity. There were no license plates on any of the vehicles, the buildings were nondescript, and the massive explosive ranges were separated by high fences and dense woods so one group couldn't see who was training on the next range. The instructors introduced themselves using innocuous first names like Bob, Jim, or some other alias. After introductions Bob asked, "So you're all FBI Agents with Top Secret clearances? That'll make my job a lot easier; I haven't taught this course in English in a really long time."

The objective was simple: learn about international terrorists' IEDs by building them, detonating them, and examining the remains. Sirens mounted atop telephone poles preceded the detonation of particularly large shots. Multiple blasts from the sirens were inevitably followed by the deep "thump, thump, thump" of successive detonations, their sound muffled by thick foliage. We brought down telecommunications towers by handcrafting powerful cutting charges capable of penetrating steel, repurposed common materials into anti-personnel mines, modified anti-tank weapons, and obliterated armored vehicles with explosively formed penetrators.

This type of training made FAC's offshore banking a little less exciting. But all the international records finally arrived and painted a bleak picture for Sulley and the five other FAC executives. I prepared a Prosecutive Report that explained the case with a step-by-step narrative and an index to the hundreds of financial documents and interviews. It was a complex financial investigation, so the AUSA would need time to assimilate the data and prepare an indictment. That delay allowed me to seize a rare opportunity to attend the British Army School of Ammunition.

Courses at the Felix Centre were designed for British and NATO soldiers. But a highly specialized course was developed for the FBI to leverage the Brits' experience with VBIEDs in Northern Ireland; this was the first class composed solely of FBI bomb techs. We arrived at the installation early Monday morning. Heavily armed guards waved us through the high, louvered gates and directed us to a small building where British Army instructors were waiting. The classroom training was brisk and punctuated with written exams. Once we had an understanding of the Brits' render safe procedures and response philosophies, the next three weeks were spent working problems in a huge Hogan's Alley–style live-fire training site.

Every morning a call would come into our staging area. With scant information, we deployed in fully equipped response trucks to resolve whatever problem awaited us. Each pass/fail scenario unfolded in elaborate cityscapes with apartment buildings and banks, industrial centers, train stations, and farming villages. Role players were randomly injected into the storyline and we had to determine if they were witnesses or terrorists. As my team was conducting the initial assessment of a reported car bomb, two masked men raced toward us in a beat-up Citroën. As they sped past, the passenger tossed a "thunder stick" at our feet, simulating a hand grenade. When the smoke cleared and our ears quit ringing, the instructor strolled over and calmly informed us, "You lads are dead. Don't get too focused on the bomb that was called in; it could just be a come along to bait you. Remember, sometimes you're the target. Ensure the perimeter is secure." Lesson learned.

Each evening the instructors met us in town to recap the day over a warm pint of beer or a little Black Bush whiskey. However, one Thursday evening we were told to stay on post and convene in the officers' mess. Once seated at a long table, the mess hall staff brought out a turkey, dressing, and all the fixings; it was Thanksgiving. Realizing we were away from home on this uniquely American holiday, the commander had his staff research the tradition, right down to the cranberries and pumpkin pie.

Training concluded in late December, so Kelly met me in London for Christmas. We enjoyed an impressive performance of Handel's *Messiah* at St. Paul's Cathedral and had cocktails in the private Yeoman Warders Club at the Tower of London. An old friend was a Beefeater there and invited us for drinks and to witness the Ceremony of the Keys.

For the last 700 years, every evening at 9:52 p.m., the Chief Warder has emerged from Byward Tower carrying a lantern and a giant ring of keys to lock the fortress gates. Escorted by a soldier of the Foot Guards, he ceremoniously moves down Water Lane toward Traitor's Gate. A guard at the Bloody Tower's archway shouts the challenge, "Who goes there?" The appropriate response at the time was "Queen Elizabeth's Keys." The rejoinder came, "Pass Queen Elizabeth's Keys. All's well." When the clock strikes ten, there's a salute to the monarch and a bugler sounds "The Last Post" as the castle falls dark and silent.

The next morning, we boarded the Eurostar for a 186 mph trip beneath the English Channel to Paris. Like London, Paris was dressed for the season. We took a dinner cruise on the Seine, attended a candlelight Christmas service at the American Church in Paris, and toured Notre-Dame; I was happy we saw it before the devastating fire of 2019.

EIGHT

Special Branch

As a new year dawned, a federal grand jury indicted all six FAC executives. Since some of the subjects had supposedly fled the country, arrest warrants were issued. The time-consuming task of tracking them down fell to a fugitive task force, so I began organizing hundreds of trial exhibits and preparing witnesses. Late one evening CIRG called. "Are you available for a TDY? We need you in Trinidad in two days." None of the fugitives had been located and trial prep was going well, so a TDY seemed like a good idea. "Sure, what's in Trinidad?"

Donald Trump had purchased the Miss Universe Pageant, which was a large, high-profile event. The island nation of Trinidad and Tobago was experiencing some political turmoil and lacked sufficient equipment and personnel to manage and mitigate the potential hazards. I landed in Port of Spain where a policeman escorted me through Customs and on to the Chaguaramas Hotel in St. James. A message from the desk clerk read, "Meet Asher at 8:00 AM."

The next morning a tall man with a very deep voice entered the lobby. "Mr. Black? I'm Asher, Special Branch. Please come with me."

Special Branch is the intelligence arm of the Trinidad and Tobago Police Service. We drove downtown for a conference in a small upstairs room; electric fans stirred the thick, hot air as neatly pressed attendants served ice water from silver trays. Government officials, representatives from Special Branch, the army, and police provided intel related to a few political groups that might see the pageant as a platform for mayhem and international media coverage. One particularly violent group had already murdered three Special Branch officers and burned a police station to the ground.

Except for the real threat of a militant uprising, this was an island paradise. Each evening, bars and hors d'oeuvres were set up under white tents for the politicians and VIPs. Steel drum bands played amid palm trees wrapped in thousands of tiny white lights as searchlights crisscrossed the night sky. Security was tight because intelligence reports predicted violent protests, but there were no major issues. The week culminated with Miss Botswana being named Miss Universe beneath a barrage of fireworks.

With that, I was looking forward to a quiet night's rest. However, the Chaguaramas had suddenly been designated as the site for the inaugural ball because a worker at the original site had been electrocuted while installing special effects. I joined Asher in the ballroom as elaborately costumed servers in sparkling body paint served bacon-wrapped bananas, curried chicken, and salmon pâté.

Over the steel drums, Asher leaned in to whisper a message received through his earpiece. "We have a suspicious package at Mr. Trump's hotel downtown." I met one of Asher's men and inspected the package, which was wrapped in brown paper and tightly overwrapped in cellophane. A quick X-ray determined it was just a gift from a local artist.

I returned to Oklahoma Friday night only to learn I was to be in Guam the following Tuesday. That 22-hour trip began with a 4:15 a.m. departure. Still adjusting to the 15-hour time change, I entered a conference room where Navy personnel and other Agents were waiting. The head of the FBI's Guam office addressed the group: "Thanks for coming. We're here to support the South Pacific Games, a precursor to the Olympics. The games are taken very seriously throughout the region and we'll have large numbers of athletes, spectators, and government officials from several nations. Local police are highly trained, but not equipped for multiple or simultaneous IED attacks. The Navy's EOD Detachment is on standby and you'll be working with them."

Each 12-hour shift passed without incident, but there was other work to do. A Navy lieutenant explained that World War II ordnance was commonly unearthed around the island and the Navy was responsible for its disposal. I was invited to assist with the demolition of some small munitions, hand grenades, shape charges, 60 pounds of C4, and a 5-inch naval shell. Once the charge was prepared, we drove out of sight and took cover in a buried concrete bunker. Standing in the doorway, I initiated the shot with a remote firing device. A tremendous detonation instantly shook the ground and sucked the air from the bunker. After ensuring all the ordnance was consumed, the lieutenant offered to show me some of the island's World War II history.

We saw a beached two-man Japanese mini-sub, toured a honeycomb of beachfront defensive tunnels with interlocking gun positions, and trekked through the jungle to the remains of a USMC Corsair that crashed in 1944. But not all the sites were on land; Japanese planes and other artifacts were submerged in Apra Harbor and beyond in the Philippine Sea.

The most interesting SCUBA dive occurred one night inside an extinct volcano; from the dive boat we could see its dark jagged vent in contrast to the sea's white sandy bottom. Once inside the volcano, about 100 feet beneath the surface, the lieutenant signaled to switch off our lights. Even at that depth, faint, fuzzy starlight was visible through the vent above. Switching the lights back on, we descended to 149 feet and glided into the open sea through a massive hole in the steep volcanic wall.

I returned to Oklahoma to learn all six FAC executives were in custody. Five had been arrested by the Bureau's Fugitive Task Force in four different states. The Mexican Federales had arrested Sulley, who was currently fighting extradition from his jail cell.

As we worked through his extradition proceedings, the Legal Attaché in Caracas advised that Niles Allread, FAC's stockbroker and key government witness, was purportedly found dead on a yacht off the coast of Bonaire. The body had been immediately cremated so there were no fingerprints or DNA to prove his identity. All we had was a grainy faxed photo from a Caribbean coroner. The circumstances of his death were suspicious, but beyond my reach and out of my control.

Sulley was eventually extradited and the six defendants stood trial; Castle and I testified for days during the three-week proceeding. It was difficult to keep the jury's interest in such a technical financial case, but all six were convicted even without Allread's testimony. The average sentence was six years in prison and $7 million in restitution.

New Year's Eve 2000, brought fears of a global Y2K computer crash. Some were convinced that complex computer programs written in the 1960s wouldn't interpret the "00" date correctly and would cause widespread failures of financial systems and power grids. Even though the new century wouldn't actually begin until January 2001, people made big plans to ring in this particular new year. Ahmed Ressam's new year's plan was to bomb LAX.

Ressam attended al-Qaeda training camps in Afghanistan and attempted to cross into the U.S. on December 14. Astute border guards at Port Angeles, Washington, thwarted his plan by discovering bomb-making materials in the trunk of his car. Ressam was convicted on terrorism charges in 2001 and, after numerous sentencing issues, sentenced to 37 years in prison. International terrorism was alive and well, but domestic terrorists posed a growing threat.

Some homegrown violent extremists feared what they called the "New World Order." Their theory was the United Nations, or some new totalitarian regime, would gain global dominion and implement an authoritarian one-world government. Their fears were fueled by the creation of global entities like the World Trade Organization (WTO).

Created in 1995, the WTO is a coalition of governments established to negotiate and liberalize international trade. In December 1999, the WTO concluded a conference in Seattle by announcing a series of trade negotiations for the new millennium. This alarmed some extremists, who responded with riots resulting in millions of dollars of damage and injuries to hundreds of police officers and civilians. Those demonstrations were followed in April 2000 by protests in Washington, D.C., at the International Monetary Fund (IMF) and World Bank. The following August saw riots at the Republican National Convention (RNC) in Philadelphia, resulting in injuries, property damage, and some 300 arrests. Threatening rhetoric and violence escalated as various extremist groups became more vocal and cohesive.

Intelligence reports indicated that the Democratic convention, scheduled a few weeks later in Los Angeles, would be even more volatile than the WTO, IMF, and RNC conventions. Many of the extremists that commonly protested throughout the country lived in California, and other more violent groups were concentrated all along the West Coast. To augment LAPD resources, the Bureau supplied analysts, SWAT teams, and 12 SABTs. Upon arrival we received detailed briefings about the ideologies of these groups and the types of weapons they often used. Some protesters were known to siphon out egg yolks and refill the shells with etching acid to throw at police. They also filled spray bottles with urine or gasoline, shot fireworks, threw Molotov cocktails, and used clubs disguised as protest signs.

Obviously there were numerous high-profile politicians at the convention, so we worked closely with the Secret Service and other specialized resources from the Department of Energy (DOE). Due to the heavy traffic and road congestion of LA, helicopters were provided by the U.S. Customs Service to augment fixed and rotary wing aircraft from the California Department of Justice and LAPD. The helicopters were dispatched from the LAPD Academy or from downtown LA, which at that time had the largest elevated aircraft platform in the world.

I was fortunate to be paired with a veteran LAPD bomb tech named Dan. He expected us to be busy since LA averaged 2.5 bomb calls per day when the President and anarchists weren't in town. Over this 10-day TDY, our team alone responded to 45 calls. The most unusual deployment was in Venice, where a bike patrol officer noticed a small car parked on the street. Hidden among assorted military gear, the officer saw yellow blocks marked TNT—DANGEROUS and what appeared to be dynamite.

Two city blocks had been evacuated by the time Dan and I arrived. Military paraphernalia, camouflage netting, camping equipment, TNT, and dynamite were visible through the rear window. There didn't appear to be a fully constructed IED, just bulk explosives. Several documents with telephone numbers were visible through the windows, so we relayed that information to the CP to flesh out. We were advised the car wasn't stolen and was registered to a 22-year-old female with no known criminal history. After assessing the threat and our available equipment, we remotely breached a rear window and began recovering what appeared to be loose blocks of TNT, several sticks of dynamite, a box of electric blasting caps, and some hand grenades. During that process, a perimeter officer reported, "I've got a lady here saying it's her car. She says it's all fake; Hollywood props for some kid's party."

Detectives interviewed the woman and confirmed her company hosted "extreme parties." The previous night she'd thrown a $20,000 GI Joe–themed birthday party for a five-year-old. She rented military equipment including a Humvee for the kids to play on and used movie props like TNT and hand grenades for realism. Only in California.

After the convention I was off to teach a post-blast school in San Juan. It was an opportunity to see old friends, as one buddy was a commander at Rosy Roads Naval Station and five of the Puerto Rican bomb techs had gone through HDS Basic with me. These 40-hour post-blast schools incorporate live IEDs and teach our state and local partners how to process and investigate bombing crime scenes. The course concluded Friday and I returned to Oklahoma, where several bank fraud and money laundering cases awaited. It would be nice to settle into a normal white-collar routine.

Nine

Major Case: PENTTBOM

As I pulled through the outer security gates at my office, a news bulletin reported a plane had crashed into the North Tower of the World Trade Center. It was September 11, 2001. Subsequent reports indicated several planes might have been hijacked. As I entered the Emergency Operations Center (EOC), United Airlines Flight 175 struck the South Tower. Thirty-four minutes later American Airlines Flight 77 flew into the Pentagon, then United Airlines Flight 93 crashed in Shanksville, Pennsylvania.

In every major incident, accurate information is critical and must be filtered through the noise and chaos. One early report stated a car bomb had detonated outside the U.S. State Department; another claimed the U.S. Capitol had been hit. These reports were later attributed to the sonic boom of fighter jets that scrambled to intercept any airborne threats over D.C. Every FBI office implemented its emergency operations plan as national assets swung into action. In an unprecedented move, the FAA ordered all commercial aircraft to land and prohibited any departures. President George W. Bush boarded *Air Force One* and was ushered to a secure facility at an old Strategic Air Command base in Nebraska. He returned to Washington later that day escorted by F-16s.

President Bush later said, "The attack took place on American soil, but it was an attack on the heart and soul of the civilized world. And the world has come together to fight a new and different war, the first, and we hope the only one, of the 21st century. A war against all those who seek to export terror, and a war against those governments that support or shelter them."

America was embroiled in a new type of war: the Global War on Terror. The FBI's New York office was in overdrive and had lost one of their own, Special Agent Bomb Technician Leonard W. Hatton. Lenny was on his way into the office when the first plane struck. A former Marine and volunteer firefighter, he ran toward the danger and, from the roof of a nearby building, reported the second plane striking the South Tower. As debris rained down, Lenny helped FDNY evacuate occupants and was inside the World Trade Center when the buildings collapsed. He was a good man and is missed.

I was ordered to be in New York City no later than September 30. Commercial planes were flying again, but most carriers had drastically reduced the number of flights. As usual I was flying armed, so after reviewing the required paperwork, a flight attendant introduced me to the captain. It's usually a quick and informal conversation, but this time was different. The captain emerged from the cockpit and shared his new personal policy. "You have my authority and permission to take whatever action you deem necessary at any time while aboard this aircraft. It's now my practice to put any armed law enforcement passenger as close to the cockpit as possible."

A hush fell over the plane as we approached LaGuardia. The Statue of Liberty stood before a skyline that was forever changed; a veil of smoke still hung over the Financial District. The only word spoken came from the man seated next to me, who breathed a barely audible "Unbelievable."

Night operations at Ground Zero of the World Trade Center (October 10, 2001).

It was a cold, misty afternoon and the streets were eerily empty. American flags were defiantly displayed everywhere, balconies and overpasses were draped in patriotic bunting, and the Empire State Building was illuminated in red, white, and blue. With no traffic, it only took 20 minutes to transit the Midtown Tunnel and arrive at the designated hotel near Times Square. The desk clerk handed me a folded note which read, "You'll be working 12-hour shifts beginning at 8:00 tonight. Report to the CP at 26th and Westside Drive."

A cavernous warehouse had been hastily converted into a maze of electronics that was roiling with activity. There were miles of computer cables, satellite equipment, and secure communications gear, not to mention hundreds of people working around the clock. Each intersection surrounding the building was blocked by dump trucks filled with sand and flanked by SWAT teams. It was all too reminiscent of the first CP established in Oklahoma City on that clear April morning six years before.

On foot, I followed the Hudson River a few blocks south toward Ground Zero and entered the Winter Garden Atrium from the river side. The facade seemed nearly intact, but the Royal Palms and lush vegetation inside were covered in a fine powdery dust. I stood alone in that massive space, looking out onto an apocalyptic scene. The entire east end of the atrium had been torn away, leaving a gaping hole that exposed a hellscape. The sheer magnitude was overwhelming, more than 14 acres of complete destruction.

The metal skeletons of the Twin Towers loomed several stories high in places, standing watch over contorted, smoldering debris that held the remains of hundreds of victims. The surrounding buildings bore their own scars; an entire corner of one building looked as if it had been shaved off with a knife. Shattered windows and buildings blackened by the inferno were visible in every direction. The sounds of jackhammers and heavy equipment, coupled with the smell of diesel fuel, concrete dust, and smoke, conspired to dredge up memories of Waco and Oklahoma City that were all too vivid.

The gravity and scale of this tragedy took its toll on everyone. When not working at the CP or Ground Zero, I supported the NYPD bomb squad and Emergency Services Unit on calls throughout the city. The pace of the work made my 12-hour night shifts pass quickly, but the off-hours were troublesome as sleep didn't come easy. I often spent the day walking around the city; exercise and fresh air helped stem the fatigue and occupy my mind with things other than the carnage of

The search for remains and evidence continued as Ground Zero smoldered (October 1, 2001).

Ground Zero. One afternoon as I walked across the Brooklyn Bridge, a plume of black smoke suddenly rose from the site; another hot spot had been uncovered by the heavy equipment. The Trade Center housed several subterranean floors and as excavation fed oxygen to the smoldering debris, fires erupted and produced that deep black smoke.

New York remained in a state of heightened security with Coast Guard cutters stationed in the Hudson River between Battery Park and the Financial Center, and in the East River near the United Nations Building. Rigid-hull inflatable boats (RIBs) sporting M-60 machine guns patrolled the waters between the larger vessels.

Standing at Ground Zero, it was astonishing to think that 2,763 of the 2,996 people killed on 9/11 died right there. Sadly, by October 6, FEMA no longer considered this a rescue effort. The deceased were systematically recovered using methods all too similar to the recovery of those Koresh left to die in Waco and the innocent lives taken in Oklahoma City.

Diversion was necessary to avoid just sitting in a hotel room dwelling on the horror and waiting for the next shift. One day I walked to Duane St. to visit FDNY Engine Company 7, where a firefighter named Tom shared his incredible story. He arrived at the Trade Center just after the first impact and stood in horror as the second plane struck.

He estimated 20 people leapt to their deaths to escape the inferno; their bodies landed on the sidewalk all around him. He recalled jets of flame blowing out the lobby glass and critically burned victims pouring into the street right in front of him.

About 10:00 a.m. he thought a bomb had gone off, but it was the sound of the South Tower crumbling. Wearing 75 pounds of gear, he couldn't outrun the wave of rubble, so he sought shelter with other firefighters behind the concrete columns of the North Bridge. A billowing cloud of dust and smoke choked out the light and debris hammered the pillar as intense heat engulfed them. Debris caught in the tempest burst into flames, starting secondary fires as far as four blocks away. Their radios were jammed with frantic traffic and they couldn't see anything, so they followed a voice calling them to safety from across the street. The fire engine he'd driven that morning was crushed under tons of rubble and his Battalion lost 25 men. Stories like his were repeated hundreds of times.

Having walked 40 blocks that day, I hailed a cab back to Midtown. The cabbie's radio and the giant screens of Times Square announced the U.S. had launched air strikes in Afghanistan; America was fighting back in a new kind of war. It wasn't going to be just a military campaign; economic, diplomatic, and criminal investigative means would be laser focused to bring justice to those responsible. On October 10, the Bureau built upon the success of its Top Ten Most Wanted list by introducing the Most Wanted Terrorists list. Once Osama bin Laden met justice a decade later, I was presented with a copy of his Most Wanted Terrorist poster stamped with the word "DECEASED" in bold red lettering.

The worldwide investigation grew as tens of millions of tainted funds were frozen and foreign nationals associated with the attacks were tracked down around the globe. But back home, heroic men and women continued the grueling task of processing the sites in New York, D.C., and Shanksville. One million tons of debris was removed from Ground Zero in just eight months. It was trucked up Riverside Drive then ferried on barges to Staten Island where victims' remains, personal belongings, and evidence could be recovered. Teams tirelessly raked and sifted the wreckage for clues, knowing that evidence can survive even an inferno like this. The Saudi Arabian passport of Satam al-Suqami, who took over American Flight 11, and the Saudi driver's license of Ahmad Saleh Said Alghamdi from United Flight 175 were recovered in the charred debris.

The same grim tasks were undertaken near the Pentagon, where American Flight 77 killed 125 people on the ground and 59 aboard the plane. Painstaking evidence collection at that scene recovered ID cards for two terrorists, Majed Moqed and Salem Alhazmi.

By all accounts, passengers aboard United Flight 93 learned of the other suicidal attacks and took heroic action. Ultimately the plane slammed into the ground in Somerset County, Pennsylvania. There were no survivors. Passports and IDs of three terrorists, Ahmed al-Nami, Saeed Alighamdi, and Ziad Jarrah, were recovered in the wreckage. The tedious, heartbreaking work at that site also recovered a letter written in Arabic containing instructions for the hijackers. The same four-page handwritten letter was recovered from a car left at Dulles International Airport by Nawaf al-Haznawi before he boarded American Flight 77. Mohammed Atta also had a copy in his suitcase; that bag didn't get transferred when he changed flights in Boston to board American Flight 11 (Kean 2024).

Mass disasters are emotionally draining, and it's helpful to be around people with similar experiences. One evening I joined a few of New York's ERT for dinner away from the site for a little diversion, but there was no escaping the sorrow that surrounded us. As we ordered, eight police motorcycles sped by in a spray of red and blue light, followed by an ambulance and a state trooper. This scene was replayed every time the body of a firefighter or police officer was transferred to the morgue.

Dinner conversation inevitably turned to personal stories which were almost identical to those from the Murrah Building. In the long overnight hours, some people wanted to talk about their experience but didn't know what to say.

One Agent asked, "So what could a blast like that do in a tunnel?"

As we talked, she began reliving her story in vivid detail; the things she saw, heard, and felt. She was in the subway beneath the Towers when the first plane struck and wondered just how close she'd come to death. Another Agent described coming up from the subway as the second tower was struck. He was nearly hit by the body of a man who'd jumped to his death escaping the flames. Often there's nothing to say, but it's important to listen and empathize with an understanding that comes from shared experience.

As I entered the hotel that morning the desk clerk motioned to me. "Mr. Black, I have a package for you."

It was a box containing letters and drawings from a fifth grade

Sunday school class back in Oklahoma; Kelly had given them the hotel's address. The simple messages were written in crayon and read, "America the Beautiful," "Thank You," or depicted the American flag.

A second stack of notes was tied with a red ribbon and came with instructions which read, "Please deliver to the rescue workers." That night at Ground Zero a group of exhausted recovery workers were taking a break near their heavy equipment. I distributed the notes and watched every eye well up with tears.

The site took on a surreal appearance at night. Oblique lighting from cranes and light towers cast odd shadows on a field of smoldering debris; the twisted skeletons of the Twin Towers still reached skyward. It was midnight when I arrived at the CP for a briefing and ERT shift change; there was a large crowd in the warehouse. When the meeting concluded, the team leader rolled in a cake and the group began singing. It was my 38th birthday. I'm not sure how they knew, but we all wanted to celebrate something in such a dark time.

Within a few weeks, the emergency response phase abated and the CP moved closer to the Bureau's office at 26 Fed. But suddenly a new threat emerged: anthrax. In mid–October, letters laden with weaponized anthrax were sent to U.S. Senators Patrick Leahy and Thomas Daschle in D.C. and news agencies in Florida and New York, including the NBC studio just steps from my Manhattan hotel. This deadly biological attack spawned the FBI's next major case, known as Amerithrax.

The Amerithrax Task Force expended more than 600,000 man-hours. Over 10,000 witnesses were interviewed across six continents, 80 sites were searched, and more than 6,000 items of evidence were seized. The FBI Lab developed new advanced genetic testing that linked the anthrax in the letters to a specific spore-batch developed and maintained by Dr. Bruce Ivins at the U.S. Army Medical Research Institute of Infectious Diseases (USAMRIID). After several interviews with Dr. Ivins, searches were conducted of his residence and USAMRIID office where incriminating evidence was discovered. Dr. Ivins took his own life before charges could be filed (FBI 2016a).

Just three months after the 9/11 attacks, Richard Reid smuggled an IED aboard American Airlines Flight 63 from Paris to Miami. Fortunately, passengers subdued him as he attempted to detonate a bomb concealed in his shoe. Like the heroes of Flight 93, the passengers averted a much wider tragedy. Reid pled guilty to eight terrorism related charges and was sentenced to life in Supermax with the likes of Eric Rudolph and Terry Nichols (FBI 2020).

My TDY in New York concluded, but PENTTBOM (the major case name for 9/11) was far from over. Leads continued to span the globe, and one was very close to home (FBI 2016b).

Zacarias Moussaoui, known to some as the 20th hijacker, was born in France in 1968. While he was in his 20s, French authorities became concerned about his association with Islamic extremists; by 1998 he was training at an al-Qaeda camp in Afghanistan. In 2001, he arrived in America and found his way to Norman, Oklahoma, where he enrolled in a beginner pilot course at Airman Flight School. This was the same flight school visited by two 9/11 hijackers just six months before.

Moussaoui didn't complete the course in Norman. But just one month before 9/11, he enrolled in a 747 simulator course designed for experienced commercial pilots at a flight school in Minneapolis. Within a matter of days, his flight instructor notified the FBI; he found it odd that Moussaoui paid in cash, had no flight experience, and was only interested in learning to take off and land a 747.

The FBI office in Minneapolis opened an investigation and learned Moussaoui had illegally overstayed his visa. In conjunction with Immigration Agents, he was arrested the next day with two knives, a money belt full of cash, and flight training materials. Unable to explain the source of $32,000 in his bank account or provide a reason for wanting to fly a 747, he was detained for the visa violation and subject to expedited deportation. As Agents were finalizing his deportation plan, the first plane struck the World Trade Center (Office of Inspector General 2006).

Exactly three months after 9/11, Moussaoui was indicted on six counts of conspiracy associated with the attacks. During years of ensuing legal delays, he claimed to be part of a second wave that would target America. That statement was supported to some degree by statements of the 9/11 "mastermind" Khalid Sheikh Mohammed, who saw Moussaoui as a participant in follow-up attacks (UMKC 2003).

A federal judge accepted Moussaoui's guilty plea in 2005, and the following year he was sentenced to life in Supermax. As he was being taken away Moussaoui declared, "God save Osama bin Laden—you will never get him" (Malone 2009). Of course he was wrong; Navy SEALs killed bin Laden in 2011.

The stress and pressure first responders face while working these types of high-profile investigations often produce intangible psychological effects that shouldn't be overlooked or diminished. But other effects are physical and can be deadly. World Trade Center Health Program

(WTCHP) records indicate that more than 63,000 first responders, recovery, and cleanup workers have been diagnosed with illnesses related to their 9/11 response (Shelby 2025). Over 23,000 responders have been certified with cancer attributed to those toxic environments (Centers for Disease Control and Prevention 2025). Eight years after returning from New York, I was diagnosed with an extremely rare form of cancer that was directly tied to my time at Ground Zero. It took three pathologists to identify the tumor, as it represented only 0.05 percent of all known cancers. I'm grateful for the medical team that successfully removed the tumor in a delicate six-hour procedure. But many first responders weren't as fortunate.

The WTCHP records reveal more survivors and first responders have died from health-related conditions than were killed in the actual attacks. Though the list will undoubtedly grow, the FBI has lost 28 of our own because of 9/11, including several of my friends.

TEN

The Million-Dollar Deal

The year 2001 had been dreadful and deadly and the 2002 Winter Olympics were on the horizon. The prospect of another terror attack like Munich or Atlanta played heavily into the security posture for venues in Salt Lake City. As a result, the Olympics were designated as a National Security Special Event for the first time. In accordance with a new Presidential directive, the FBI became responsible for crisis response, while the U.S. Secret Service would be in charge of physical security at all Olympic sites. This joint responsibility came with growing pains as there were operational and logistical questions related to armed FBI Agents conducting explosive render safe missions within a secure Secret Service perimeter. The protocols developed in Salt Lake City served as a model for future joint operations.

The International Olympic Committee (IOC) realized the state of Utah didn't have enough law enforcement personnel to staff an event of this scale, given the heightened global security concerns. In an unprecedented solution, local police from across the country were hired by the IOC to supplement Utah's existing law enforcement. Officers took six weeks off from their respective departments and were deputized as part of the Utah Olympic Public Safety Command. Two local bomb techs from Colorado joined my team, which was assigned to the small resort towns of the Wasatch Back. We received mountain rescue training and were provided with snowmobiles to access the remote regions. Our main area of responsibility covered the venues of Park City, Soldier Hollow, and the athletes' Olympic Village. Except for some routine suspicious package calls, the six-week assignment concluded without incident.

I returned from Salt Lake City to a new bank fraud case. It centered on a flamboyant man named Gary Anderson who lived in a mansion outside Aspen, Colorado. He owned a bank in Oklahoma City, which is what brought him to the FBI's attention. Once a wealthy man, he'd squandered his fortune and was now solely dependent on dividend income generated from his bank. As the supermajority shareholder, he typically took 90 percent of the bank's profits as dividends for himself.

When visiting Oklahoma, ostensibly on bank business, Anderson spent his time with Joel McNeil, a low-level drug dealer with a string of strippers who were eager to keep the banker company. In return, Anderson personally approved unsecured loans for the girls, which of course were never repaid. The scheme went unnoticed until a diligent bank examiner began asking questions. Under the examiner's scrutiny, Anderson's access to bank funds was curtailed and he filed personal bankruptcy. Desperate for cash, his only hope was to artificially inflate the bank's profits in order to increase his dividend income.

His most elaborate scheme involved a complex real estate shell game. Anderson learned that the state intended to buy some rural farmland as part of a turnpike expansion. His bankruptcy prevented him from buying the land personally, so he conspired to have the bank buy it. The plan was simple: buy it cheap, sell it to the state for an inflated price, then reap dividends from the sale. However, banks can't buy land speculatively, so he enlisted the help of his old friend McNeil.

McNeil was to apply for a $750,000 loan at Anderson's bank. He would use that money to buy the land, listing the property as collateral. There was no way McNeil would qualify for such a loan, so Anderson would ramrod it through the loan committee, a group that owed their jobs to him. Once McNeil purchased the property, he would immediately default on the loan. The bank would foreclose, take title to the land, and sell it to the state for a huge profit, thereby increasing the bank's income, which benefited Anderson as dividends.

But Anderson didn't count on the courage of the loan committee. They might have turned a blind eye to some of Anderson's prior conduct, but loaning McNeil three-quarters of a million dollars was a bridge too far. Confident Anderson couldn't fire them all at once, McNeil's application was denied in a rowdy and contentious loan committee meeting.

But Anderson wasn't deterred; he just needed a better shill. McNeil had an idea. "Look, I know this guy in the payday loan business. I owe him a lot of money and there's no way I can repay him. He's a CPA who looks great on paper, so the loan committee will approve him. Let's cut him in on the land deal and get me off the hook at the same time."

Oscar Owsley didn't mind bending a few rules to get his money from McNeil. After a brief introduction, Anderson laid it all out. "You know I own a bank. I want you to apply for a personal $750,000 line of credit; say you need the money to buy some land for a housing development. Once you get approved, start submitting invoices for materials or something to make it look like you're building out there; I'll approve the draws myself. After you've recovered the money McNeil owes you, just walk away. The bank will foreclose on the land and you won't owe a thing."

Owsley agreed and Anderson fast-tracked his application. Once the line of credit was approved, Owsley created a paper company called Helena Land Development (HLD) and McNeil opened a front company called the Shelby Company; they wanted company names on the documents to hide their personal involvement from casual observers.

In a bizarre third-party double-escrow closing, Shelby Co. bought the land for $300,000 using funds that actually came from Owsley's line of credit. HLD immediately "bought" the land from Shelby using nothing more than a $1,000,000 promissory note secured by the property. Shelby then sold the $1,000,000 note to the bank for $10,000 in cash, which was McNeil's payment for participating in the scheme. Anderson entered the promissory note on the bank's books at face value, believing it would increase the bank's income by $1,000,000, thereby increasing his dividend.

As planned, Owsley began submitting false monthly invoices against the line of credit, which Anderson personally approved. The plan was working until the bank's Board of Directors, in an unprecedented move, fired Anderson. With Anderson gone, the bank discovered that all of Owsley's invoices were fraudulent. When confronted, Owsley claimed Anderson had somehow defrauded him. That's when the bank called the FBI.

After an extensive investigation, Owsley flipped as a government witness, resulting in an indictment against Anderson and McNeil. Anderson was arrested at his mansion in Colorado, but McNeil fled. Within days, I located him in a cheap airport motel registered under a woman's name. At their initial court appearance, McNeil was detained as a flight risk, but Anderson was released on bond.

To elongate Anderson's freedom, his attorney, Leland Kaufman, filed a motion for a six-month continuance. "Your Honor, there are over 5,000 financial documents to review. This delay is necessary to ensure my client receives a vigorous defense." Recognizing the complexities of the case, the judge granted the continuance.

Trial began the following January with the judge asking, "Mr. Kaufman, where is your client?"

Sheepishly, Kaufman replied, "Your Honor, he must have had some difficulty flying back from … Hawaii."

McNeil flew into a rage when he realized Anderson had been on the beach while he sat in jail. Displeased, the judge issued a bench warrant for Anderson's arrest and within hours a Deputy U.S. Marshal called me.

"Well, we got him when he deplaned. He supposedly forgot to reset his watch from island time. The judge set a hearing for 3:30 this afternoon and Anderson will be there in handcuffs."

Over McNeil's profane outburst, Kaufman opened the hearing with a bombshell. "Your Honor, it's my duty to advise the court that Mr. McNeil's attorney has a significant conflict of interest and should be removed."

Forcing McNeil to get a new attorney would inevitably postpone the trial and result in Anderson remaining free on bond.

"It has come to my attention that Mr. Elmore, counsel for the defense, has sued his own client and even filed a victim's protection order [VPO] against him. Such animus may raise the argument of ineffective counsel. Additionally, my investigator discovered Mr. Elmore had a business relationship with one of the government's witnesses which may impact his ability to cross examine that witness."

Looking at McNeil's attorney, the judge demanded, "Well, Mr. Elmore, what say you?"

Yes, Elmore had sued McNeil civilly, but the suit had been settled. He had petitioned for a VPO, but never pursued it. He once had a business relationship with a witness, but the company in question was now defunct. However, concerned over potential appellate issues, the judge removed Elmore, which elicited a string of profanity from McNeil.

"I won't rot in jail while Anderson is out on bond. I'll represent myself and insist on a speedy trial."

He had a right to represent himself, but the judge had to ensure the defense would be effective. A public defender was assigned as co-counsel, and her first move was to ship McNeil off for a psychiatric evaluation. Due to his extremely violent nature, he spent the next year in solitary confinement until doctors finally concluded he was mentally incompetent to stand trial. Given that diagnosis, the charges against him were dropped.

Anderson now faced a litany of charges alone: bank fraud,

misapplication of bank funds, and falsifying bank records. It was a very technical financial case that required the government to prove Anderson's unique knowledge of the banking industry and his intent to defraud. Twenty-eight witnesses, including forensic accountants, testified for seven days before Anderson took the stand as the only defense witness. For two days he smugly insisted every government witness was wrong and the jury just didn't understand the complexities of the transactions.

But the jury wasn't fooled. After only three hours of deliberation the bailiff appeared and announced, "They have a verdict."

Anderson's superior demeanor vanished as the jury foreman announced, "We find the defendant guilty on all counts." He was later sentenced to eight years in federal prison and $200,000 in restitution.

It wasn't uncommon for me to manage several financial cases at once. As Anderson's trial was underway, the Secret Service provided information about a group that was defrauding banks with counterfeit cashier's checks. A legitimate cashier's check is guaranteed by the issuing bank, so other institutions honor them as cash. In this scheme, a low-level player would open a new bank account using a false identity. After a few small cash deposits, they deposited a large cashier's check ostensibly drawn on another bank. Their account was instantly credited for the entire amount, which they subsequently withdrew. The MICR encoding and other security features embedded in the fake checks passed scrutiny at the local bank, but couldn't fool the verification processes at the Federal Reserve System. By the time the checks were returned, the money was gone.

This particular crew was responsible for passing nearly $10,000,000 in worthless checks. I traced the proceeds through accounts in Oklahoma, Texas, Louisiana, and California, and ultimately to an extensive drug operation. Physical and electronic surveillance of the group revealed LeBron Beck was producing the checks. Armed with some very compelling evidence, I interviewed him with a Secret Service agent. The interview started as expected with him saying, "Look, I don't know what you're talking about. I don't know anything about any counterfeit checks."

I nodded to the Secret Service agent, who pressed the play button on a digital recorder. We had wiretapped his phones and queued up a particularly damning conversation where he and some unknown woman were discussing the scheme in detail. Beck's demeanor changed instantly. "All right, yeah. I created the checks. But that's all I know.

This girl named Erin calls the shots; that's her on the tape. I don't know anything else about her, but you can take my computer, or whatever. Everything's on there; all the checks, everything."

The mystery woman was identified as Erin Copeland, a con artist and drug dealer well known to local police. Most recently she'd stolen the identity of a woman in Wisconsin and used it to finance a $59,000 Lexus. One afternoon a local District Attorney called. "I hear you have a federal case on Erin Copeland; do you know where she is? We got her a couple of weeks ago in a hand-to-hand crack deal with an undercover cop, but she took off when the arrest team moved in."

"Was she driving a new Lexus?"

"Yeah. During the pursuit she threw the bait money out the window and crashed into a phone pole. We arrested her, but she got bailed out and now she's gone. Think you could open a UFAP?"

Unlawful Flight to Avoid Prosecution (UFAP) is a federal crime that allows federal agents to track down local fugitives. My AUSA was still preparing the bank fraud indictment, so a UFAP charge would expedite Copeland's arrest.

Armed with the UFAP warrant, the FBI Fugitive Task Force almost caught her in Little Rock when she stabbed her boyfriend, mistaking him for an informant. Neighbors had called 911, but she vanished before local police arrived. As the Task Force investigated the stabbing, they discovered several documents and a photo ID in the name of Sheri Delavan, Copeland's latest alias. Investigation determined Sheri Delavan was currently running an elaborate investment scam at a hotel in Baton Rouge.

An astute detective, Claude Benoît, attended one of Delavan's investment seminars at a Baton Rouge Holiday Inn. "Ms. Delavan, I've been listenin' to your proposal and I'm afraid I have a few questions. My name is Detective Benoît. Let's begin with your ID, please."

She gave him a California driver's license with her picture, but a different name. "Who's Sheri Newell?" Benoît asked.

"Oh, yeah. Sheri is my middle name. I go by that sometimes and Newell is my maiden name. I just got married and haven't had time to get a new license."

Benoît ran the name and found Sheri Newell was wanted for bogus checks in New Orleans. Seeming stunned by that news, she exclaimed, "Bogus checks? That's not me; there's some mistake. I'll show you my passport, it's in my associate's car. I'll run right outside and get it."

"Of course, I'll just walk with you."

As they walked through the conference center Delavan burst into tears, pleading, "Detective, can I please have a minute in the ladies' room? This is all so embarrassing."

Suspicious, Benoît stood outside the door, not realizing there were multiple restroom exits. Delavan bolted down the hall and made her way to the parking lot where she sped away in her partner's Jaguar. Benoît stormed back into the ballroom. "You! Was that your green Jag in the parking lot?"

Feigning surprise, Delavan's partner gasped, "Yes, why? What's happening?"

"I've been sittin' here for days listenin' to y'all talk people out of their money. I believe you gave that woman your keys so she could abscond. In my book, that's aidin' and abettin' and somebody's fixin' to go to jail. However, if you didn't authorize her to use your vehicle, then maybe we can help each other."

Sensing an opportunity, the partner said, "Um no, no. I didn't authorize anybody to use my car. She stole it and I want to help you get it back."

With that, Benoît used the Jag's InControl tracking feature to locate Delavan. She was in West Feliciana Parish when the local sheriff arrested her. That night her crew tried to bail her out, but the jailer thought something was odd and called Benoît at home.

"No, I'm glad you called. Don't let her go. We need to talk to the judge first 'cause I'm not sure who she really is. Let's wait 'til we get somethin' back from the FBI."

When Delavan was arrested, her fingerprints were sent electronically to the FBI's Criminal Justice Information Center (CJIS), where she was positively identified as Erin Copeland. CJIS called me at 1:00 a.m. advising Copeland was sitting in the West Feliciana Parish jail under the name Sheri Delavan aka Sheri Newell. I placed a federal hold on her so she didn't slip away again, and within 48 hours she was on the U.S. Marshals jet known as "Con Air" for a free flight back to Oklahoma City.

The UFAP charge was dropped in favor of a multimillion-dollar federal indictment. Arrest warrants were issued for the remaining subjects, including Copeland's brother who was quickly arrested hiding in his invalid grandmother's basement. He provided the location of his old college roommate who was arrested next. The last fugitive was arrested in Dallas, living under his deceased father's name. All three pled guilty and agreed to testify against Copeland. Facing overwhelming evidence, she pled guilty four days later and was sentenced to 12 years in prison and $500,000 in restitution.

Eleven

Mother of Satan

The Anchorage Police Bomb Squad celebrated its 30th anniversary by hosting a counter–IED summit. Seventeen hours of daylight offered plenty of time to demonstrate the newest explosive render safe tools and still hike Matanuska Glacier or ski the bowls of Alyeska. One evening, the class was debriefing in a local bar when the news reported three time bombs had detonated at a police station in Athens, Greece. This was newsworthy because the Olympics were to open there in exactly 100 days.

Greece had its share of anarchists and terrorists, with the 17 November group being the most notorious. In anticipation of the 2004 Olympics, 17N was eradicated only to be replaced by a new terrorist cell called Revolutionary Struggle. Since its emergence in 2003, this group had conducted several terror attacks on Greek and Western interests to include bombing a judicial center with time bombs like those just used at the police station (Voice of America 2009).

I met a team of about 100 Agents and scientists at a cargo terminal near Dulles and loaded a chartered 737. We'd been assigned to assist Greek authorities at the Olympics. After refueling in Iceland, it was a six-hour flight to Athens, where buses took us to the embassy. The Legal Attaché assigned four SABTs to the Hellenic National Police in the north and four to the Hellenic Coast Guard (HCG) in the south.

My team arrived at the Port of Piraeus to meet HCG commander, Ioannis Angeledes. The men of Strike Team Zeus welcomed us and provided a comprehensive tour of the port and its enhanced Olympic security features. The facility was an attractive target as 13 cruise ships were docked there to serve as floating hotels for Olympic athletes and officials. Anti-intrusion barriers were stretched across the mouth of the harbor and layers of technical security such as chemical sniffers, radiation detectors, and encrypted communications were installed. Blimps with high-resolution cameras remained overhead as the Coast Guard and Navy patrolled the sea. For 10- to 12-hour shifts, we integrated with HCG teams aboard their vessels, or staffed the southern Olympic venues.

One night Ioannis said, "You've been working many long shifts, but you can't be in Greece for six weeks and only work. We'll make sure you see our country. Do you SCUBA? My friends are former Marines and they now have a dive shop; we'll dive together." As our schedule allowed, we explored World War II shipwrecks in the Aegean Sea and toured ancient sites from Cape Sounion to Delphi.

One evening I was sitting in the ancient Panathenaic Stadium at the finish line for the gold medal marathon event. The race began in the village of Marathon and traced the route Pheidippides took to announce the Athenians' defeat of the Persians in 490 BC. As runners entered the white marble stadium, a man next to me began railing about all the police in the venue. He had no idea who I was when he demanded, "Why do we need all this security?"

As if on cue, some lunatic jumped onto the track and tried to grab one of the runners, but was immediately mobbed by Greek police.

I said wryly, "Maybe that's why there's so much security."

The Games concluded with no major incidents, perhaps due to the $1.5 billion spent on security and the 70,000 Greek police and military personnel assigned to the mission (NBCNews.com 2004). After the elaborate closing ceremonies, we bid farewell to our Greek partners and boarded the plane at 4:30 a.m. for the 25-hour trip back home.

Improvised explosives, often referred to as homemade explosives (HME), are commonly used by terrorists and criminals. The 1993 World Trade Center bombers manufactured urea nitrate in an apartment complex; McVeigh and Nichols mixed ANFO at a state park. These types of bulk explosives are relatively insensitive and require the explosive shock of a booster to make them detonate. A booster is a more sensitive high explosive that can detonate with just the explosive force of a blasting cap.

Blasting caps, also known as initiators or detonators, incorporate small quantities of very sensitive and powerful primary explosives which serve as the first step in an "explosive train"; detonator to booster, then booster to main charge. It's a dangerous undertaking, but detonators can be improvised just like main charges. Ted Kaczynski, the Unabomber, created detonators in his remote Montana cabin.

One particularly dangerous and powerful HME used in detonators is triacetone triperoxide. Known as TATP, it's exceptionally volatile, easy to produce with common household chemicals, and possesses roughly 80 percent of the power of TNT. Discovered in 1895, it had no practical application due to its extreme instability. However, terrorists like it because it makes excellent detonators; just a few grams can initiate much larger IEDs.

But that power comes with a price. Many terrorists have died manufacturing or mishandling TATP, which has earned it the name "Mother of Satan." Its first reported use was in a 1980 terrorist attack in Israel. Until then it was thought to be too unstable for use in IEDs, but that attack proved terrorists were undeterred and the trend continued.

Over time this highly sensitive white crystalline powder began to be used in larger quantities. A series of bombings in Paris used TATP in suicide belts. A few months later, suitcases laden with TATP detonated in Brussels. Those explosions led investigators to a bomb factory where 33 pounds of TATP was recovered along with an ISIS flag.

Clearly this unstable compound had advantages for terrorists. It was difficult to detect with current screening technology, it's extremely powerful, and it's relatively simple to synthesize with inexpensive precursors that are readily available. The intelligence community anticipated its use would increase, and that assessment was borne out on July 7, 2005. Four coordinated attacks targeted London's transit system: 56 people were killed and 775 injured. British authorities discovered TATP in a bomb factory in Leeds. The Mother of Satan was moving west. Thankfully, awareness, training, and evolving technology have made TATP less of an enigma.

After 9/11, terrorists redefined acceptable targets. Airports became harder targets so they shifted to more vulnerable sites like shopping malls, concert halls, public transit, and sporting events. When a bomb detonated at a University of Oklahoma football game 12 weeks after the London attack, it was immediately presumed to be terrorism.

The detonation thundered over the din of 82,000 fans, including the governor and other VIPs. The venue fit the new terrorist targeting parameters: large public event, onsite media coverage, and high-profile attendees. The location of the blast indicated prior planning; it detonated on the west side of the stadium seven minutes before halftime. A well-known practice for this particular stadium allowed spectators to leave at halftime and congregate along the west side for food, drinks, and souvenirs. Also noteworthy was the description of the blast provided by bomb techs working inside the stadium.

The most common type of IED in America utilizes low explosives, like gunpowder. But the local techs working inside the stadium reported the sound of this blast as a sharp "crack," which is more readily associated with high explosives.

They called me at home and provided details. "The seat of the blast is approximately 100 yards from the stadium's west gate. We usually open that gate at halftime, but we're locking it down and setting a perimeter."

I arrived just as their robot "disrupted" a backpack found at the bomber's feet. It was a grisly scene; the lower half of a human body was seated on a park bench. The rest was in small pieces scattered across the South Oval.

The blast bowled over a nearby pedestrian and blew out windows 148 feet away. But an initial post-blast survey didn't reveal the usual remnants of an IED: no bomb fragments, shrapnel, power source, or wiring. This looked like raw, bulk explosives had detonated with enough power to tear the bomber apart from the waist up, shattering bones and crushing teeth.

As K9s searched for secondary devices, we inspected what was left of the body and found a wallet containing two IDs. The CP quickly confirmed the bomber's identity, an engineering student with a nearby address. Interviews with friends revealed he was a loner with a penchant for making HME.

Agents located the bomber's roommate who happened to be from Afghanistan. He'd left the apartment earlier that evening and hadn't heard about the blast. When asked about his roommate, he just shook his head.

"We met online and both just needed a roommate. I don't know much about him, but there was always a strange smell coming from his bedroom; he'd never let me in there. You can search the apartment if you'd like."

At 4:34 a.m., two local bomb techs and I entered the small second-floor apartment. We hit the door and did a quick sweep for people, weapons, and IEDs. A chemical odor hung in the air and through the open door of the subject's bedroom we saw a disconcerting scene. Strewn among 20mm and .50 caliber ammo cans were bottles of hydrogen peroxide, acetone, and acid, precursors for TATP. Containers with a white crystalline powder, laboratory beakers, a functional fusing system, and an IED were readily visible. In the predawn silence I tried to make sense of what we saw. TATP had never been used as a main charge in the U.S., but there was almost a pound of white powder in this bedroom and the precursors were unmistakable.

Since TATP was so uncommon at the time, there were no field tests available to safely determine if this was actually the Mother of Satan. As the sun rose I called Dr. Kirk Yeager, a Bureau PhD and the preeminent authority on TATP. After hearing what happened and the volume of HME in the apartment, Kirk and another chemist boarded a Bureau jet. They brought the latest cutting-edge tech, including a portable Raman spectrometer which could interrogate the powder at a molecular level without causing it to detonate. The spectrometer's first histogram confirmed our initial suspicion: it was TATP.

After remotely removing and countercharging the bulk HME, we continued a detailed search as the broader investigation began. In less than two days, over 200 interviews were conducted. Video surveillance from local DIY stores had captured the subject purchasing precursors just days before the blast. Inspection of his laptop revealed downloads of *The Terrorist Handbook*, HME recipes, and a rambling, angry Word document which FBI's profilers concluded was a suicide note, but from its syntax, they couldn't rule out the possibility that he also intended to kill others. Had the blast occurred seven minutes later, the bomber might well have been surrounded by hundreds of people.

Due to the unstable nature of TATP, it's conceivable that the device detonated prematurely. His true intentions will never be known, but the investigation painted a picture of a lonely, angry man with no ties to any terrorist groups.

Given the burgeoning use of TATP and its use at the OU ballgame and recent London attacks, I was asked to meet with Scotland Yard's Counter Terrorism Command, known as SO15. This highly specialized unit was created by merging Special Branch and the Anti-Terrorist Branch after the London transit attacks.

Weeks later, a man associated with a group called the Glass Desert Underground was killed while making TATP in Texas. Texas City joined Norman, Paris, Brussels, Manchester, Surabaya, Sri Lanka, Hong Kong, and other locations where peroxide explosives were used. TATP and its chemical cousin, hexamethylene triperoxide diamine (HMTD), were now an undeniable domestic threat.

Most explosives used in IEDs are chemically based on nitrates, not peroxides. So detection systems, including explosives-detection K9s, weren't geared to detect peroxide HME. That was an attractive attribute exploited by terrorists.

Peroxide explosives' extreme sensitivity to heat, shock, and friction, coupled with diminished detection capabilities, required a new approach to security and search techniques. Public safety professionals and private security screeners at sporting events, concerts, and other arenas would have to adapt to the new threat. In February, I spoke at the Professional Sports Security Summit in Chicago. Attendees included bomb squads, tactical teams, venue managers, and security directors for the NBA, NFL, U.S. Soccer, and other organizations. I discussed security protocols employed at the Olympics in Salt Lake and Athens, the threat of peroxide HME, and lessons learned from the OU and London bombings.

The following month saw the Southeastern Conference Chiefs of Police convention in Gainesville, Florida. My flight left on Easter Sunday with a connection in Memphis. As I deplaned, the gate agent pulled me aside.

"Mr. Black, aren't you heading to Gainesville? There's been a fatal plane crash at the terminal and the airport's closed. I can get you down there by tomorrow afternoon, but that's the best we can do."

A TV in the baggage area confirmed a twin-engine plane had crashed into the west side of the terminal, killing everyone on board. By 8:00 p.m. a cab delivered me to a motel on the south side of Memphis; it had one of the few rooms available. I hadn't eaten, so the desk clerk suggested a local BBQ place. Picking up the phone she winked and whispered, "I've gotcha, honey. Just wait right here."

Within 10 minutes a long pink Cadillac limousine pulled up in front of the lobby. It was a short ride down Elvis Presley Boulevard, past Graceland, then a right turn at a huge BBQ smoker painted like a pig.

The conference was postponed until Tuesday morning, as many other attendees had been delayed by the plane crash. After opening remarks, I gave a presentation on the unique threat posed by peroxide explosives, an overview of the OU bombing, and new security procedures being implemented around the country.

The following year I provided a similar presentation at the Atlantic Coast Conference Chiefs of Police symposium in Tallahassee. College campuses and sporting events remained viable targets, so the agenda for this three-day seminar focused on campus security and special event management. As I deplaned in Tallahassee, news of a mass murder at Virginia Tech was unfolding; 32 were dead. The conference opened with a moment of silence. Virginia Tech's police chief was understandably absent. Frequent classroom breaks allowed the chiefs to meet with a sea of reporters waiting in the hallway. The irony of holding a campus security conference as this horrible event occurred was lost on no one.

Twelve

Weapons of Mass Destruction

A weapon of mass destruction (WMD) is loosely defined as a nuclear, radiological, chemical, biological, or other device intended to create significant damage and a high number of casualties. Conventional explosives may be considered a WMD, as in the case of the Oklahoma City bombing. It's a matter of scale.

The term "car bomb" was historically used to describe an IED placed in or under a vehicle designed to kill its occupants, a favorite tool of the Mafia. A VBIED is a much larger device designed to create widespread damage; the vehicle is merely a delivery system. The first VBIED in modern America was a horse-drawn cart detonated on Wall Street in 1920. It incorporated dynamite and iron window sash weights, killing more than 30 people.

Rarely encountered in the U.S., VBIEDs gained prominence in the 1970s during Northern Ireland's "Troubles." They've also been employed by drug cartels in South America. Over time, they've grown in size and complexity. Sadly, they're now routinely used in Europe and Asia, and throughout the war-torn Middle East.

Recognizing the unique challenges of collecting evidence at a VBIED scene, a good friend and forward thinking SABT in Los Angeles asked if I'd be an instructor for a new course he was developing; VBIED post-blast. The first class was in 1998, three years after the Oklahoma City bombing. Kevin's course was a tremendous success; I was pleased to be a frequent instructor and honored to be present for the 143rd iteration marking its 20th anniversary.

The 40-hour course provided case studies and hands-on experience in collecting evidence at large bombing scenes. We detonated VBIEDs ranging from 600 to 1,500 pounds and deployed smaller secondary devices as part of each weeklong scenario. The story unfolded as physical evidence recovered from the scene, coupled with "witness statements" provided by instructors, led students to storage units and hotel rooms in nearby towns. Mock search warrants recovered "evidence" that tied those sites to the bombing scene. The week concluded with teams presenting their findings to a federal prosecutor in moot court.

Due to the size of the explosions, classes were held in remote locations like the Marine Corps Air Station in Yuma, Arizona, the Navy's Air Station Fallon in Nevada, or Eglin AFB in the Florida Panhandle. Public information officers at each site worked with the media to quell public concern when the thunderous detonations rattled windows in town. After a particularly large blast at Francis E. Warren AFB in Wyoming, the front page of the *Laramie Daily Boomerang* featured the enormous fireball and the headline "Ka-boooom."

Post-blast evidence collection is important, but preventing the blast is preferable. Scientific research and development continuously takes advantage of technological advancements to produce effective VBIED countermeasures. I was fortunate to attend the Bureau's newest VBIED Countermeasure course at the Army's Yakima Training Center in Washington. The 510 square miles of barren high desert, often referred to as "Yakistan," provided a perfect location to test the latest tools on massive live devices. One evening over dinner, the news led with an all too familiar story; the UN headquarters in Baghdad had been destroyed by a bomb-laden cement truck. It was the first time an international humanitarian organization had been targeted. The world remained a dangerous place.

Explosives weren't the only WMD threat. The U.S. had seen unconventional weapons such as anthrax, ricin, toxic industrial chemicals, and even radiological "dirty bombs." Expecting the trend to continue, the Bureau created its WMD Directorate in 2006. To enhance my knowledge base as Oklahoma City's WMD Coordinator, I was certified as a hazardous materials technician and attended highly classified and restricted training provided by the Department of Defense, DOE, and other specialized agencies.

The Naval Surface Warfare Center in Indian Head, Maryland, was established in 1890 and was the oldest joint military school in the country. The unique training curriculum at the "University of Bombs and Bullets" required a Q clearance from the DOE in addition to the Top Secret clearance every FBI Agent possessed. The Q clearance allowed access to special nuclear material (SNM) data and nuclear weapons designs, subjects that could only be discussed in a Sensitive Compartmented Information Facility (SCIF). The class at Indian Head, known as the Advanced Access and Disablement course, incorporated written exams and pass/fail practical exercises that employed advanced technology to defeat extremely sophisticated unconventional weapons.

The hands-on scenarios evolved in the deep woods of the installation or in multistory buildings called "kill houses." Each kill house was constructed within cavernous, windowless warehouses so hostile satellites couldn't observe the sensitive techniques being used against realistic, though inert, devices. Each scenario centered on an improvised nuclear weapon, dirty bomb, or chemical delivery system with penalties for failure. "Fatalities" were immediately tallied on a football-style scoreboard as sirens wailed and strobe lights announced another catastrophic detonation. The logistical and technical solutions were complex and captured in the school's unofficial motto, "I stared into the eyes of the beast … then it ate me."

The weeks in Maryland were followed by additional training at CIA's secretive site known as "The Farm." After rolling to a stop at the outer perimeter, an armed guard checked my credentials against his clipboard and provided an alphanumeric code granting access to the living quarters, conference rooms, and demo ranges that would be home for next week. Passing through the main gate, a series of popup security bollards created a serpentine route along a narrow road leading through the heavily wooded facility. I arrived about dusk and noted there were no street lights and few street signs. All intersecting roads were designed with sharp curves to prevent a direct line of sight. The dorm was a three-story cinder-block building set in a circular clearing only accessible by a one-lane road. Though students had private rooms, there was no way to lock the door from the inside. Except for days on the explosives range, everything we needed was in that building: a SCIF for classes, a restaurant, TV lounges, and exactly two hard-line telephones. No cameras, cell phones, internet devices, or weapons were allowed.

The course delved deeply into chemical, biological, and nuclear weapons, as well as terrorist TTPs (tactics, techniques, and procedures). Lecturers included MDs, PhDs, weapons engineers, military specialists, and experts from every three-letter agency in the government.

The next training evolution occurred at the Navy's Training and Evaluation Unit at Fort Story, Virginia. Some of the nation's top scientists lectured on radiological dispersal devices, improvised nuclear weapons, and other horrific threats that face our nation.

Driving home the reality of those threats, the next course was held at a nondescript DOE facility in Kansas. The World War II–era building appeared antiquated from the street, but the two-million-square-foot labyrinth housed some of the latest tech related to America's nuclear arsenal. The hallways were 20 feet wide and hundreds of yards long, with periodic bulletproof checkpoints manned by armed guards. Cavernous storage rooms ran perpendicular to the halls, their massive doors studded with warning lights and strobes. Chokepoints were under constant CCTV surveillance and required key swipes, cipher locks, and positive ID checks for passage. Nuclear physicists as well as electrical, chemical, and mechanical engineers provided theoretical and hands-on training related to the types of materials and facilities terrorists would need to create a nuclear weapon.

I next traveled to the deserts of New Mexico for a course known only as Block X. Located at Sandia and Los Alamos National Laboratories, the security was obvious and impressive. At the initial security briefing we were each given an encoded badge and a 2" × 2"sealed envelope. Inside was a slip of paper that read, "Do Not Read Contents Aloud. Your Personal Identification Code Is…" The slip of paper was then returned to the registrar. Both the encoded badge and memorized code were required for access through any door; the most highly restricted areas also required clearance through biometric scanners.

The instructors were brilliant nuclear scientists and weapons designers. They never used notes and patiently answered every conceivable question from a group of accountants and lawyers. It was nearly impossible to simplify beta decay and other technical concepts, but they tried with statements like "Think of it this way: in a nuclear reaction tiny particles must interact very quickly. So we take extremely accurate measurements of time and space. For instance, a 'shake' is 10 nanoseconds and a 'barn' is simply a unit of area that measures the reaction cross section of subatomic particles. It's equal to 10^{-24} square cm."

The oldest instructor wore a bowtie and had the tone and inflection of Paul Harvey, a familiar radio commentator from childhood. He used a long wooden pointer instead of a laser and freely admitted he was from the slide rule era. His discipline was particle physics and he clearly loved his work. Discussing thermal and electromagnetic pulse effects, his speech quickened: "I mean, these things will hit you like a step function." I never knew what that meant, but it sounded really bad.

Classes concluded with a tour of a classified museum locally referred to as the Defense Threat Reduction University. It contained full-size replicas of every atomic weapon from Little Boy to the latest, most highly classified systems. An IMAX-style theater displayed incredible 3D images of detonation waves in super slow-motion to show a comparative analysis of how minute and impossibly precise calculations can alter the effects of nuclear blasts. The technology was fascinating, if not a little terrifying.

WMD training continued in the Great Plains at the nation's first International Symposium on Agroterrorism. Speakers included the FBI Director, as well as senators and governors from across the Wheat Belt. World-renowned experts lectured on the intentional transmission of mad cow disease, foot and mouth disease, and the use of plant pathogens designed to destroy crops. An attack of this type could be devastating. A 1986 natural outbreak of bovine spongiform encephalopathy (mad cow disease) in the United Kingdom resulted in an estimated economic loss of $980 million.

Terrorists clearly understand the potential of agroterrorism. Among the thousands of documents recovered in the caves of Afghanistan were training manuals specifically targeting U.S. agriculture. A successful agroterrorism attack on our food supply could result in significant economic loss, social violence, and loss of public confidence in the government.

Next came a block of chemical weapons training at Aberdeen Proving Ground (APG), an Army facility tasked with designing and testing chemical warfare agents since World War I. It's a highly modern defensive research facility now, but some of the old weapons factories active during the Cold War still stand, too hazardous to demolish. Shuttered and sealed behind barricades, razor wire, and very explicit warning signs, they would make the perfect set for some postapocalyptic movie.

Classes were held in a small SCIF, secluded in the woods and surrounded by 10-foot razor wire fences. The instructors were PhDs, chemists, biologists, former Navy SEALs, and members of the Army's Technical Escort group. As with most of the other courses, classes began with the phrase, "OK, no notes."

The Edgewood Chemical Biological Center, part of APG, is one of the few places that still deal with live chemical agents. Deep inside the facility, amid extremely robust security, was the Level III Bio Security Lab. Another nondescript fortress housed the chemical agents; a sign by the only gate read in large red letters, Use of Deadly Force Is Authorized. Inside was a long, well-lit corridor with heavy color-coded doors on each side. Each door had a red rotating light above it, multiple cipher locks, and block letters clearly identifying the agent inside. Small blast-proof windows allowed a glimpse of horrifying nerve agents like VX and sarin. The chemist accompanying us spoke loudly over the hum of massive positive pressure systems and multiple air filtration units used to ensure these deadly agents could never escape the building.

This wide array of training on conventional and unconventional weapons allows FBI SABTs to assess threats in the field and accurately relay critical data to other highly specialized FBI teams strategically deployed throughout the country. These teams routinely work with the Nuclear Emergency Support Team (NEST), the Department of Defense, DOE, and other agencies to provide a "whole of government" approach to address any threat.

Information is critical, so in the 1990s, FBI Director Louis Freeh increased the number of Legal Attachés housed in embassies around the world to enhance global liaison. In conjunction with the FBI's International Operations Division, Legal Attachés work with partner nations to advance FBI investigations and provide specialized counterterrorism training abroad. The training fosters excellent interagency relationships and has an added benefit: if terrorists are effectively addressed overseas, we won't have to deal with them on American shores.

In June, I met three agents in San Francisco for a 5,500-mile trip to Seoul. That 13-hour flight was followed by another six-hour leg, which arrived in Kuala Lumpur at 2:30 a.m. local time. Our first meeting with the Royal Malaysian Police (RMP) commenced five hours later.

Malaysia was a destination country for al-Qaeda, ISIS, Abu Sayyaf, and Jemaah Islamiyah fighters en route to the Philippines and the Middle East. After introductions at RMP headquarters, we began an 80-hour block related to the exploitation of terrorist crime scenes. We covered collection techniques for forensic evidence and the unique requirements of processing a post-blast crime scene.

Obviously we can't travel with explosives, so we utilize whatever is available in country. In this case, I used PP-01, a Yugoslavian plastic explosive to build IEDs for a simulated attack on a VIP motorcade. Target vehicles were delivered to a remote jungle clearing along with a motorcycle which would deliver the IED, a scenario taken from real world events.

After a morning of range preparation, the RMP commander took me to the nearby village of Kuala Kabu Baru. While dining on chicken hearts, beef curry, and durian, he got a call. The conversation ended in English with him saying, "All right, scramble two helicopters and two full teams."

"Do you need to go?" I asked.

He casually responded, "Oh no, it's just pirates."

Saturday's morning paper confirmed a cargo ship had been seized by pirates in the Strait of Malacca. That news was personally disconcerting, as I planned to dive in those waters later that weekend. Fortunately, no pirates were encountered during my 90-minute ferry ride to Paulau Payar. A young man on the dock spotted me as an American and approached me on the dock.

"Good morning, I'm Ali, your dive master. It'll be just the two of us; would you like to see sharks?"

His small boat dropped anchor east of Langkawi and we rolled into the warm, tan water. Visibility was marginal; like diving in weak tea. Swimming against a slight current at about 40 feet, a blacktip reef shark began trailing behind us; soon six more sharks appeared, circling overhead. Ali descended, kneeling on the sandy bottom, and motioned for me to follow. He pulled several fist-sized pieces of fish from his BCD (buoyancy control device); that's what the sharks had been sensing. He tossed each like an underhand softball, but the water's resistance left them hanging perilously close to us. An array of small fish darted in before the large sharks converged and began writhing in a feeding frenzy right in front of us.

Class resumed on the RMP range Monday morning. Before the students arrived, I riddled the VIP motorcade with AK-47 fire and positioned the bomb-laden motorcycle beside the dignitary's vehicle. Birds took flight and monkeys howled as the powerful explosion reverberated through the jungle. RMP teams arrived later to process the scene, collecting the spent casings and conducting bullet trajectory analysis, post-blast swabbing, and other evidence collection techniques taught in class. Media from across the Malay Peninsula watched the exercise with great interest. The class ended Friday with a very formal ceremony and tea, a nod to Malaysia's British roots.

Crime on the high seas wasn't limited to pirates. In 2000, suicide terrorists detonated a boat alongside the USS *Cole* as it refueled in Yemen. The blast ripped a 40-foot-wide hole in the guided-missile destroyer and killed 17 American sailors. Navy and FBI divers worked under extremely difficult conditions and linked the attack to al-Qaeda. This waterborne threat now required IED sweeps for at-risk ships, domestic piers, and harbors.

An unnamed Royal Malaysian Police commander translates a Chinese newspaper for me on a remote jungle range in Kuala Kubu Baru. The headline reads, "FBI Anti-Terrorism Experts Give Advice" (June 2005).

Recognizing the unique challenges of submerged crime scenes, another forward-thinking SABT in Los Angeles developed an underwater post-blast course. I was a Master SCUBA diver with a series of technical certifications and was humbled to be part of the first international iteration of Greg's course in Victoria, Australia. Logistics were an issue given the need for SCUBA gear and marine support in addition to all the standard classroom materials and explosives. Students included police SAR (search and rescue) divers and Royal Navy Clearance Divers from across the nation. This was the first time Australian police and navy divers had trained together in a joint exercise.

As lectures began in the classroom, another diver and I loaded inert explosives and other "evidence" aboard a small vessel named *Hucklebuck*. We then rigged her hull with live C4 and sent her to the bottom of Hobsons Bay. An elaborate fact scenario was provided to the teams, who were tasked with locating the vessel and recovering evidence. Instructors served as "witnesses" who could provide critical information if properly interviewed.

Based on information gleaned from interviews, a RIB was deployed with side-scan sonar. Once *Hucklebuck* was located, a remotely operated vehicle (ROV) revealed grainy images of what appeared to be hundreds of pounds of unexploded plastic explosives. The Royal Navy divers inspected the scene first and determined the terrorist device must have "low ordered" because only some of the explosives had detonated, scattering the rest in and around the wreck. Once the Navy deemed the scene reasonably safe, police divers began their underwater photography and evidence recovery. Afterward, the vessel was raised using lift bags and towed to shore for further processing.

At the end of the first week, a gregarious diver from the Queensland Police Service known as "Rooster" met us at the bar; all the Aussies had nicknames. Rooster was a burly, affable diver from Far North Queensland who was not fond of the cool waters of Melbourne.

"You know, mate, diving this far south isn't really diving. You boys should take a trip up to Cairns where I'm from and dive the Great Barrier Reef; go up for the weekend."

Flying within 24 hours of diving is dangerous, so Saturday would be our only day to dive. "Isn't Queensland about 1,500 miles from here?" I asked.

"Yeah, no worries. There's a red-eye that'll have you there before sunrise."

During dinner, Rooster made a few calls. "OK, mate; I made a booking for you boys and arranged a flat across from the Cairns police station. A minibus from Down Under Adventures will collect you at 0800 tomorrow."

By 9:00 a.m. we were boarding an 80-foot catamaran called *Silverswift*. Cruising at 27 knots, we reached the outer reef in about an hour. Between dives off Flynn Reef, the captain stopped to chat. "Have you been in this business long?" I asked.

"Well, I got a good deal on the boat a few years back. She used to be *Outer Edge*."

"*Outer Edge*? Isn't that the boat that left some divers out here? They never found them."

"That's right; bloody awful. I bought her out of bankruptcy. It's bad luck to change a boat's name, but I had to. Nobody would ever dive on *Outer Edge* again."

The diving was amazing, but we had to get back to work. Rooster was waiting for us when we arrived in Victoria Sunday evening. "Well, how was the dive? The boys want to hear about it; they're waiting at the yacht club."

The Royal Yacht Club shared a dock with the Victoria Water Police. We met the Aussies and were recounting the dives over a couple of beers when Rooster asked, "You blokes ready for dinner?"

At 7:00 sharp a 42-foot custom Cougar catamaran roared alongside the dock. They fired up its two big diesels for a trip up the Yarra River and into Victoria Harbor. "Hope you like Indian. Bhōj is the best, but it's pretty hot."

The final practical problem centered on a sunken terrorist's fast boat. The scenario stated the vessel was in the restricted waters of a naval shipyard when it was sunk by security forces. The team had to locate, inspect, and process the vessel before lifting and towing it to shore.

As the exercise concluded that evening, Rooster asked, "That's the last problem, right? Why don't we have our debrief back at the yacht club?"

After an hour of discussion and a few drinks, Rooster motioned to the group. "C'mon, mates, the boys have somethin' for you. We know you're away from your families and today's one of your holidays, right?"

We walked into the main dining room where the staff served a complete Thanksgiving dinner. Just as in England, they'd prepared a huge turkey, dressing, cranberry sauce, and pumpkin pie. After dinner another Aussie named Matty "the Hammer" pulled me aside.

"The Australian Federal Police are hosting an international counterterrorism conference at headquarters in Melbourne. We asked up the chain and your embassy suggested you'd be willing to give us a talk about that federal building bombing. If you are, I'll take you up tomorrow, then we'll have a look around."

The conference attendees came from across the South Pacific and were interested not only in OKBOMB, but also the underwater school. When the conference concluded and all the questions were answered, Hammer and I began walking toward the garage.

"Thanks for the talk, mate; bloody interesting. While we're in the city I wondered if you'd be up for a little dive this evening. I've arranged some time in the Melbourne Aquarium."

The 580,000-gallon aquarium offered something called the Shark Dive Xtreme. As we donned wetsuits and SCUBA gear, the guide provided one simple instruction.

"The important thing is to go straight to the bottom … avoid interaction with the big animals."

It was amazing to be in a glass box surrounded by 14-foot wide stingrays and a host of huge sharks. The largest was a 550-pound sand tiger named Georgie; her beady black eyes and rows of jagged teeth left quite an impression.

The underwater curriculum was a success and was subsequently scheduled for other exotic venues in Hawaii and Southeast Asia. Our contact at Pearl Harbor was a Senior Chief assigned to the Navy's Special Operations Command, Mobile Unit 3. We worked out of their facilities along the West Loch and conducted dive operations within sight of the USS *Missouri*. Students included divers from the U.S. and Australian Navy, as well as U.S. Army and police bomb techs. The days were long, but it's SCUBA diving in Hawaii; how bad could it be?

One night we took a small boat off Hawaii Kai; the moon was out and the water was crystal clear. Trailing behind the group in the dark warm water, it seemed as if someone was beside me. I moved my light to the right to find a curious, seven-foot long Hawaiian monk seal. They're an endangered species and this one was close enough for me to read the tracking tag on his flipper: W-22. He stayed with me for the rest of the dive and broke the surface to watch me climb over the gunnel into the dive boat.

Another iteration of the underwater school was scheduled in Malaysia. After a 7,255-mile flight, I met the team in Hong Kong for a short leg into Kuala Lumpur. Three vans were waiting at the curb and took us to a hotel near the embassy; it was Saturday, 2:45 p.m. local time and I'd been in transit for 48 hours. A message at the desk revealed the Legal Attaché wanted to meet us at the bar within the hour.

"Thanks for coming. I'm sure you're all tired, so I'll be brief. The Navy just finished a two-week block with the RMP yesterday. A driver will pick you up at 7:00 AM and take you to Ipoh, about 197 kilometers north of here. First we'd like a weeklong post-blast class course. The classroom and demo ranges are at a remote camp belonging to the RMP Field Force, a paramilitary unit responsible for internal security. In addition to RMP, you'll also have five counterterrorism colonels from the Royal Thai Police. Try to get some rest."

During class introductions in Ipoh, a couple of students kept smiling in my direction. On a break the two men approached and nodded politely.

"You may not remember us, but I am Ong and this is Soo from the forensics lab. We were students in your site exploitation class years ago. I am now the bomb squad commander and will assist you on the range."

"Of course I remember. It's great to see you again. Is Nasir here, too?"

"No, he was promoted to Superintendent in Penang. But these three officers work directly for him."

Ong insisted on calling Nasir and, after a brief exchange in Malay, handed me the phone. As stern as ever, Nasir began the conversation with a tongue in cheek reprimand.

"You failed to report to me upon your arrival in Malaysia."

Ong met us that night in the Emergency Bar, located in the hotel's gleaming marble lobby. "This is Nahthin; he will drive you to New Town for food. Go, you go now."

Within 45 minutes we stopped at Restoran Onn Kee Tauge Ayam, where Ong was already seated at a small plastic table; I couldn't help but notice we were actually sitting in the street. Always smiling, Ong assured us it was OK and placed an order for the group. We enjoyed steaming bowls of pho and some sort of very spicy chicken, followed by a stroll through the busy street market. It was an early night as we had to be on the range before sunrise.

The demo range was a jungle clearing near the Field Force's remote camp. As we set our explosives, the crack of rifle fire from Vat 69 commandos rang through the dense vegetation. Like the Field Forces, Vat 69 is a paramilitary commando unit attached to Malaysia's Internal Security Branch. Many of the students, including Ong, served in these specialized units. More than one conversation began with "When we were fighting Communists in the jungle…" Until 1989, Communist insurgents waged war in the mountains and jungles of Malaysia; the newest threat was Islamic extremism.

Our first range day consisted of nine detonations to demonstrate the effects of different types of explosives. The training progressed to incorporate scenarios based on recent local attacks and culminated with four VBIEDs. The students were broken into teams, each charged with processing a crime scene, identifying the IED components, and preparing a report to be presented to the class.

One afternoon Ong took us to lunch at a Chinese restaurant where we selected our entrée from a selection of ducks hung by their necks in the window. Afterward we drove into the Cameron Highlands through the thick jungle of the Banjaran Titiwangsa Mountains. Along a mountainous jungle road, we encountered a group of Orang Asli, the "original people" of peninsular Malaysia. They were dressed in traditional clothing: loincloths, tree bark, and vines. Each of the men carried blowguns with poison-tipped darts. Meeting them was an incredible experience, but we had to get back for a briefing at the Emergency Bar in Ipoh.

The following evening, some RMP officers invited us for authentic Indian food at Samy's in the small town of Chemor. Our driver was late and the restaurant was farther than expected, so local officers were waiting outside upon our arrival. We entered the cinder-block building through its small kitchen and were escorted to a private room in the back where we sat at a long marble table and ate off banana leaves instead of plates; there were no utensils. The menu was mutton, fish, and a variety of other very spicy dishes. At the end of the meal I committed an etiquette faux pas by folding my banana leaf toward me to cover the fish bones. Ong smiled and softly whispered, "No, fold the other way if you enjoyed the meal."

Class concluded Friday with a formal ceremony followed by high tea. Afterward we packed our gear and departed for Lumut, a coastal town about 84 kilometers southwest of Ipoh where we would present the underwater post-blast course. Our quarters and classroom were on a secluded beach surrounded by jungle on three sides and the Strait of Malacca to the south. The weekend was spent preparing the classroom, our dive gear, and the RIBs needed for Monday. As in Ipoh, the instructor staff included two of us from the FBI, three highly skilled divers from the U.S. Navy's Mobile Unit, police divers from Los Angeles, and Ong as the RMP commander; it was an impressive cadre of instructors with a wealth of knowledge and experience. The schedule called for lectures Monday morning followed by an explosives demonstration that afternoon.

Sergeant Singh, a tall Sikh wearing the traditional turban and a fabulously long beard, approached. "I have been assigned to accompany you in search of a suitable range. I have an area in mind if you will allow me."

We crossed a dirt road and were following a narrow jungle path when Singh casually mentioned something that seemed important. "If I may, a word of caution. Beware of the pit viper; they drop from trees. Very deadly."

The path opened into a large clearing with nothing but unpopulated jungle in every direction; it would suffice for a demo range. Throughout the next week, echoes of our explosions could be heard rolling along the high cliffs surrounding the clearing. As the sun set one evening, Ong pointed to some animal tracks along the woodline. Smiling, he asked, "Do you know wild boar?"

I wasn't sure what he meant, but before I could ask he nodded and walked away. The following evening, Ong met the team outside our quarters.

"I will take you all for dinner. The van will meet us here."

Author with unnamed Royal Malaysian Police bomb technician in the jungles of Lumut, Malaysia (2007).

The van soon arrived for a long drive on remote jungle roads. About an hour into the trip, we stopped and picked up a man standing on the roadside in the small fishing village of Pantai Remis. As the older man climbed in, Ong made the introduction: "This is my uncle."

Following the river, we finally came to a restaurant called Tur Kee Restoran. As we walked inside the small cinder-block building, Ong whispered, "Those boar tracks on the range? I asked Uncle to hunt one for dinner."

The cook was preparing the boar and two wild chickens Uncle had shot that afternoon, along with salted shark, pork, prawns, and fresh crabs. The beverage of the evening was toddy—local moonshine made from fermented coconut tree sap.

The following morning, as instructors lectured in the classroom, I rigged a boat with explosives and sank it in the calm bay. Once the boat settled to the bottom, I seeded the site with IED circuitry, modeling clay to represent bulk plastic explosives, and an IED made from a propane cylinder full of inert HME.

When the lecture concluded, the day's scenario was revealed to the students: terrorists opened fire from a speedboat racing toward a crowded market pier. As Vat 69 commandos returned fire, there was an explosion aboard the vessel and it sank. The class had to conduct necessary interviews, determine the boat's location, and formulate a plan to recover any evidence that might have survived the blast.

Using their search and interview skills, the boat was quickly located and a dive plan established to document the scene and recover evidence. When police divers found the explosives, they called in bomb techs, who used remote techniques and lift bags to recover the large propane cylinder. Once it was rendered safe, the remaining explosives were recovered and the entire vessel was raised.

Class concluded that evening with a cookout on the beach. There was a pig roasting in a pit, prawns, lamb, beef, fish, rice, and a 4.5-liter bottle of 12-year-old scotch, which made the karaoke a little more amusing. The night was cut short by strong coastal winds that drove sheets of heavy rain under the tin roof of our bamboo shelter.

The next morning each team presented their reports in a moot court. They provided detailed sketches and photographs and were "cross-examined" by instructors. After a formal closing ceremony, we loaded our gear for a three-hour trip back to Kuala Lumpur.

The quirks of government travel determined it was $1,700 cheaper for each of us to spend the weekend in Singapore instead of flying straight back to America, so we checked into the Intercontinental for some much needed rest. After dinner we toured Marina Bay with its iconic Merlion and had drinks at the Long Bar, where the Singapore Sling was invented. Sunday we flew from Singapore to Hong Kong, then another 7,300 miles to Los Angeles, which was home for the other instructors. Unfortunately, I had a long layover before a flight to Oklahoma rounded out my 32 hours in transit.

The pace of international terrorism training continued, but I was still working various domestic investigations. On Palm Sunday, I flew to Baltimore to testify in a hearing on a case that had begun the previous September. A private pilot had attempted to board a commercial plane with an IED in his backpack; TSA screeners discovered the device and detained him. When I arrived at the airport, local police already had the man in custody. In a lengthy interview, the man confessed.

"Look.... OK, yes, it's mine. But this is all just a big mistake. I forgot it was in my backpack. Come on, it's really just a small noise maker. I make 'em all the time for fun."

The 9/11 terrorists took over four planes with box cutters; Richard Reid's bomb was small enough to hide in a shoe. This man had a metal

CO_2 cylinder filled with a low explosive, an initiator, and a battery. By every definition his "small noise maker" was an IED that a licensed pilot was trying to carry aboard a commercial aircraft. Over his objections, I arrested him for attempting to board a plane with a destructive device.

Within a day, his politically connected family and friends were making phone calls. A former local politician appeared on television saying, "I know this young man; he's no terrorist. He'd never use a bomb on a plane. He just builds them for fun, as a curiosity."

I asked the FBI Explosives Unit to build several identical devices and test them on aircraft fuselages. The effects were predictable: the device was more than capable of blowing a hole in the pressurized cabin of an aircraft. So I was stunned when the U.S. Attorney's Office refused to file felony charges. The subject eagerly accepted a misdemeanor plea requiring just two years' probation and a $1,000 fine.

TSA wasn't happy with the plea deal. After researching the matter, TSA attorneys concluded the misdemeanor plea could preclude the man from working in the aviation industry and jeopardize his pilot's license. It was the first time TSA moved to take a pilot's license from a U.S. citizen. I was summoned to Baltimore to testify as an expert on the device and its effects on an aircraft. After an eight-hour hearing in the old Customs House, a judge decided the subject posed a threat to aviation and revoked his license to fly. At least that was something.

Thirteen

Snake Charmers and Sanjo

It was 4:00 a.m. and 25°F when the plane departed Oklahoma City in February 2008. By noon I was in sunny Daytona Beach for the 50th anniversary of the Daytona 500, an NSSE due to heightened security concerns. I joined three other SABTs and the Volusia County bomb squad as part of an "all hazards" response team with emphasis placed on the counter–IED mission.

The week was full of activity. Thursday saw the Gatorade Duels, Friday had time trials and truck racing, and Saturday was the Camping World 300. My team's area of responsibility for those events included the track, Pit Road, and an entertainment area known as the Fan Zone.

Organizers pulled out all the stops for the golden anniversary. Fans could meet Daytona 500 winners and NASCAR legends and see iconic cars like Richard Petty's 1970 Superbird. The entire city was geared for die-hard race fans. One evening while buying batteries at a Kmart, I noticed a large and rowdy crowd seated in the patio furniture section. The store manager was holding a cash auction for life-sized cardboard cutouts of NASCAR drivers holding their sponsor's products: Doritos, M&Ms, and motor oil. These folks were true racing fanatics.

Long before the main event on Sunday afternoon, the faithful poured in for pre-race activities. Most paid $60 to park in a strip mall and walk a mile to the Speedway, but high rollers paid thousands of dollars to park million-dollar motorhomes in the infield. About noon, an announcer introduced the official Mayor of the Infield, who'd spent his honeymoon at the first Daytona 500 in 1959 and attended every race since.

My team's area of responsibility for race day was the section along Turn 1, which was where I met Lee, a NASCAR spotter manning the turn's watchtower. If he saw a crash or any other hazard, he'd radio the main tower and drop the yellow caution flag.

"I've been calling this race for 26 years from the best seat in the house. Why don't you come up and watch a few laps?"

Soon the announcer bellowed those famous words, "Gentlemen, start your engines." Once the pace car left the track, Richard Petty waved the green flag and the tower shook as cars thundered below at nearly 200 mph. I reluctantly climbed down and met the rest of the team along the thick white wall of Turn 1.

With just six laps to go, Casey Mears's Number 5 car slammed into the wall, showering us with sparks; four minutes later, Ryan Newman crossed the finish line under a barrage of fireworks. Once the helicopters, blimps, motorhomes, and 200,000 spectators cleared the track, I loaded my gear for the trip home.

The following month I was at Nellis Air Force Base in Nevada for another HME school. Surprisingly, instead of housing the class on base, our group was booked in the MGM Grand on the Vegas Strip. We spent our days synthesizing HME in the desert and the evenings exploring Sin City's casinos, shows, and the highest thrill rides in the world atop the Stratosphere Hotel. The 40-hour class was successful and I was home in time for Memorial Day weekend.

Taking advantage of the holiday, I took the family to Disney World. While standing in line at Space Mountain, the Counter–IED Unit (CIEDU) at headquarters called my cell. "Hey, ITOS [International Terrorism Operation Section] needs a hand with some training. Can you be in the Maldives in two weeks? From there you'd go to India."

"Uh, sure. Where are the Maldives?"

"It's an island nation in the Indian Ocean, straddling the equator about 435 miles southwest of Sri Lanka. Have your office FedEx me your official passport and I'll get Danielle at OIO [Office of International Operations] to secure your visa for India. We'll let the embassies know you're coming."

Upon my return from the Magic Kingdom there were plane tickets to Malé on my desk, but no passport or visa. I called Danielle at OIO.

"Yeah, there was a little snag at the Indian embassy. But you should have your passport with the visa by the third."

"That's cutting it a little close; I leave on the fifth."

Of course it didn't arrive and Danielle called early on the morning of my departure. "All right, the good news is I have your visa. But it and your passport are still in D.C.; there was a delay with FedEx. How about you fly to headquarters and pick it up?"

There was no time for that, so I emailed the Legal Attaché in India from my breakfast table. Within an hour an instructor from Quantico called. "Here's the plan. I'm on this TDY, too. I'll drive into D.C., pick up your official passport with the Indian visa, and bring it to you in Malé. Since the Maldives doesn't require a visa, just use your tourist passport when you land there."

I left the house at 1:00 a.m. and met some of the team at LAX. After a six-hour delay, we settled in for a 7,300-mile, 15-hour flight to Hong Kong where we changed planes for a four-hour hop to Singapore. An overnight stay in Changi afforded us some real food, a hot shower, and much-needed rest. The next day saw an eight-hour flight to Kuala Lumpur, then a four-hour flight to Malé where we finally arrived at 9:00 p.m. local time.

The Legal Attaché and five Maldivian policemen met us on the tarmac to usher us through Customs. We gathered our gear and followed them to a dock about 100 yards away, where a police boat was waiting. The country is made up of about 1,200 small islands; the airport was on one and our hotel on another. It took 20 minutes to motor across the calm sea to Bandos Island, where resort reps met us with fresh mango drinks and maps to our bungalows. It was a muggy 15-minute walk along winding raked-sand paths to Room 225, where I took a shower and fell into bed.

At sunrise, bright red parrots chattered in the palm trees and crystal-clear waves lapped the white sand a few feet from my door. Since it was Sunday, I arranged for a couple of morning SCUBA dives before motoring over to Girifushi Island to meet the police and inspect the explosives range.

This course would center on post-blast evidence collection and highlight the types of technical assistance the U.S. could offer in terrorist investigations. It came on the heels of the Maldives' first real terror attack. An IED had injured a dozen Western tourists just eight months earlier at Sultan Park near the iconic gold domed mosque. Both were common tourist attractions (BBC News 2007), and this country needed tourist dollars. Subsequent attacks included stabbings and arsons which were attributed to ISIS. Three men were quickly arrested for the Sultan Park bombing and admitted their goal was to target non–Muslims as part of a jihad. The FBI provided forensic assistance for that investigation and wanted to strengthen relationships with Maldivian authorities.

The Maldives stretch 1,000 kilometers across the equator, making class logistics difficult. Each morning we were picked up by a police launch and taken to whichever island we'd be training on that day. Though I taught a few topics in the classroom, my primary responsibility was the explosives portion of the class. Nahid, a senior officer, ensured I had access to the necessary explosives, in this case British PE4. Using those explosives and locally obtained components, I constructed several IEDs, which we detonated at the Girifushi Training Centre. The size of the shots was limited as the range was fairly small, just a white sandy patch surrounded by an earthen berm in the middle of the Indian Ocean. The largest IED destroyed a SUV that the class later processed for evidence.

The Maldives civilian police force had only been in existence for about four years; law enforcement had previously been a military function. Nahid, a former soldier, was now a policeman with the Ministry of Home Affairs. He'd been integral to the transition from military to civilian policing, even serving as a member of his president's protective detail.

One morning we were wiring in IEDs when Nahid began sharing an interesting story. "Not long ago on this range I was burning dynamite. Something went wrong and it exploded." He stood and pointed to the ocean beyond the sandy berm. "The blast picked me up and threw me over the berm. I landed unconscious in the sea; my clothes were ripped apart and I had lost some hearing. My friends thought, 'Nahid is no more.' But Javid came and pulled me from the sea and I'm alive to tell the tale." Javid was in the class as part of Malé's Quick Reaction Force (QRF) and his quick reaction that day saved Nahid's life.

One evening after range operations were complete, a speed launch pulled alongside the Girifushi dock. Nahid spoke to the captain, jumped aboard, and motioned for me to follow. We cruised into the open ocean and rendezvoused with a much larger boat. After a warm welcome, we handline fished from the decks until the sun disappeared in an orange blaze. The crew lit a wood grill on the bow of the vessel and cooked everything we caught right there; it was delicious.

The Maldives are truly an island paradise, surrounded by beautiful reefs and dozens of dive sites just a boat ride away. On Friday the 13th we seized the opportunity for a night dive on the wreck of the *Maldives Victory*. It was dark and stormy as we rolled into the sea above the 270-foot freighter. From the wheelhouse, about 100 feet below the surface, we could see her sprawling deck and coral-covered railings.

Inside, her cavernous cargo holds and eerie living quarters were pitch black except for the narrow beams of our dive lights.

Class concluded the following Friday with glowing remarks from a Member of Parliament who discussed the changing role of the new civilian police force. He mentioned that Article 30, an amendment to the Constitution, was being proposed that would give Maldivian citizens new civil rights that many Americans take for granted.

A police boat picked us up at 7:15 Saturday morning. Nahid and four other officers escorted our group through the airport, pushing crowds aside and expediting us through Customs as other passengers looked on curiously. We flew from Malé to Colombo, Sri Lanka, and after a four-hour layover boarded a flight to New Delhi.

India has struggled with violent extremism since 1947 when British India was divided into India and Pakistan. Sikhs and Hindus departed newly formed Pakistan for India, which put them in conflict with Indian Muslims. The situation grew particularly violent in the Jammu and Kashmir region where a Muslim majority was ruled by a Hindu maharaja.

In 1989, the Pakistani-backed Jammu and Kashmir Liberation Front (JKLF) stoked a revolution that produced numerous militant groups. Lashkar-e-Tayyiba (LeT) formed in the early 1990s, and Jaysh-i-Muhammad (JEM) followed in 2000. JEM made efficient use of IEDs, suicide bombers, and VBIEDs in India and allied with the Taliban against U.S. forces in Afghanistan.

When the plane landed in New Delhi, an embassy expediter escorted us through Customs and onto a waiting van. Once the bags were loaded, we sped to a hotel near the embassy. By 11:00 p.m., the team was checked in and had booked a tour for the next morning, our only day off.

The alarm rang early, as it was a 500-kilometer trip to Agra. The roads were paved, but the pace was slow due to camels pulling overstacked carts, three-wheeled tuk-tuks, tiny scooters carrying entire families, and brightly decorated trucks rumbling along in questionable states of operability. Roadside stands were replete with macaques and snake charmers coaxing cobras from wicker baskets. The roundtrip took 15 hours, but seeing the Taj Mahal was worth it.

Monday morning, we met at the Indian Central Bureau of Investigation Academy in Ghaziabad. Attendees included senior police inspectors from the various Indian states, Special Forces officers, and Army EOD technicians. The opening ceremony was quite formal with dignitaries giving speeches as the instructors were presented with large, colorful bouquets. After morning tea, my partner and I ducked into a conference room and began constructing circuitry for the IEDs we'd detonate later that week.

The following morning, I met Major Ajmal at the embassy. He was a National Security Guard (NSG) bomb technician assigned to assist me on a remote explosives range in Manesar. NSG is India's counter-terrorism commando force more commonly known as the Black Cats. Once at the range, Ajmal introduced me to Major Kumar, who assigned six more Black Cats to assist with logistics for Thursday's Field Training Exercise (FTX).

Just as classes began, several instructors were struck with a variety of maladies, mostly of an intestinal nature. By Wednesday, three of the five were too sick to work. They rallied by Thursday's FTX, though the sweltering bus ride to the remote jungle range was unforgiving.

As I was wiring in the explosives early that morning, a mongoose ran out from the woodline. One of the commandos pointed and smiled.

"Ah, tradition says a mongoose in the morning brings good luck."

"Really? Why is that?" I asked.

He answered nonchalantly, "They kill the cobras."

Once the class arrived, we detonated a series of shots so they could see, hear, and feel the blasts. As I began to lecture in a small jungle clearing, the students started walking away, gathering at the woodline. I asked the major, "Where is everyone going?"

Kumar looked at me incredulously and explained it was tea time. Soon a young man wearing a white starched long-sleeved shirt and bowtie peddled up on a large tricycle. Though the jungle humidity was stifling, he began serving cookies and hot tea from a silver tray resting on the trike's basket. Once tea time concluded, we detonated several VBIEDs and the class began their post-blast crime scene processing.

Closing ceremonies at NSG headquarters were hosted by the commanding general. He noted that this was the first time the FBI had provided training in India and he wanted the collaboration to continue, which pleased the embassy personnel. Our 7,477-mile flight departed at midnight, transiting the Middle East, Greenland, and Canada before finally landing at O'Hare. The 10½ hour time change should have put me in Oklahoma City by midafternoon, but my Chicago departure was delayed by an intoxicated, belligerent passenger who had to be removed by airport police.

Author with Indian Black Cat commandos on a sweltering jungle range near Manesar, India (2008).

I'm often asked why we teach these types of international schools; why is the FBI training people overseas? The reason became apparent about one month later. I was dead asleep when my cell phone rang. Fumbling for the phone, I heard the Legal Attaché in New Delhi say, "Hello ... hey, yeah, it's Steve. Who were the best NSG guys in your class?"

"Umm, well, it's like three in the morning here. I don't have their names. Can I call you tomorrow?"

"There's been a series of bombings in Mumbai. Looks like maybe a couple of hundred dead and hundreds more injured. NSG wants to send the guys you trained to take charge of the investigation. I'm sending you the student roster now; let me know who the top performers were."

Running through the names sparked my memory: Majors Ajmal and Kumar would be ideal for this mission. With that recommendation, they were dispatched to Mumbai to oversee multiple horrific crime scenes. It was humbling to know the lessons taught in our course would be used to investigate one of the largest terrorist attacks in India's history. Their investigation revealed 10 LeT jihadists had launched coordinated attacks that killed over 160 people, including six Americans, and wounded hundreds more. The only terrorist who survived the 60-hour siege was subsequently convicted and hanged (CNN 2022).

The following year, Chicago's Joint Terrorism Task Force (JTTF) arrested David Headley, an American citizen who helped plan the attack. He pled guilty to 12 terrorism charges, including six counts of aiding and abetting the murder of U.S. citizens in India and conspiracy to provide material support to terrorists. In return for his full cooperation, the Department of Justice didn't seek the death penalty. Instead he was sentenced to 35 years in prison (Department of Justice 2015).

My next TDY began with a sunrise flight to Chicago, followed by a 6,300-mile trip over the Bering Sea. A merciful ticket agent offered an upgrade to the upper deck, or hump, of an aging 747 that provided extra space for the 13-hour trip to Tokyo, where I met the rest of the team. By the time we landed in Thailand, I'd flown over 10,000 miles and was happy to learn we'd spend the night in Bangkok.

Our next flight didn't depart until late the following afternoon, which gave me a chance to shake off the jetlag. Wat Pho, one of the largest Buddhist temples in Bangkok, was a short walk from the hotel. I toured the entire 20-acre site, including the famous Reclining Buddha and then the Grand Palace; some exercise and sunshine were rejuvenating. After a late lunch at Hard Rock Café, I hailed a tuk-tuk back to the hotel, showered off the humidity, and left for the airport.

The flight to Cambodia was a mere 50 minutes and the Thai Air flight crew was impossibly polite, giving each of us an orchid as we deplaned. Once inside the airport we purchased visas, cleared Customs, and loaded our bags into a waiting van. Our first conference was scheduled at 8:00 p.m., just two hours after arrival; the Legal Attaché was already waiting at the hotel.

"Welcome to Phnom Penh. Some associates from the embassy would like to meet you at the Foreign Correspondents' Club. It's just a short walk."

The old building had mosaic tile floors and slow ceiling fans that strained against the thick night air. We opted to sit outside on the upper deck, where a breeze from the Tonlé Sap River made things a little cooler. It's an unfortunate reality, but Americans abroad must constantly be aware of their surroundings to mitigate potential threats. At restaurants, I tend to select a table away from the street, especially if the business is known to cater to westerners. The farther from the door the better, in case someone comes in shooting or tosses a grenade in from the street. A table on an upper floor toward the back is better yet, presuming there's a handy exit.

Within minutes, embassy personnel and local Cambodian authorities joined us. We became fast friends over duck cakes and a few cold

Angkors. As the evening wore on, about half the group wanted to go out for the night, but I was still reeling from the travel and 14-hour time change. I walked to the hotel and had just fallen asleep when the phone rang. It was another instructor who said ominously, "Turn on the TV." A quick look at BBC World News revealed that the Marriott in Islamabad had just been destroyed by a VBIED. Globally speaking we were in the neighborhood, but after several conversations with headquarters it was decided our team would stay in Cambodia and teach the post-blast course as planned.

The class was hosted by the Royal Cambodian Air Force (RCAF) and designed to assist them in forming Cambodia's first civilian bomb squad. Students ranged from very young Special Forces soldiers to senior high-ranking officers. There were even two generals who had fought against the communist Khmer Rouge; over dinner they recounted atrocities committed by that brutal regime. We toured the infamous S-21 prison, the Tuol Sleng Genocide Museum, and the Killing Fields at Choeng Ek. Cambodia was liberated from Pol Pot in 1979 when Vietnamese forces overthrew the Khmer Rouge.

As is often the case, blowing things up in foreign countries poses logistical issues. When asked about the location of an explosives range, my RCAF counterpart motioned to the nicely manicured soccer pitch of Battalion 70. I explained it was much too small and the private homes located just beyond its modest eight-foot walls would be damaged, not to mention the large craters we'd leave on the pitch.

After some robust conversation in what I believe was French, another option was presented. It was a remote facility called Mango Range in Kampong Spue, 80 kilometers from the classroom, which posed transportation problems for the students. Another option was mentioned, a range at Kampong Chhnang where a former USMC master sergeant ran a civilian demining operation. After separating from the Corps, this Marine accepted the challenge of ridding Cambodia of the thousands of landmines left over from decades of war. He generously offered the use of his range facilities, which made planning and logistics much simpler. However, the RCAF commanders hastily removed that option as they didn't want to appear incapable of providing the infrastructure required for the class. We settled on Mango Range, but enlisted the former Marine's assistance to oversee logistics and ensure the explosives were safely delivered to the isolated jungle site.

The time change and jet lag woke me at 4:00 a.m., so I started soldering the week's IED circuitry, or TPUs (time and power units), in my room. Once at the range, we coupled those TPUs with raw explosives the Marine had reclaimed from recovered landmines. The plastic explosives were mainly of Russian and Chinese origin, while the detonating cord and blasting caps were Indian. Our day on the range progressed from several smaller shots to a significant VBIED, which the class then processed for evidence.

One evening just before sunset, I walked to the Wat Phnom temple near the hotel. In a wooded area near the ancient temple's steps stood Sanjo, an Indian elephant. For 15 U.S. dollars, I climbed atop Sanjo for what I presumed would be a short ride along a dirt path surrounding the temple. But Sanjo had other plans; he veered off the trail and lumbered through the trees as monkeys scattered and children laughed and pointed. He then stepped over the cable barrier encircling the park and meandered through the streets of Phnom Penh, literally stopping traffic. It was quite a spectacle.

Once class concluded Friday, we checked out of the hotel and briefed the ambassador. After hearing a report on the week's activities he said, "You're here for the weekend, right? You need to see Angkor Wat."

Embassy staffers recommended a reliable guide that could depart immediately. It was supposed to be a five-hour drive along National Road 6, but our pace was slowed by water buffalo constantly ambling along the blacktop. Once the sun set, we were plunged into darkness, which further reduced our speed; thankfully the hotel held our rooms for a very late arrival. We departed for Siem Reap at sunrise.

Angkor Wat is the largest religious monument in the world and one of the most important archaeological sites in Southeast Asia. Built in the 12th century, the jungle reclaimed this magnificent UNESCO World Heritage site after it was abandoned in 1431, and it remained unknown until French explorers discovered it in the 19th century. The 400-acre complex was amazing, with intricately carved scenes covering massive sandstone structures. The ruins of a royal monastery, Ta Prohm, were left just as they were discovered, enveloped by huge strangler figs, banyan trees, and hanging vines. It was literally a scene from *Lara Croft: Tomb Raider* which was filmed there. We spent the entire day strolling among hundreds of temples, but barely scratched the surface. Sadly, our time was up.

After a six-hour drive to Phnom Penh, we flew to Bangkok and got a few hours' sleep. The concierge arranged for Mr. Chin to take us to the airport at 5:00 a.m. Weaving through traffic like an Indy driver, his Mercedes S430 screeched to a stop at Suvarnabhumi Airport a mere 25 minutes later. The flight to Japan took six hours, after which a lengthy layover provided enough time for a good meal and a shower before boarding the hump of another 747. I'd been in transit for 34 hours when the last flight landed in Oklahoma City.

Fourteen

Joint Terrorism Task Force

The FBI is a huge bureaucracy funded by Congress. Budgets and manpower are tied to national crime trends and anticipated workloads. For accountability, each Agent's work hour is captured and categorized through a system called TURK (Time Utilization and Record Keeping), which is used for Congressional funding requests. For instance, in the 1980s, Congress passed the Financial Institutions Reform, Recovery, and Enforcement Act (FIRREA). FBI Agents hired with FIRREA funding were expected to work only financial crimes. In a perfect world, Agents assigned to white-collar squads would only work financial crimes and Agents on reactive squads would only work bank robberies or kidnappings. But the world is imperfect.

I was hired under the Bureau's accounting program and had always been assigned to a white-collar squad. But TURK revealed that much of my time was spent on international and domestic terrorism. The government had invested a great deal of money training me as a bomb technician, hazardous materials technician, and WMD first responder. Yet my local supervisor was under pressure to keep me working only financial cases. I'd already stepped down from the SWAT team due to the training time associated with being a sniper, but something else had to give.

After 9/11, every FBI office was directed to form a Joint Terrorism Task Force (JTTF). New York developed the model in 1980 and it was adopted nationwide. Though I enjoyed the challenge of financial crimes, moving to JTTF made more sense. The white-collar supervisor would no longer have to complain about my TURK and I'd be free to focus exclusively on the Bureau's counterterrorism and counter–IED missions. There was no shortage of work.

In January I got a call from the Federal Protective Service (FPS), which provides security for federal facilities. The message was simple.

"We have an issue at the new federal building."

After the Murrah Building was destroyed in 1995, a new facility was constructed that overlooked the bombing memorial. Even though the new building incorporated all the latest blast-resistant technologies, it was difficult for some bombing survivors to return to an office that close to the original Murrah site.

While en route to the new federal building, FPS provided updates on the current situation. An unknown man had entered the building, left two notes and a large duffel bag in the lobby, then fled on foot. One note railed against the IRS and stated there was a bomb in the duffel bag. The second note claimed there was a larger bomb in the suspect's car, which had been abandoned just outside. A 12-block perimeter was established and several buildings evacuated; some evacuees were survivors of the Murrah Building.

Using security camera footage, police quickly located and arrested the subject a few blocks away. He'd been convicted of making bomb threats before, but this was the first time he'd actually left something tangible associated with a threat. As JTTF Agents interrogated him, the bomb squad began addressing the IED threats. The bag was quickly cleared with X-rays; no bomb. The car would take a little more time, as explosives can be easily concealed almost anywhere within a vehicle. We remotely opened the old Oldsmobile and searched it with a robot. There was a large ice chest in the trunk, but X-rays revealed no IED. The entire episode was a hoax.

The new year's first international TDY began with a request from the U.S. State Department's Antiterrorism Assistance Program (ATA), which works with partner nations to further American interests abroad. This assignment was in the Kingdom of Bahrain, a small island nation strategically situated in the Persian Gulf. Home to the U.S. Navy's Fifth Fleet, Bahrain has hosted a U.S. naval command since 1948. During the Gulf War, approximately one-third of allied sorties originated there. More recently, Bahrain supported U.S. and British airstrikes targeting the Houthis, who were menacing Red Sea shipping lanes from bases in Yemen. Needless to say, Bahrain is a strategic partner in a volatile part of the world.

The kingdom suffers from a questionable civil rights record and significant political unrest; the Shia majority opposes the Sunni-dominated monarchy. Terrorist groups such as the Iranian-backed al-Ashtar

Brigades (AAB) routinely deploy IEDs against government facilities in an effort to overthrow the government. Once America designated AAB as a foreign terrorist organization, it threatened direct attacks against U.S. and U.K. interests. The goal of this TDY was to determine the efficacy of U.S. counter–IED training and equipment we'd previously provided, and assess the need for further technical support for Bahrain's war on terror.

I arrived in D.C. and took a cab to a nondescript off-site facility maintained by the State Department. The four men I'd be working with introduced themselves as we walked into a geopolitical and threat assessment briefing. The team leader was a 75-year-old former Marine and Diplomatic Security Agent. He'd been operating in the Middle East since I was in high school. Each team member was a subject matter expert (SME) in their field: land border security, port security, and cyber security. I was there as an SME on forensics and counter–IED capabilities. Strangely enough, the rest of the group were all private contractors who'd worked together before. I was an outsider, but the long flights and layovers gave us time to get acquainted.

The final flight from Frankfurt was on Gulf Air, a carrier whose financial woes had been in the news. The plane's peeling paint and rusty rivets didn't go unnoticed. As we bounced down the runway, the illuminated "Exit" sign fell from the ceiling; a sheepish flight attendant nonchalantly kicked it under her seat. Halfway through the flight she gently woke me and seemed to whisper the entrée choices. I was half asleep and thought I heard, "Would you like pasta or ham?"

"I'll try the … ham." As the word left my mouth, I remembered pork is considered unclean in this part of the world. Getting ham on the flag carrier of the Kingdom of Bahrain was highly unlikely. With a rather stern look she clarified in a louder voice, "Pasta or *lamb*?"

"Of course. The lamb would be great."

The embassy's Regional Security Officer (RSO) was waiting on the jet bridge when we arrived in Manama late that night. He was a young, efficient West Pointer who had everything perfectly organized. I signed for an embassy SUV and followed the RSO to our hotel. After checking in, we had a quick meeting by the pool; it was a cool, clear night and scented shisha smoke filled the air.

"I know you're all tired, so I'll make this quick. Even though it's the weekend, we don't have you in country very long. So your first conference is at the Joint Counter Terrorism Center at 0800."

The next morning, we met a highly competent and professional colonel in command of Bahrain's paramilitary Special Security Forces and his British advisor. Though no longer a British protectorate, the Brits maintain a strong influence in Bahrain; residuals like roundabouts and a foot stomping, flat-handed salute remained.

Colonel Hassan soon introduced me to Major Ali Saleh, who oversaw the Kingdom's relatively new EOD unit. Ali would serve as my point of contact for an assessment of his team's capabilities and Bahrain's forensics lab. He was extremely helpful and eager to provide any necessary information, often meeting me in the evenings to provide details of recent IED attacks. One morning we went to a training camp in Safrah to review the team's equipment and observe a training evolution. The new unit was functioning quite well under Ali's leadership.

Similarly dedicated officers ran the nation's forensics lab. Built in the 1980s, it was due for an update to incorporate the latest technology America would provide. Local case presentations highlighted how U.S. equipment had already been used to successfully thwart several terrorist plots within the kingdom.

The RSO maximized our time by splitting the team in half to cover more ground. We'd convene each evening by the pool to review the day's accomplishments and discuss the remaining objectives. Bahrainis have a highly social culture, and informal "working dinners" occurred most every night. The first affair was at Zahle in the elaborate Gulf Hotel. Our hosts arrived wearing traditional Arab attire; their flowing thobes and ghutras were an interesting departure from the crisp, paramilitary uniforms worn during the day.

After formalities, we took our seats at a long table in the rear of the restaurant. Immediately, Lebanese appetizers of every description appeared, followed by a mixed grill of fish, chicken, lamb, and beef, presented on hammered metal grills filled with burning embers to keep the food warm. The embassy reciprocated their hospitality with dinner at Monsoons, a Thai restaurant near the palace in Manama. The restaurant was dimly lit by hundreds of candles freely floating in a meandering stream cut into the stone floor. The last banquet was at Al Yacout, an octagonal Moroccan restaurant designed to resemble a Bedouin tent. We were seated on cushions around low tables. A waterfall spilled from the wall, open flames cast long shadows on the floor, and thin, billowing veils offered vistas of the Arabian Gulf. In the center of the room, a belly dancer performed as imdyazn (musicians) played traditional Moroccan music.

The work week concluded with tours of the Bahrain Coast Guard,

Royal Academy of Police, and various QRFs located at highly sensitive sites. To demonstrate their preparedness, Ali sounded a klaxon at one of the facilities and instantly a large, well-organized contingent of black-clad men fell into formation in front of a fleet of armored vehicles, shoulder weapons at the "ready gun" position.

Once back in the U.S., each SME would prepare a report detailing their respective findings. The report would make its way through the State Department, the embassy, and eventually to the end users in Bahrain. Realizing the written report would take some time, the major general overseeing all law enforcement in the kingdom requested an oral briefing. Before we finished, the RSO leaned over and whispered, "The ambo wants a briefing, too."

The embassy's outer security zone was a maze of concrete Jersey barriers which funneled us to a checkpoint. Nepalese Gurkhas physically searched our vehicle before we moved through layered screening sites using K9s, fluoroscopes, and magnetometers. Once inside, we surrendered our passports to the Marine stationed in a bulletproof cube, then met the ambassador in his large top-floor office. He listened

Author with an unnamed Bahraini EOD technician inspecting a bunker in the Sakhir Desert, Kingdom of Bahrain (January 2010).

intently and seemed sincerely interested in our findings; it appeared more State Department training dollars would be allocated to this strategic island kingdom.

Being in Bahrain for only 10 days, I never really adjusted to Arabian Standard Time. Crossing the Prime Meridian and five time zones, I often awoke after just four hours of sleep. One morning I watched the sun rise over the 15th-century Arad Fort on Muharraq Island. I toured Qal'at al-Bahrain, a World Heritage Site dating back to 2,300 BC, and made the obligatory excursion to the Tree of Life, a 400-year-old mesquite tree standing alone in the Sakhir Desert about two kilometers from Jebel Dukhan.

Just as I became accustomed to the local time zone, the trek home began. My first leg was an hour hop to the United Arab Emirates (UAE), followed by a brutal 15-hour flight from Dubai to D.C. I cleared Customs, flew to Dallas, and finally arrived in Oklahoma City on Friday night after 30 hours in transit.

That weekend gave me time to refine a WMD scenario for OHP's bomb squad. Monday morning, just as Troopers were executing their render safe plan, the commander's phone rang. After a brief conversation he looked at me and relayed the message.

"There's a problem in Boise City. A bank robber left a bomb at the bank."

The small town of 1,500 people occupies the crossroads of two highways in Oklahoma's far northwestern Panhandle. It's actually closer to Denver than Oklahoma City, and from the center of town you could be in four states within an hour.

The chief of police was the sole officer on duty when a man walked into the town's only bank, put a bomb on the counter, and demanded all the cash. There hadn't been a bank robbery in Boise City in recent memory, and never one involving an IED. The chief evacuated the bank and established a 100-yard perimeter around the building. Unfortunately, the perimeter closed the intersection of the only major roads in that part of the state.

Bank robbery is a federal crime that falls under the FBI's jurisdiction, but the nearest FBI Agent was several hours away, so the chief called the closest OHP Trooper. There was only one Trooper anywhere near Boise City, and he immediately called OHP's bomb squad commander in Oklahoma City.

After notifying my office of the robbery, the commander and I called the police chief for more information. As he described the situation, some of the details sounded familiar. The verbiage of the threat was similar to another robbery and the description of the device was almost identical to a hoax IED we had encountered during another bank robbery just two weeks earlier.

The immediate issue for the chief was time and distance; Main Street was closed and that was backing up traffic on two highways. The news media from Amarillo, Texas, was already on scene and everybody wanted the bomb to go away. OHP's commander estimated it would take seven hours for a response team to arrive from Oklahoma City, which wasn't welcome news to the chief. I knew the Bureau had small surveillance aircraft, but nothing big enough to transport bomb techs and their necessary equipment. So I called a friend at the U.S. Customs aviation unit in Oklahoma City.

"Stan, we have an unusual situation. The police chief out in Boise City says he has a bomb in his bank; the whole town and two major highways are shut down. I think this may be a serial bank robber we've dealt with before, but I'm having trouble getting assets up there to assess the device and open things up. Do you think you could get us out there?"

Within 30 minutes, Customs pilots were helping me and two Troopers load gear into a Beechcraft King Air. The local Trooper met us at a very short airstrip outside Boise City, loaded our gear into his SUV, and sped us into town. Within a half hour we confirmed the device was a well-designed hoax attributed to the serial robber. The chief reopened the highways and we flew back to OKC. The lone FBI Agent in Woodward would take the case from there.

Fifteen

The Mola Mola

The specter of nuclear proliferation and nuclear terrorism was now a serious threat to international security. In 2010, President Barack Obama convened the first Nuclear Security Summit in Washington, D.C. World leaders from 47 countries and three international organizations attended to discuss the global nuclear threat, techniques to deter nuclear terrorism, and how to thwart SNM (special nuclear material) smuggling. A conference like this was a tempting target for terrorists, so security was tight.

I arrived at Reagan National, rented a car, and drove to the FBI's Washington Field Office. Home to the National Capital Response Team, the initial briefing took place in its state-of-the-art Command and Tactical Operational Center. Live feeds from various street cameras were displayed on dozens of flat screens along with local and national news. Secure communication links, world clocks, and enough computing power for a space launch were arrayed in this custom-built command center.

I was assigned to one of the summit's multi-agency "all hazard" response teams. Similar teams were formed specifically for intelligence gathering and tactical response. Fifty-two days of preplanning delineated 24-hour security schedules, road closures, and interagency response protocols, including evacuation contingencies for every head of state. Each world leader would have their own security package similar to President Obama's, and all those motorcades and personal security movements had to be closely coordinated. The Secret Service was responsible for physical security, the FBI was responsible for the counterterrorism mission, and FEMA would handle "consequence management" if that need arose. There were a lot of moving parts, but the throng of federal and local agencies came together with only a few wrinkles.

The high-profile nature of this assignment often required rapid and discreet resolutions. One afternoon a surveillance team at the intersection of 11th and L streets near the convention center called in a suspicious package.

"It looks like the utility door at the base of a streetlamp has been pried open. There's some type of case wedged in there. We've got a large group of protesters and a motorcade is just a few minutes out."

Like most suspicious package calls, this item was cleared without incident; X-rays and a physical search revealed the package contained the personal effects of a homeless person. But in that threat environment, nothing could be left to chance.

The following month took me to Batavia, New York, to teach a VBIED countermeasures course. After checking into a quaint hotel, I met the other instructors at State Police headquarters. A nearby rock quarry would serve as the explosives range where we constructed a series of live VBIEDs inside delivery trucks. The quarry's remote location allowed us to demonstrate large countermeasure tools that incorporated an appreciable amount of explosives themselves. Students learned how to build and deploy these specially designed "energetic tools" to successfully defeat the VBIEDs. Though the tools themselves produce significant blast effects, they create much less damage than allowing the device to function as designed.

Each evening the local officers drove us into Buffalo to settle a fiercely contested debate: who had the best Buffalo wings? Though supposedly invented at Anchor Bar, many argued Duff's wings were better. Their motto is "Medium is hot and hot is very, very hot."

Late one evening after some very hot wings, I strolled through the charming town of Batavia, founded in 1801 at the junction of two Iroquois foot trails. It was 9:00 p.m., but the sun was just setting as a huge orange ball at the end of Main Street. It was like a Norman Rockwell painting; the lane was lined with old stone churches, ice cream shops, and beautiful Victorian homes. As the sun sank lower, families gathered on flag-draped porches to enjoy the cool evening air. Kids rode bikes in the street and young couples strolled hand in hand along Tonawanda Creek.

I got home Friday evening and celebrated Father's Day early because my next flight departed at sunrise Sunday. It didn't seem possible, but I was already eligible to attend a retirement conference in Sacramento: three days of lectures on annuities, long-term health insurance, and qualified retirement plans. Due to the rigors of the job, federal law enforcement agents are required to retire at age 57. However, they're *eligible* to retire at age 50 with 20 years of service, or at any age with 25 years of service. Under those rules, I could theoretically retire at age 49.

The relatively young mandatory retirement age complicated normal retirement and Social Security plans. So these seminars were offered a couple of years prior to retirement eligibility to explain the financial nuances. The speaker began with some basic questions: "Are you comfortable managing your own assets or should you hire an expert? If you hire someone, can you trust them with your life's savings?"

I'd heard some of this before; as the Training Coordinator in Oklahoma City, I occasionally brought in speakers to provide this type of training for office personnel. Months before the Sacramento conference, I hosted a widely touted financial advisor named Wayne McLeod, who specialized in the unique provisions of the federal law enforcement retirement system. He came highly recommended by other federal agencies and had a long list of impressive credentials. As his host, I took him to dinner and we naturally discussed retirement planning.

"So you're an accountant? Well, I'm sure you have a pretty good grasp of how this all works, but you're not a Certified Financial Planner. My company manages portfolios for several other agencies and even your former Director. The staff handles most accounts, but after getting to know you, I'd be willing to invest your funds personally. Think it over and let me know."

I'd always managed my own financial affairs. But as retirement drew closer, maybe it was time to let a professional take over. So my ears perked up when the Sacramento speaker began Day Two by saying, "Let's talk about financial advisors. Has anyone heard of FEB Group?"

That was McLeod's company. The speaker projected a newspaper article from that morning's *The Florida Times-Union* which read in part, "Investment adviser ran a Ponzi scheme that raised at least $34 million from federal employees across the nation. McLeod killed himself Tuesday four days after telling investors the fund was closed and no more money would be paid out. In a complaint filed Thursday, the SEC charged McLeod's firms with fraudulently soliciting investors for a government bond fund that never existed" (Harding 2010).

This was stunning news; just a few weeks before, McLeod had magnanimously offered to personally manage my life's savings. I'd dodged a bullet and decided to continue managing my own money.

After a few weeks back in Oklahoma, I was scheduled to speak at a conference in Atlanta. Don, my good friend and counterpart, was the host. Like any good host he rolled out the red carpet.

"Tammy and I would like you to come to the house for dinner one evening. And if I recall correctly, you're an avid SCUBA diver, right? I arranged a little tour of the Georgia Aquarium for you."

The Security Director met me at the gate early one evening. As we walked through the various exhibit levels, the scale of the facility became apparent.

"I thought the Melbourne Aquarium was big, but this place is enormous."

He just smiled. "Melbourne is about half a million gallons. We're over eight million, the largest aquarium in the world. What'd you think of Melbourne?"

"It was impressive—they let me dive with the sharks."

"Don mentioned that. Want to dive with our whale sharks? They're about the size of a city bus and we're the only place outside of Asia that has them." He didn't have to ask twice; it was an amazing experience.

Once the security conference at the Georgia Dome concluded, I gave a presentation for Georgia Tech's campus security team. Violence at universities, like the OU bombing and Virginia Tech's shooting, were on the rise and most universities were updating their response protocols. I got home Friday evening and packed for Monday's departure to LAX.

The rest of the team was waiting in LA when I arrived. We had a working dinner in Hermosa Beach and spent the next day checking our gear before a 1:55 a.m. flight to Indonesia. The terrorist group Jemaah Islamiyah and various violent splinter groups associated with al-Qaeda had a long track record of bombings in Indonesia, which was why we were going. The State Department wanted us to provide post-blast training for the nation's crime scene investigators, forensics lab personnel, and counterterrorism command.

After 27 hours in transit, an embassy expediter met us in Jakarta. As drivers loaded our bags into two armored Suburbans he said, "Mr. Black, we have your accommodations ready. You may choose between the Ritz-Carlton or the JW Marriott. Which do you prefer?"

"There must be some mistake. You know we're on government per diem, right? We can't go over the approved lodging rate."

"Yes, of course. Both hotels have been bombed at least once, so we get rates well under per diem."

"In that case, let's go to the Ritz."

Both hotels were controlled by U.S. interests, which made them viable terrorist targets. In the latest attacks, just 11 months before, suicide bombers killed nine and injured more than 50 people eating breakfast in the hotels' restaurants. Their IEDs detonated just five minutes apart and a subsequent search located a time bomb in a hotel room; it would have detonated, but the timer malfunctioned. Since those attacks, security had been enhanced at both properties. Before entering the Ritz's parking lot, our vehicles were searched by guards and K9s. Once through the barricades, we were physically searched and our baggage X-rayed prior to entering the lobby.

The first day in Jakarta was spent on logistics: meeting the interpreters who helped us purchase materials needed to construct the IEDs, and finding an appropriate explosives range. The best facility was in Bogor, about an hour's drive from Jakarta. Driving back from the range, the Legal Attaché offered a little diversion.

"We have you on a pretty tight schedule and tomorrow is your only day off. If you don't mind getting on another airplane, you should really get over to Java. It's beautiful and there's a lot of history there."

"Sounds good. Can you get us a flight?"

"I've been several times and know a good tour company. Let me make a few calls."

John, an SABT from Kansas City, and I left at 6:00 a.m. on a Lion Air 737 to Yogyakarta; the 600-kilometer flight took about an hour. Rika, the tour guide, and a driver were waiting when we landed. We spent several hours stopping at small temples and the Sultan's Palace en route to Prambanan, one of the largest Hindu temples in Southeast Asia. Built during the ninth century, it was rediscovered in 1733 by a Dutch explorer.

The next World Heritage site was Borobudur, a single colossal building that's the largest Buddhist temple in the world. Built around 800 AD in the center of a giant lake, it was buried in ash from the massive eruption of Mount Merapi in 1006 AD, then slowly consumed by the jungle. An Englishman rediscovered the site in 1814 and it was restored to its former glory in the early 1900s. After that tour, we stopped at an open air market for dinner with some locals before returning to the airport. The flight to Jakarta was an hour late, but we were back at the Ritz by 9:00 p.m.

The week's work schedule was full. I spent most of the time in Bogor, but was scheduled to lecture Monday and Wednesday in one of the hotel conference rooms. A check of the calendar caused a little concern. Some terrorists plan attacks in clusters and see anniversaries or key dates as attractive times to strike. Our conference room was directly above the restaurant that had been destroyed by a suicide bomber a few months before, and the anniversary of a prior attack would occur that week. This particular conference would have Indonesia's counterterrorism commanders, leading forensic scientists, top crime scene investigators, and a handful of FBI experts together in one room.

Fortunately, the hotel's security contractor was a former Green Beret who was never far away. After discussing the timing of the conference, he came up with a plan.

"Tell you what, I'll have a Special Action Unit stationed in the lobby and around the hotel perimeter. They're heavily armed and hard to miss; that should deter any threats. I'll post outside the conference room myself."

As promised, there was a very high security presence when class began on Monday. That evening the Legal Attaché stopped by and said, "Day One went well. I'd like you guys to join me for a little working dinner over at the JW Marriott. Meet me in the Pearl about 8:00 PM."

The hotel was a block away and had also been bombed several times. We were ushered into a private room where the chef presented the evening's menu: chilled jellyfish rolls, pumpkin soup with seafood and quail eggs, Peking duck, and steamed Soon Hock. The nine-course meal lasted over two hours, which afforded plenty of time to talk shop with the other guests, commanders of Detachment 88.

Established as Indonesia's elite counterterrorism unit after the bombing in Bali, they provided a comprehensive briefing of Indonesia's counterterrorism capabilities. As the evening concluded, the commander leaned in and whispered, "Please advise me prior to any detonations in Bogor. The president's residence is nearby and I should alert his security staff."

Each morning I notified the commander before detonating a series of window-rattling VBIEDs, which the students then processed for evidence. The course was successful and concluded late Friday afternoon with each team presenting its findings to a panel from the Attorney General's Office. After a series of photos and hearty goodbyes, I headed straight to the airport for a flight to Bali; it was time for a little vacation.

Things didn't start well. My flight was delayed, then combined with another flight. I was assigned the very last seat on the very last row of an aging Garuda Air 737. To make matters worse, the diminutive man in front of me decided to fully recline his seat; I spent the next 93 minutes with his head in my lap. We landed about 10:00 p.m. and I hired a "fixed price" taxi to take me to the hotel in Nusa Dua. Apparently there were two properties with the same name and he took me to the wrong one. It was approaching midnight as the soft-spoken receptionist apologized and offered to call their sister property. With a warm island smile she said, "Mr. Barry, your room will not be ready until tomorrow. Our properties are oversold."

"Tomorrow? I'm only here for two nights." I produced a confirmation number and receipt showing advance payment in full.

"Oh, I see. Yes, we will make accommodation for you here."

A driver from Atlantis Divers picked me up at 7:00 a.m. After a four-hour journey we arrived in Tulamben on Bali's east coast in the shadow of the Gunung Agung volcano. Porters carried my gear down a cliff and across the black volcanic sand; the sloping sea floor offered a perfect spot for shore entry and access to the wreck of USAT *Liberty*. The 400-foot-long Army transport was sunk by a Japanese torpedo in 1942.

The wreck was impressive, but my primary reason to dive in Bali was a chance to see the elusive Mola mola. They're the largest bony fish on earth and live at extreme depths, but once a year they can be found in relatively shallow water near Bali. I booked a boat out of Sanur and told the guide, Kristine, my objective.

She smiled knowingly and said, "Yes, everyone wants to see the Mola mola and they're spectacular. But in all my diving here, I've only seen one. It was two days ago near Nusa Penida, about an hour away. We will go there and maybe get lucky."

There were several boats already at anchor when we arrived at Crystal Bay. We hastily donned our gear and descended to the spot where Kristine had seen the huge fish. The water was crystal clear and the sandy bottom sloped away from the boat almost immediately; even without Mola mola, this was a stunning site with abundant marine life. We hit a thermocline at 100 feet and the water temperature dropped dramatically. At about 130 feet, Kristine noticed a flash of silver. She motioned to me and we descended for a closer look.

It was amazing; hanging there nearly motionless at the edge of a steep wall were not one, but six Mola mola. I checked my dive computer; we were 150 feet below the surface, so there wasn't much time to linger. Just as we began our ascent, two dozen divers feverishly descended upon us, causing the fish to slowly turn and fade into the abyss. Kristine and I compared notes back aboard the *My Darling*; she had remained a few meters above me and saw only four of the six I'd seen. The boat captain was amazed; spotting more than one was rare, but six was now the local record.

Our second dive site was aptly named Manta Point. We settled near the seafloor along a shallow reef and watched several manta rays glide overhead. They were enormous, about 12 feet across, and weighed more than a ton.

The next day I hired a local guide, Widi, to show me Bali's other highlights. We trekked the trails of Ubud's Sacred Monkey Forest and saw a temple purification ritual that occurs once every 30 years. Villagers dressed in white made special offerings as chaotic gamelan rhythms played and monkeys howled in the jungle canopy. Next we crossed the central part of the island, passing the terraced rice fields of Tegallalang on the way to the volcanic peaks of Batur. There was no GPS, but the driver confidently told Widi he knew a shortcut that would save us hours en route to the temples of Danua Bratan.

I became skeptical as the van crept along steep, single-lane dirt "roads" with acute switchbacks hewn from the thick jungle. There were few other cars and definitely no tourists. When we finally stumbled across a little village, Widi got out and asked for directions; we were lost. As they talked, village kids gathered and stared, pointing curiously at me sitting alone in the back of the large van.

Two harrowing hours later we arrived at Bedugul in a light mist. The site was surrounded by cloud-shrouded mountains, and thick fog hugged Lake Beratan where 400-year-old temples rose from the water. It's easy to see why locals thought spirits lived here.

It had been a fun few days, but I needed to get back home. As we wound our way to the hotel, I asked Widi to stop at Kuta Beach, where Bali's deadliest terror attack had occurred seven years before. The well-coordinated Jemaah Islamiyah attack began with an IED outside the U.S. Consulate in Denpasar, then a suicide bomber detonated a backpack inside Paddy's Pub. About 20 seconds later, a VBIED leveled the popular Sari Club and destroyed several other buildings. A makeshift memorial was eventually replaced with a huge marble plaque etched with the victims' names (Australian Federal Police 2024).

At 3:45 a.m., a cab dropped me at I Gusti Ngurah Rai International Airport. In the predawn darkness, a porter advised it would cost 750,000 rupiahs to get my SCUBA gear on the plane. That sounded like a lot until I did a quick conversion in my head; it was about 52 USD. Shaking his head, he emphatically exclaimed, "No, no dollars. No credit card. Rupiahs only."

I didn't have that much local currency and the only money changer in the small airport had forgotten his cash drawer key. I explained to him that missing this flight would delay my departure by at least a day.

"My home not far. I return in time, you see."

He did and I caught the flight to Java, transferred to a Boeing 777 to Hong Kong, then went on to Singapore. After 19 hours I landed in Chicago, cleared Customs, and boarded a two-hour flight to Oklahoma City.

The next TDY was much closer to home, in Arlington, Texas. Super Bowl XLV had been designated as an NSSE and I was assigned to assist. Cowboys Stadium was amazing, the largest domed stadium in the world with the fourth-largest HD video screen on the planet. Intelligence and actual attacks around the world indicated that this type of venue was an attractive terrorist target. Interagency response teams were deployed to the game and all pregame activities.

The Super Bowl itself was just the culmination of a weeklong party with concerts and activities for throngs of fans at the NFL Experience. It was like Mardi Gras, with Steelers fans wearing top hats and beads and Packers in huge foam cheeseheads.

My team spent the week supporting the counter–IED mission at various sites and conducting radiological assessments with the DOE. Having DOE onsite may seem excessive, but NSSE plans must consider every possibility. Radiological Dispersal Devices, or "dirty bombs," and improvised nuclear weapons are actively sought by terrorists, and no one wanted a *Sum of All Fears* moment like Jack Ryan faced at that championship game.

Beyond the spectacle of the big game itself, the news was dominated by inclement weather. A freak winter storm delayed hundreds of flights to Dallas and played havoc with every aspect of the pregame activities. Even I wasn't spared. The Bureau had just shipped me a brand new, fully equipped F-250 response vehicle, and this was its first deployment. My team of state police bomb techs, DOE assessors, a K9, and a medic were inside the stadium when we heard a low rumble. Instantly the medic's radio crackled: "…several injured outside."

We rushed out to see huge, jagged pieces of ice covering the ground. It wasn't a terrorist attack; the arena's heaters had warmed the enormous retractable roof to the point where all the snow and ice avalanched, crashing 292 feet to the ground below. A local news helicopter captured the massive ice sheet sliding off the roof and showering workers below; six people were sent to the hospital (ESPN.com 2011). The video also captured dozens of frozen missiles shattering my truck's windshield and puncturing holes in the body. The news footage was played back home, clearly showing the avalanche engulfing my truck. As expected, the good-natured harassment began immediately. Once Green Bay accepted the Lombardi Trophy, I got the windshield replaced and drove back to Oklahoma City in several inches of snow and –5°F temperatures.

Unusual weather continued to plague me during the next assignment. High winds and mechanical failures put me in Savannah, Georgia, shortly before 1:00 a.m.; it took another hour to gather my gear and rent a Suburban. About 2:30 a.m., fighting sleep and mindlessly obeying the GPS, I noticed some flashing lights in the rearview. On a lonely stretch of blacktop, a local officer informed me that the speed limit on Georgia Highway 21 is only 45 mph. After explaining all the weapons and stacks of Pelican cases weighing down the Suburban, I was on my way with a polite warning.

Savannah had been selected as an alternate site for the domestic underwater post-blast course usually taught in LA. Having an east coast location would reduce costs and travel time for divers from that half of the country. Not only did we "train the trainers" for future courses, we had a full class of divers and bomb techs from the U.S. Navy, Coast Guard, and police units from New York, Florida, South Carolina, and Georgia. The class concluded Friday afternoon with presentations and a recap of the week's events. I returned the Suburban, checked my bags, and was home by midnight.

Sixteen

Just Another Day

When I was an accountant in the private sector, or even working financial crimes for the Bureau, one day was pretty much like another. But the move to JTTF gave each day a new potential. One morning my phone rang. It was the watch commander at the Norman Police Department.

"We just had a bomb threat at the station. We know who did it because he gave us his name."

Making a telephonic bomb threat is a federal felony which gives the FBI jurisdiction. But it's also a state crime, so I had to ask. "I'm happy to help. But if you know who it is, can't you pick him up?"

"Well, here's the thing. This guy, Ellis, is a fugitive with warrants for violating a VPO. He says if we don't stop asking all his buddies about him, he'll toss a bomb in the station. He's threatened to kill a judge and some other people, but also made references to being like Timothy McVeigh and killing women and children. We traced this last call to his aunt's house in Tulsa and thought the Bureau could expedite things."

The FBI had a small office in Tulsa, but the fastest way to apprehend this fugitive would be the local police. A Tulsa detective was on JTTF, so he sent officers to Ellis's aunt's house. As patrol cars pulled up, Ellis bolted through the back door and a foot chase ensued. Of course he was caught and arrested on the outstanding local warrants. Within a week I filed federal charges against him for the bomb threat and took him into custody. He pled guilty and was sentenced to 30 months in prison. I thought I'd never hear about him again, but he resurfaced years later in a domestic terrorism investigation.

Another unusual call came in one day just before lunch. A young sergeant with the Military Police at Fort Sill called, saying, "Sir, EOD thought we should give you a call. An AWOL soldier showed up on post with a bag of weapons and an IED."

Police stations and military bases had proven to be attractive targets for terrorists domestically and abroad. Insider threats were a real possibility, and nothing could be dismissed as "impossible." Given the gravity of the situation, Fort Sill was locked down until the subject was subdued. We X-rayed the package, which revealed an elaborate hoax device; subsequent searches of his quarters and vehicle turned up nothing incriminating. He was charged with a litany of federal violations to enhance his AWOL status.

In another instance, the FBI office in Jacksonville sent a lead to our JTTF regarding a fugitive wanted for bombing a mosque in Florida. Information was developed that he might be hiding in the remote, windswept prairie of northwest Oklahoma. Aerial surveillance confirmed a small campsite on a rugged butte in the Gloss Mountains that afforded a commanding view of the barren plains below. That vantage made any approach dangerous, so two SWAT teams made their way in the predawn hours. As they discreetly scaled the rocky butte, the fugitive emerged from his tent brandishing an AK-47; a sniper terminated that threat.

OHP bomb techs and I checked his body for explosives, then began a search of his camp and vehicle in hopes of finding evidence that would tie him to the mosque bombing. No explosive threats were discovered, so we turned the scene over to ERT. Their search was followed by a shooting review investigation which exonerated our personnel.

In another case, FBI Puerto Rico developed an informant who said a former Army commando had stolen a cache of military explosives and was storing them in an old farmhouse in rural Oklahoma. Though many informants provide vague information, this source gave the soldier's name and specified the type of ordnance he stole: Claymore mines.

There was a time when such a crazy-sounding tip might not have garnered much attention. But in the current threat environment, nothing could be ignored. We checked the information against military records and learned there was a former Green Beret with that name. His military specialty was explosives, which would have given him access to Claymore mines. Public records revealed he owned a farmhouse in rural Jackson County, Oklahoma, and the IRS was about to seize it for back taxes. The prospect of a highly trained man equipped with anti-personnel mines awaiting an IRS seizure team was a recipe for disaster, regardless of how bizarre the situation sounded. We determined the subject was now a private contractor working in

Afghanistan, but was scheduled to return home in 10 days. The totality of these circumstances gave sufficient probable cause for a search warrant.

A pre-raid briefing occurred in the early morning hours at the Jackson County Sheriff's office. Local police, EMTs, FBI ERT, and OHP bomb techs and K9s gathered to support the search. This was an unusual situation. Military ordnance falls under the purview of the U.S. military, but due to the Posse Comitatus Act, the military can't perform domestic law enforcement functions. However, they can provide technical assistance.

I'd already looped in Captain Gates at Fort Sill's 761st EOD unit, who agreed to have a team on standby; the post commander wouldn't allow his men to deploy unless military ordnance was actually discovered. The last step was to confirm the whereabouts of the suspect. We didn't want an angry commando stumbling into the search scene. I contacted an FBI Agent embedded at the same Afghan camp where the suspect was working. He had eyes on the contractor and would attempt an interview once our search began.

The initial entry would be made by bomb techs supported by K9 teams. We left the blacktop and drove for several miles down the rural dirt roads with nothing but wheat fields as far as the eye could see. It had rained overnight and the muddy roads were nearly impassable; I switched the big F-250 into 4WD and clawed my way past each section line. OHP's response trucks were fishtailing and sliding as they tried to stay in my tracks. We finally reached the farm sitting alone in an open field, apparently unoccupied.

Booby traps were a concern, so after clearing the outbuildings we made entry through a laundry room window. Most of the furniture had been removed, but we found numerous weapons, about two dozen military ammunition cans, and 10 footlockers. As expected, the K9s alerted on the ammo cans, but they also hit on the footlockers. We X-rayed and cleared each item as it was discovered. Throughout the morning we found standard issue gear: helmets, body armor, and thousands of rounds of military ammo in various calibers. Then things got interesting. X-rays revealed what appeared to be grenades in one of the footlockers. We carefully opened the case and discovered hand grenade simulators, several military smoke grenades, and riot grenades containing tear gas. There were also explosive artillery ground burst simulators, fusing assemblies, grenade bodies, and binary explosive mixtures. Then, buried in a locked footlocker under the dining room table, we found what we'd come for: an M18A1 Claymore directional anti-personnel mine complete with its military detonator, firing wire, and clacker.

These mines are brutal killing machines containing a pound and a half of C4 that propels hundreds of steel balls in a 60-degree spread. It didn't appear to be modified, so this was a military matter. I briefed Captain Gates over the phone and securely transferred our digital images and X-rays.

"Well, that's a fully functional, live Claymore. I don't see any modifications, so it's safe to handle. It'll take several hours for us to get way up there, so just store it in your bunker if you'd like. But looking at all that other stuff, you may have a problem. Many of those simulators, the CS grenades, and that binary are in pretty rough shape. All of that together has an appreciable net explosive weight. Just to be safe, I'd BIP it."

"BIP" is an acronym for "blow in place." Instead of destroying the farmhouse with a countercharge, we remotely moved the unstable ordnance into a deep bar ditch and destroyed it with a liberal application of C4. As ERT began their search for documentary evidence, I secured the Claymore and started the 180-mile trip back to Oklahoma City.

In order to charge the suspect with possession of stolen military ordnance, we had to be absolutely certain it was authentic. Short of detonating it, the only way to be sure was to have the lab chemically test the explosive filler material. Since this evidence was very hazardous by definition, we couldn't just FedEx it to Quantico. The Bureau's aviation unit advised that the Dash 8 was flying HRT back to Manassas from a mission out west. They could divert the jet to Oklahoma City to take me and the Claymore back to Virginia.

A scientist from the Explosives Unit met me at the Bureau's airstrip, took custody of the mine, then drove me to Dulles for a commercial flight home. Chemical analysis determined the Claymore and detonator were live. Even more damning, the Latent Fingerprint Section lifted the subject's prints from the mine's plastic case. The contractor ultimately admitted to stealing the ordnance while on active duty, but only to keep as a souvenir. He pled guilty to federal charges and was sentenced to two years in prison. But as a result of the conviction, he lost his security clearance and that lucrative job as a defense contractor.

In another case, a man entered a bank brandishing a pistol. He approached a young teller and placed a brown briefcase on the counter. He opened the case to reveal a complex-looking device and shouted, "This is a remote control bomb. Give me all the money, now!" The terrified teller emptied her cash drawer into a bag and breathed a sigh of relief when the robber fled, taking the bomb with him.

Despite being visibly shaken, the teller was able to describe the pistol and IED, gave a remarkably good description of the bandit, and even recalled that a Ford Fiesta was waiting for him in the parking lot. We put a BOLO (be on the lookout) out for the vehicle and soon a local officer spotted a car matching the description driving erratically. He fell in behind the Fiesta and attempted to pull it over, but the driver wouldn't yield. After a short chase through a residential neighborhood, two men bailed out and ran. A police helicopter directed officers and K9s to the pair, who were hiding in a backyard shed. Desperate to avoid being mauled by the German Shepherd, they surrendered.

Both men refused to talk, so we had to go with the information provided by the teller. A robot was used to visually inspect the car. Its black-and-white cameras revealed that the doors were locked and the key was in the ignition. A large knife and pistol were visible on the passenger floorboard and a brown briefcase was on the backseat. The teller specifically recalled the robber saying this was a remote control device, yet neither man possessed a transmitter. Could a third person have the trigger, or did they discard it during the chase?

The robot had been deployed with a specialized tool already loaded and ready to fire. Recognizing the need to target the briefcase in a specific area, we used a laser to designate the point of impact, then fired a focused, high-velocity jet of water through the car door. The shot had the desired effect, opening the briefcase and expelling its contents. Electrical components and a detonator were separated from the explosive main charge, which tumbled out the other side of the tiny car. As the robot moved around to inspect what had been ejected, its cameras focused on banded stacks of cash: $27,000 of soaking wet bank robbery loot. Who puts bank robbery money in with a bomb? Analysis of the components revealed it to be an elaborate inert device. The bumbling pair were soon identified by fingerprints that revealed the robber had been released from prison just nine days before.

Working dogs, like the German Shepherd that nabbed the bank robbers, are amazing assets used by both law enforcement and the military. Explosive-detection K9s are specifically trained to alert on unique chemical signatures of explosives. Historically, dogs weren't trained on peroxide-based explosives like TATP or HMTD because they were deemed too unstable for use in IEDs. But recent TATP cases identified that as a significant training gap which had to be corrected.

As a result, the FBI and our military partners entered into a memorandum of understanding (MOU) whereby chemists in the FBI Explosives Unit would create TATP and HMTD and safely ship the samples to FBI SABTs across the country. We would then make the material available in a controlled environment so military and police trainers could safely "imprint" their canines, giving them that new detection capability.

During one of the peroxide training sessions, an Air Force kennel master mentioned something surprising. His military working dogs (MWD) were routinely deployed overseas in helicopters, but most of them had never been exposed to the noise and sensation of combat flight. Without practice, getting a German shepherd or highly strung Belgian Malinois to board a flight-ready Blackhawk was tricky, especially in a combat zone. Other trainers from Air Force and Army kennels confirmed this was an issue and opined it would take just two or three iterations of boarding, flying, and landing to acclimate the dogs.

It seemed like a simple fix. I had friends at the Army National Guard's Aviation Support Facility near Lexington, Oklahoma, that routinely flew CH-47s and Blackhawks, the same airframes used to deploy MWD teams in theater. After a series of emails with a captain, two majors, and three colonels, it was all set. Most of the unit's training missions were flown with no passengers, or "pax," so it wouldn't cost anything to place MWD teams aboard the empty flights. I drafted a MOU which was readily approved by all the necessary officials.

Many see the twin rotor CH-47s as slow, lumbering machines used only for hauling equipment, but their size is deceiving. The Chinook is actually one of the fastest and most powerful helicopters in the U.S. fleet. Their tremendous lift made them perfect for combat missions in the high altitudes of Afghanistan, while Blackhawks were better suited to operate in Iraq. The new K9 Combat Flight Acclimation Program would use both.

As the crew chief for the first test flight read off the pre-flight checklist, each sentence seemed to begin with the phrase, "If we catch on fire…" Since I was the only one not wearing a flame-retardant Nomex flight suit, I had to ask if fires were that common.

He laughed. "No, we just have to cover it. And remember not to go in front when the blades are turning, they dip to within four feet of the ground. You don't want to be there."

The first flight needed to go smoothly, so we selected an experienced dog team just back from the desert. Neither Rex nor his handler had any problems pushing through the rotor wash and boarding the back ramp of the cavernous Chinook. However, the next two dogs had never flown. The flight maneuvers and altitude changes weren't the problem; the issue was acclimating the dogs to loading and unloading quickly in a simulated combat environment with deafening noise and gale-force rotor wash. But as the trainers predicted, each team was perfectly at ease after just two or three attempts.

The Army's caveat for the MWD flights was we couldn't alter their preset flight plans. That made for some pretty wild rides as Blackhawk pilots honed their nap-of-the-earth skills, jerking and banking low and fast over the local terrain. The first "confined space" landing occurred as a young pilot dropped the giant Chinook straight down through the woods into a clearing the size of a postage stamp. Next came a pinnacle landing on a two-story flat-topped mound of dirt used to simulate an urban rooftop assault. The pilot adeptly flared the nose and lightly rested the rear ramp on the edge of the makeshift roof. The dog teams disembarked and reloaded before the final exercise, a 60 mph touch-and-go landing. The close working relationship that was

(From left): USAF Staff Sgt. Jesse Galvan with K9 Cita, author, and Staff Sgt. Dwight Veon with K9 Blackie preparing for K9 combat flight orientation training (February 2012).

developed with the military led to open discussions for additional unique training opportunities.

Some MWDs are trained to detect explosives and others alert on narcotics. But due to safety and security concerns, handlers' kits are made up of small training aides often measured in grams or ounces and the training occurs in highly controlled, often unrealistic environments. As a result, some trainers reported their dogs seemed overwhelmed in the field when confronted with large quantities of drugs. They felt if the dogs were exposed to larger amounts in training, they would alert more reliably on actual calls.

Understanding the training gap, I devised a solution. OHP had massive quantities of seized narcotics along with smugglers' vehicles. Both were held by OHP awaiting regularly scheduled destruction. I located a huge, disused state facility on the outskirts of town and proposed we utilize it and the seized drugs and vehicles for "mass narcotics odor" training.

Without disrupting the destruction schedule, OHP agreed to maintain custody of the narcotics and vehicles and provide Troopers as security at the abandoned facility. We concealed pounds of seized meth, heroin, and cocaine inside the hidden compartments of actual smugglers' vehicles, which provided a much more realistic training environment for the K9s. The program was an amazing success, with dog teams from the USAF, Army, and police interdiction units from across the southwest participating.

With a desire to expand the training possibilities, some military trainers and kennel masters asked if we could also provide mass odor training for explosive detection. They reported MWDs were often overwhelmed by large amounts of explosives encountered in caches overseas or in buried IEDs. The K9's behavior would change, but it wasn't the standard "alert" associated with smaller quantities. So we expanded the mass narcotics training to include explosives. Given unfettered access to the state's secure remote facility, we buried cases of TNT on the surrounding grounds and hid large quantities of C4, detonating cord, and other stable explosives within the cavernous warehouses of the complex.

As word of this unique quarterly training spread, teams traveled from across Oklahoma, Texas, New Mexico, Kansas, and Arkansas. To ease logistical concerns and train as many K9s as possible, we held the peroxide and mass explosives training the same day as the mass narcotics training. OHP was an integral partner, supplying bomb techs and security throughout the sprawling complex. Making explosives and narcotics training available at one location on the same day allowed military kennels to fully load a trailer with both types of specialized K9s and maximize their training time.

The partnerships and realistic training were a huge success. One Air Force inspection report cited the distinctive training as a benchmark other bases throughout the country should adopt. Its value was also credited in a USAF After Action Review. While patrolling a village near a U.S. FOB (forward operating base) in Afghanistan, the handler noticed a change in his dog's behavior outside a mud brick building. It was subtle, but identical to the change detected in the mass odor training. A team searched the building and discovered a large hoard of explosives which EOD blew in place, denying terrorists access to that cache.

The character and professionalism of our military partners were always impressive and it was an honor to work with them in any capacity. It was a pleasure to develop training tailored to their needs, and those efforts didn't go unnoticed. I was humbled to be selected as the keynote speaker at the first "Dining Out" event for Fort Sill's 761st EOD unit. These black-tie affairs predate the Revolutionary War and are designed to foster esprit de corps amid strictly prescribed pomp and circumstance. The evening was very impressive with a formal receiving

U.S. Army First Sgt. Brett Fisher (left) and Capt. Brandon Gates presenting me with the inaugural 761st EOD Dining Out speaker's award (November 2012).

line, the national anthem, and toasts to the President. As was the custom, no one began eating until a designated taster announced, "The meal is fit to eat." I was also privileged to later be named an honorary Air Force Commander due to my close relationship with the kennels, Security Forces, and Office of Special Investigations.

Seventeen

Jesse James

The next VBIED post-blast course was scheduled at Eglin Air Force Base in Florida's Panhandle, where 53 military and police bomb techs joined crime scene personnel from 18 different agencies. The scenarios began with a briefing from the Security Forces commander, who advised that a 1,500-pound VBIED had detonated at the main gate that morning. The explosion was immediately followed by a series of smaller bombings throughout the surrounding town. As usual, the class was then broken into teams and tasked with simultaneously processing each scene. Instructors gave "witness" interviews, which led to my hotel room, where incriminating evidence was discovered during a late-night search.

Once the class in Pensacola concluded, I flew to Quantico for a WMD conference. A CIRG supervisor called Tuesday morning, saying, "Hey, State Department would like your help with a capabilities assessment in Pakistan. You'll head out in about three weeks. OIO is working on the visa now."

U.S. relations with Pakistan were still tepid. This was 2012; it had barely been a year since Navy SEALs killed bin Laden in Abbottabad during Operation Neptune Spear. The raid caught Pakistan's Inter-Services Intelligence by surprise and soured relationships.

Once back from Quantico, Air Force doctors reviewed my medical records and provided necessary boosters for DTaP, pre-exposure rabies, and malaria prophylaxis. I was almost packed when Danielle from OIO called.

"Hey, the Pakistanis are dragging their feet on your visa. The TDY is still a go, so just sit tight and I'll keep you posted." Nineteen hours before departure, the entire assignment was canceled.

A few days later she called again. "OK, we just got your official passport back from the Pakistanis. That trip is still off, but CIRG could use you in Libya. Are you available?"

"I already cleared my calendar for Islamabad, so sure."

"Great, the RSO in Tripoli will contact you directly about the assignment parameters." Several emails and phone calls were exchanged outlining the current threat environment and what to expect in Libya. As the date grew closer, the RSO expressed some security concerns.

"I think we're going to have you stay on the embassy compound instead of a hotel in town. I'll assign you a driver, an armored Land Rover, and a small security detail. Things seem a little sketchy right now."

The TDY was scheduled to last through September 1. But like the assignment in Islamabad, the RSO canceled the tour just hours before departure.

"Things are too unstable here. We'll reschedule down the road."

Nobody could know that Ambassador Christopher Stevens and three other Americans would be assassinated in Benghazi, Libya on September 11. American interests were under attack throughout North Africa and the Middle East.

In mid–October CIRG called again. "Those last two cancellations were unfortunate and unexpected. Would you be willing to teach a couple of courses at the police academy in Trinidad? We can promise this one won't get canceled."

The tropical islands of Trinidad and Tobago were a far cry from Pakistan and Libya, even though Trinidad had one of the highest murder rates in the Caribbean. With fond memories of the Miss Universe pageant, I flew to Houston and boarded a 737 for the 2,600-mile flight to Piarco International Airport. Thanks to a short diplomatic line, I cleared Customs and walked outside in a matter of minutes. Just beyond the glass doors of baggage claim stood a smiling man holding a sign with my name.

"Good evening, Mr. Black, I'm Jesse James. Your embassy hired me as your driver for the week. The rest of your group has been delayed by the storm." Tropical Storm Rafael had grounded all flights from Miami.

It was 10:00 p.m. and I hadn't eaten, so Jesse stopped at a street vendor for some "hot doubles," curried chickpeas in paper-thin flatbread. A wild Saturday night was underway in Port of Spain, but I just wanted to get some rest. At check-in, the hotel clerk provided a note saying the rest of the team would arrive by morning.

I was pleased to see Bret, an old friend and talented instructor from Quantico, arrive the next morning. We ordered breakfast and discussed the week's itinerary. We would present Major Case Management and the Incident Command System (ICS), and the other instructors would cover violent crimes and homicide investigations. Rafael hadn't reached the islands yet, so Jesse suggested a sunny Sunday drive up the North Coast Road to Maracas.

As the afternoon wore on, Jesse pointed to a shanty across from the beach. "Richard's Bake and Shark Shack is very good; we'll eat there." We each had fried hammerhead sandwiches with spicy pineapple chow that Jesse whipped up in the back of the van. I drew the line when he ordered a Styrofoam cup full of chicken feet; iguana and opossum were also on the menu.

Class started Monday morning at the National Police Academy in St. James, where the Superintendent of Police and several representatives from the U.S. Embassy gave opening remarks. The students comprised a new unit established to prepare the Trinidad and Tobago Police Service (TTPS) to manage complex, major cases. I provided an overview and lessons learned from WACMUR and OKBOMB, and outlined the best practices for managing protracted, high-profile, multi-agency investigations. Classes on how to implement the standardized, all-risk incident management system known as ICS followed. The TTPS officers were friendly and enthusiastic, which made the days pass quickly. After class each evening, the group often went to Queen's Park Savannah to hear steel drum bands and enjoy "buss-up-shut roti" from street vendors.

Class concluded Friday at noon and the instructors met at a tiny Greek restaurant for lunch. Out of the corner of my eye I noticed a flame just as the woman at the counter, four feet away, shrieked and dove to the floor. As I tried to process what was happening, we heard a loud "whoosh" and the entire counter area was engulfed in a bright orange fireball. The gas line supplying the gyro rotisserie had broken loose and fallen onto the gas stove's burner. The cook screamed, "Gas! Get out!" and ran for the shutoff valve as customers fled into the street. I've seen gas explosions before and didn't want to be remembered as the bomb technician that got blown up by a gyro machine in Trinidad.

But with the turn of a valve, the flames subsided and we were invited back inside to finish lunch. Though the cook sustained some minor burns, no one called the fire department or paramedics; everyone just got back to work. The infamous Jesse James took me to the airport at 4:45 the next morning.

Another year was ending and a request from ATA had me traveling again. I was supposed to meet the group from the failed Islamabad

TDY in Houston, but flight delays made that connection seem impossible. I deplaned and jogged to Concourse E, but the boarding area was empty. I heard, "Hey, come on!"

It was George, the affable team lead from ATA, standing on the jet bridge with a mildly agitated flight attendant. "You must be Barry; I was beginning to think you wouldn't make it. The rest of the team is already on board. I'll introduce you when we land."

The 3,200-mile flight ended six hours later at Lima's Jorge Chavez International Airport; it was 11:40 p.m. local time. George introduced the team as we waited in baggage claim. It consisted of a retired Marine colonel with more than 30 years of service, a former SWAT commander for a major U.S. city, a former high-ranking DEA official, and a senior agent with the Diplomatic Security Service. We cleared Customs and climbed into a waiting van that took us to Miraflores, a commercial center about an hour south of Lima along Peru's Pacific coast. By 2:00 a.m. we arrived at the designated hotel for a short night's sleep; our initial meeting was scheduled for 7:00 a.m.

The RSO provided a briefing on local events, national crime trends, and Peru's terrorism concerns. The primary terrorist organization, Sendero Luminoso (SL) or Shining Path, sees the U.S. as a principal enemy. But its domestic goal is to overthrow Peru's government and replace it with a radical Marxist-Maoist regime. Their prolonged terror campaign had killed tens of thousands of people, usually in rural areas and often with machetes to save the cost of ammunition. The group's structure made SL difficult to infiltrate; individual cells were highly compartmentalized and loyal to a lone, local commander. Iranian-backed Hezbollah was also gaining a toehold in the country.

Once the initial briefing concluded, we departed the embassy and met with the country's top counterterrorism agencies and scientists. Tours of various sensitive sites were provided as well as capability demonstrations by highly specialized maritime, urban, and jungle warfare teams that work directly with the military to combat SL terrorists.

The days were filled with equipment assessments and practical demonstrations such as sniper insertions, a "hostage rescue" in a live-fire shoot house, and IED render safe drills. At the end of each day, instructors would meet to compare notes over dinner. One evening the interpreter suggested authentic Peruvian food.

"You must try the cuy; it's an Andean delicacy."

The small restaurant wasn't crowded, so the cuy arrived quickly; it was a pair of roasted guinea pigs. Skeptical, I ordered ceviche (raw fish

Author with three unnamed Peruvian National Police bomb technicians at a remote training site near Lima, Peru (2012).

marinated in chili and lime juice) just in case. To my surprise, the little guys were pretty good; they had the taste and texture of a tough turkey leg.

Just as in Bahrain, each SME was to draft a report detailing the capabilities and training gaps for the specialized units reviewed. Based on those reports, America would then provide the recommended training and equipment to enhance Peru's capabilities. The intelligence gathered and relationships established during these assessments are mutually beneficial. For instance, information gleaned about Shining Path's reemergence, its diverging branches, and new tactics allowed the U.S and Peru to modify their ongoing joint counterterrorism strategy. Other threats identified during the TDY included an increase in narcoterrorism related to the burgeoning cocaine trade and highly sophisticated groups of counterfeiters producing Peruvian soles and U.S. dollars.

The assessment concluded Friday and most of the team departed, but I was too close to another item on my bucket list. After a long discussion, the RSO offered some good advice.

"Let me arrange a reputable car service to get you out of Lima; we have what we call 'express muggings' here. Unscrupulous cabbies drive tourists to a predetermined location where waiting gangs rob them. I'll also arrange a vetted tour group that specializes in the Andes. You'll have a great time."

As the sun rose Saturday, a Taca Air flight departed for the 3,000-year-old city of Cusco. Once on the ground, a driver took me to the Ruinas Hotel. It was a far cry from Lima's JW Marriott, but quite adequate. The desk clerk was waiting in the lobby with a cup of hot coca tea. Coca leaves are illegal in the U.S., but "mate de coca" has been used by indigenous Andean people for thousands of years.

"Good morning and welcome. Please enjoy—the coca helps with altitude sickness."

Cusco was once the heart of the Inca Empire and is located over 11,000 feet above sea level. Spending a day or two there lets tourists acclimate to the altitude and enjoy the local history. That evening I walked around the Plaza de Armas to get my bearings and found Cicciolina, a restaurant the translator recommended. The huge wooden doors opened into a California-style kitchen with polished wood floors and cinnabar walls; there were white linen tablecloths and red velvet chairs, and the wait staff wore crisp black uniforms. An appetizer of causa (mashed yellow potatoes with chilies and guinea pig confit) was followed by a spicy alpaca filet. A light rain began to fall as I followed the dark and empty cobblestone streets back to the hotel.

I'm not Catholic, but Sunday morning service at the 400-year-old La Catedral del Cusco was a memorable experience. The entire mass was in Latin, but as it was late December I recognized some familiar Christmas hymns. Afterward, I met Enrique the tour guide at Norton's Rat, a bar in Cusco, to discuss the day's tour over lunch. Our first stop was the massive complex of Sacsayhuamán, where a small number of armored Spanish cavalry decimated the Inca. Next was the subterranean altar at Q'enqo, accessed through a labyrinth cut deep into the stone. Perhaps the most impressive site was the Temple of the Sun at Qorikancha. Its walls were once completely covered in gold; a single ceremonial font was crafted from 120 pounds of the precious metal. In 1533, the Spanish conquered Cusco and looted its temples; over 100 tons of golden artifacts were melted down and shipped to Spain.

At 5:30 the next morning, Enrique drove me to Poroy to catch a train. Along the mountainous road he pointed out a bungee jumping platform and asked, "Shall I stop? They say it's only 60 U.S. dollars … or free if you jump naked."

As much as I love a good deal, PeruRail's *Expedition* wouldn't wait. It's a comfortable narrow-gauge train with skylights and huge windows offering views of towering mountains as it negotiates "El Zig-Zag" through the Sacred Valley. *Expedition* is a step above the spartan backpacker's train, but much less luxurious than the *Hiram Bingham* line. The four-course meals and open bar of the all-inclusive *Hiram Bingham* offered a different culinary experience than the banana chips, salted beans, and warm can of Coke included with my *Expedition* ticket.

After three and a half hours, the train arrived in the ramshackle town of Aguas Calientes, where my guide was waiting. A 20-minute walk led to a bus stop for an eight-kilometer ride to the gates of Machu Picchu; it was spectacular. Located among the clouds high in the Andes, the scale of this ancient city was magnificent. I lost track of time and nearly missed the last train back to Poroy.

My alarm rang at 4:30 a.m. for a flight to Lima, where a driver took me back to Miraflores for a long nap, hot shower, and a good meal. The flight to Houston departed at 8:30 p.m. and I was safely home by December 21, the day the Maya Long Count calendar predicted the world would end.

Eighteen

Tagaligtas

January 2013 took me to Arizona for the 135th VBIED post-blast school at Marine Corps Air Station Yuma. The exercises were staged on a live bombing range known as Yoda-ville, a mock village in the high desert complete with streets, buildings, and vehicles. As in the past, the scenario-based exercise centered on a series of IED attacks culminating with a 1000-pound bomb secreted in a motorhome. Forty-two FBI, USMC, and police bomb techs participated along with crime scene investigators from across the nation.

In February, the NFL decided to hold Super Bowl XLVII in New Orleans during Mardi Gras. Given the international media attention and anticipated crowds, the game was designated an NSSE. I arrived in New Orleans at 7:00 p.m. and drove directly to a secure off-site for a briefing with New Orleans PD. Hotel rooms were at a premium, so I was assigned a small, windowless room in a 19th-century warehouse near the French Quarter.

In the days leading up to the game, my team was assigned to the NFL Experience and the TV broadcast headquarters in Jackson Square. As always, the French Quarter was crazy; crowds were a mix of NFL fans and Mardi Gras revelers, which made getting from one venue to another challenging. After a final security sweep, we locked down the Superdome early Saturday morning and established concentric rings of security as kick-off drew closer.

Just as in Dallas, the threat of an ice storm in New Orleans was remote. So I parked the response vehicle near Fan Plaza and met my team inside the stadium. The group consisted of two state troopers, a K9, members of the National Guard Civil Support Team, and a DOE Radiological Assessment Team. It's impossible to hide a team like this, and no staging rooms were available within the stadium. Mindful that roaming around with a bomb dog and radiological detection equipment might unnerve some people, we found a spot behind a beer vendor in the lower bowl on the 50-yard line. We were out of the way, not blocking anyone's view, and still had easy access if we were needed.

During the game, an irate and inebriated 49ers fan seated in front of us turned and sarcastically mumbled, "Well, that must be nice. I paid $20,000 for this seat and you're just standing there for free."

Within minutes of his statement, the stadium suddenly went dark. There was a collective gasp, then a hush fell across the crowd. The man turned around again and whispered, "Hey, I'm really glad you guys are here. What's going on?"

The thought of terrorism was suddenly on his mind. Teams on the outer perimeter confirmed it was just an electrical failure, but the 34-minute delay made this the longest game in Super Bowl history.

The game ended without incident, but the next major athletic event did not. On April 15, 2013, terrorists detonated two IEDs at the Boston Marathon. The FBI mobilized regional resources to join state and local partners in a fast-moving case that dominated the 24-hour news cycle for days. I remained in Oklahoma City and was at the firing range when Doug, a good friend and fellow "old guy," walked over.

"Well, it's April 19. Twenty years ago we were standing in Waco at the Branch Davidian compound and 18 years ago at the Murrah Building. It's a pretty significant date."

It was also a significant date for the Boston terrorists. After a massive manhunt, the Tsarnaev brothers were engaged by police in the early morning hours of April 19. Tamerlan was shot by officers, then dragged under a car driven by his brother, Dzhokhar, who fled the scene. At 8:30 that night, Dzhokhar was discovered hiding in a boat behind a house in Watertown, Massachusetts. He was reluctant to surrender but, encouraged by some flashbangs, eventually gave up, bloody from previous gunshot wounds. He was convicted two years later in a 30-count federal indictment and sentenced to await the death penalty in a Supermax prison cell (FBI 2023).

In September, OIO asked if I'd teach the ICS and Major Case Management course which had been so well received in Trinidad. I immediately agreed when they mentioned the venue was in Cape Town. A buddy serving in Afghanistan had been to South Africa on R&R and suggested I go a few days early for great white shark diving in Gansbaai.

The flight from Oklahoma City to Houston was uneventful. From there it was a 9.5-hour trip to Amsterdam, followed by the final

11.5-hour leg. As I deplaned late that night, a text from the dive master appeared on my phone.

"Apologies—there's a huge storm blowing up the southwest coast and all shark dives out of Gansbaai have been canceled. I took the liberty of canceling your driver and coastal hotel accommodation as well. Please advise if you'd like to reschedule."

Suddenly I had no transportation and no place to sleep. The ICS course was scheduled at the Southern Sun Hotel and Conference Center near the Victoria and Alfred Waterfront. The desk clerk advised they had a room available for the night and offered to send a car for me. Soon a black Mercedes pulled to the curb and a friendly, well-dressed young man got out and introduced himself.

"Mr. Black? I am Klolisa from Southern Sun."

His name was pronounced with a clicking sound that was part of his Khoisan tribal language. The long drive into town afforded an opportunity to book a safari for the next morning since all dives were canceled. Twelve hours later I was in the arid Little Karoo valley.

Located on the dry side of the Hottentot Mountains, the private Aquila game reserve encompasses 19,000 acres and only allows 96 guests per night. When the van arrived at the main lodge, a ranger grabbed my backpack as the receptionist poured a glass of Old Branch brandy.

"Enjoy your brandy, then Graham will show you to your chalet."

The small freestanding cabin was built into a rocky hillside with a thatch roof, exposed beams, and rough stone walls. The center of the room had a huge fireplace, which was essential this time of year; I wasn't expecting Africa to be so cold. A hot tub was sunk into the flagstone floor, but the shower was outside, tucked into a rock outcropping, which proved to be an exhilarating experience.

I unpacked and sat on the deck overlooking a vast expanse of brush ringed by low, rocky mountains. Within minutes, two elephants lumbered by just yards away. About 1:00 p.m. we mounted an open safari truck for the afternoon game drive. There were giraffes, buffalo, hippos, and rhinos, but the best was a pride of lions that came alarmingly close to inspect our high clearance vehicle. It was a long day and dinner was waiting by the time we returned to camp. Walking back to the chalet along a narrow footpath, the Southern Cross hung low in a crystal clear sky. Graham had already started a roaring fire and left a bottle of Dr. Robertson's local Shiraz, which was a welcome surprise. There was no TV, radio, internet, or central heat, so I steeled myself for a brisk outdoor shower and settled in by the fire.

The morning game drive departed at sunrise, followed by breakfast in the lodge and a trip back to Cape Town. As we passed through the vineyards and shanty towns along the N1, sheets of blowing rain began to fall. Torrents of water ran off the mountains, creating white waterfalls that filled the shallow creek beds along the roadside. This was the leading edge of the storm that canceled my dive. After a 115-mile drive through blinding rain, I took a steaming hot *indoor* shower and got some rest.

Monday morning there were 30 high-ranking law enforcement officials from across South Africa waiting in the Southern Sun conference room. Some units had recently undergone a great deal of change and were often vulnerable to political pressure due to a negative public perception. Sadly, real world events played into our class discussions. During the first week, international news reported 12 people had been killed by an active shooter at the Naval Sea Systems Command at the Washington Navy Yard. Other than the Fort Hood attack, this was the deadliest mass murder to occur at a U.S. military facility.

Days later, al-Shabaab terrorists attacked Nairobi's Westgate mall, killing 71 and wounding 200 in a rampage that lasted 80 hours. These events were becoming all too frequent and served as the impetus for the ICS and Major Case Management training we were providing. Breaking news reports were incorporated into class discussions to spark debate on how ICS could be used to manage these protracted, high-profile incidents.

As is routine, discussions spilled into off-duty hours in the infamous Long Street bars and restaurants. Tribal musicians were performing as we arrived at Mama Africa for dinner. We were seated at a long table and presented with an unusual menu. I chose a platter of crocodile, ostrich, springbok, and kudu.

Our only day off allowed a tour of Table Mountain via its famous revolving cable car. It offered an impressive 360° view of Table Bay and Robben Island, where Nelson Mandela had been imprisoned. Apartheid was still a hot topic of discussion as were Mandela's achievements. He passed away just three months after the class.

The course concluded Friday evening with a brief ceremony. As we said our goodbyes, one of the students, Nigel, insisted we get together if I was ever in South Africa again. He was a fascinating man assigned to the nation's anti–rhino poaching unit.

South Africa is home to most of the world's rhino population and it's estimated that 1,000 are illegally killed each year. Poachers use military-style equipment, including high-powered rifles and helicopters, to locate and slaughter their prey only to cut off its horn. The black market demand for rhino horns originates in Asia, where many believe the horns are an aphrodisiac, and it's a big business. A single horn can be worth over $180,000. Many park rangers have been murdered trying to stop poachers.

The only flights home didn't depart until Saturday night. So Bret, my buddy from Quantico, booked us a day trip along the Coast Road, past the Twelve Apostles, and on to the Cape of Good Hope. After dinner, the driver took us directly to the airport where Bret and I parted ways. My flight to Johannesburg was delayed, nearly causing me to miss a 16-hour connecting flight to Atlanta. From there I flew directly to Huntsville for a 40-hour course on improvised nuclear weapons and radiological dispersal devices.

The new year began with a call from George, the ATA team leader from the Peru assessment. Finding a group that can work well together, collaborating for long hours in an overseas environment, can be challenging.

"Hey, I was able to pull together the rest of the team from Lima. We'd like you to join us for a counterterrorism assessment in the Philippines. The FBI folks at CIRG and OIO agreed to support it if you're willing to go."

I left the house at 4:00 a.m.; since the State Department was paying the bill, they specified the travel itinerary, which was not ideal. I had a six-hour layover in Detroit before taking a seat in the very back of a packed 747 for a 12-hour flight over Canada, the Bering Straits, and the coast of Russia before finally landing in Japan. After two hours in line at Customs at Nagoya, I boarded the same plane, reclaimed seat 65H, and settled in for the next 2,000 miles.

The plane landed in Manila just before midnight local time; an embassy expediter was waiting on the jet bridge. I stepped outside into the humid night air as an armored van with diplomatic plates pulled to the curb. The driver, Ken, unlocked the heavy vault door in the rear and loaded my bags. It was 1:15 a.m., but the streets were packed and fireworks filled the sky. "What's all this?" I asked.

Ken replied, "It's Chinese New Year, the Year of the Horse."

As we pulled through the hotel's outer checkpoint, a guard waved us through with a sharp salute aimed more at the diplomatic plates than the van's blacked-out windows.

"The rest of the group was delayed and should arrive tomorrow evening. But I'll be back to pick you up at 0800 for briefings at the embassy."

It was already 2:30 a.m. and I'd been in transit for 30 hours; the 14-hour time change was going to make the morning meetings rough. But the RSO and his analysts did a great job explaining the national threat environment, beginning with a rather long history of Islamic terrorism. The main organizations currently operating in the Philippines were the Moro Islamic Liberation Front, the Abu Sayyaf Group, Jemaah Islamiyah, and the Bangsamoro Islamic Freedom Fighters. However, ISIS was making inroads throughout the island chain.

Kidnappings, hijackings, beheadings, and bombings had become standard fare. As a result, the Philippine National Police (PNP) created a Special Action Force (SAF) modeled after the British SAS. Known as Tagaligtas, the unit was primarily created to conduct high-risk counterterrorism operations. As the briefing concluded, the RSO offered a welcome suggestion.

"I'm sure you're tired from the trip. Since the rest of the group isn't here yet, why don't you take tomorrow to get acclimated? We'll start again Monday morning."

I spoke with the embassy's Community Liaison Officer, who recommended a vetted tour guide; I needed to stay awake and shake off the jet lag. The guide arrived early Sunday for a daylong tour of Luzon, beginning with a 50-kilometer trip to Taal Volcano, one of the most active volcanoes in the Ring of Fire. A series of prehistoric eruptions produced a second volcano inside the original caldera; both craters eventually filled with water, creating a lake within a lake. Six years after my visit, a major eruption vaporized the 15-mile-wide lake and leveled the surrounding villages. The tour continued at the 16th-century Spanish citadel of Intramuros and the beautiful, yet somber Manila American Cemetery honoring 16,859 World War II heroes killed in operations across the Philippines and New Guinea.

The rest of the team arrived Sunday night and we set the agenda over drinks. I was to provide capability assessments for the PNP bomb squads, crime scene investigators, and forensic laboratories. The others would cover border security, cybercrime, and hostage rescue. Our schedule was aggressive given the wide geographic area, so we split up to cover more ground. A driver picked me up at 4:30 a.m. to catch a plane to Mindanao at the archipelago's southern tip. The destination was General Santos City (GenSan), a hotbed of terrorist activity about 1,000 miles south of Manila.

A private contractor and two heavily armed Tagaligtas were waiting on the airstrip. The soldiers sat on either side of me as our armored vehicle navigated rough jungle trails to a secluded FOB. Passing through the first fortified checkpoint, the contractor warned, "Mr. Black, we'll be stopping soon. Abu Sayyaf and Jemaah Islamiyah are very active in this area; I suggest you don't stray far into the jungle." No worries; there was plenty of firepower in the van.

Tagaligtas commanders and their counterterrorism commandos were waiting at the FOB. Each briefing was professional, thorough, and timely; a terrorist IED had killed a child and police officer in GenSan just that morning. We inspected equipment, assessed their TTPs, and toured the K9 kennels. The assessment concluded with presentations from forensic scientists outlining their current lab capabilities and a wish list for more modern equipment. I spent the final night in Mindanao with one eye open in a small, dicey motel on GenSan's outskirts; my flight to Manila departed at dawn.

The weekend was free, so another SABT assigned to Manila arranged a 5:00 a.m. diving excursion in Oriental Mindoro. A driver took us to the coastal city of Batangas, where we boarded an overloaded outrigger for a precarious trip through the Verde Island passage. A porter met us at Puerto Galera and showed us to a small hotel adjoining the dive shop where Rick, an affable Brit, was waiting.

"Hello, mates, sorry to say your room isn't quite ready. So just drop your kit and we'll go diving."

The first site was a wreck lying in 88 feet of crystal clear, 80°F water. It was followed by two beautiful shallow reef dives off Sabang Beach. Motoring back to the dock, Rick radioed ahead to make some arrangements.

"I've got you lads booked at Hemingway's for dinner right on the beach. Your bags are in your room; enjoy the evening."

We took the first outrigger back to Batangas the next morning and got to work. The rest of the assignment would be at Cuartel de Santo Domingo, a remote SAF training camp. We evaluated live-fire sniper demonstrations, hostage rescues, close quarters combat, and counter–IED scenarios. I noticed each masked operator's uniform had a name tape with a moniker like "Cobra" or "Viper."

The commander explained, "When we are on operations, we don't want terrorists to know our family name. They will find our families and kill them in retribution, so we display only these names."

This was a very dangerous business. But as with all the special operators I've met, a high degree of professionalism and personal pride were evident. The assignment concluded and Ken shuttled me to the airport at 3:30 a.m. Bleary-eyed, I made my way through the queue to the gate agent.

"Sorry to inform you, but the 6:00 a.m. flight has been delayed by 12 hours. The plane was diverted to accommodate a group of tourists snowbound in Japan." No alternate flights were available, but I eventually made it back to Oklahoma.

Nineteen

Purgatory and Transylvania

Purgatory, actually Purgatory Flats, lies at the northern edge of the Mojave Desert. The lectures for this VBIED course would be presented in the dayroom of the Purgatory prison with a makeshift explosives range located in the vast, open desert outside the security fence. Students included Marine and Army EOD, state and local bomb techs, and FBI ERT from as far away as Hawaii. We detonated several devices, including a 600-pound IED hidden in an airport shuttle. As always, the class honed interview and evidence-collection skills before executing search warrants in my hotel room. On Friday their findings were presented to a federal prosecutor in moot court. The long summer days provided time for evening team-building hikes to ancient petroglyphs along Anasazi Ridge and the trails of Zion National Park.

Several weeks passed before the next TDY to Bucharest, Romania. A driver ferried me to a 100-year-old hotel located just blocks from the former Central Committee of the Communist Party Building. In 1989, Nicolae Ceauşescu gave his final speech from the building's balcony shortly before being overthrown and executed by firing squad.

After unpacking, I took a walk around Revolution Square to shake the jetlag. Of interest was the former headquarters of Directia V Securitate, the brutal secret police of communist Romania. A modern glass building protrudes from the remains of the original 1890 structure, which is pockmarked with bullet holes from the revolution. Beyond the enormous Palace of Parliament were the medieval remains of Curtea Veche, the palace of Vlad the Impaler.

I was to train a group at the embassy before addressing a counter-IED symposium for former Soviet Bloc nations. The training began Monday morning with embassy personnel and representatives from

Romania's Brigada Antiteroristă, the highly specialized counterterrorism brigade. A simultaneous interpreter translated the lectures to a full house. Afterward, one of the commandos invited me to Old Town Lipscani for a dinner of fried pork fat, potatoes, cabbage, and racituri, a type of jellied pig hoof with garlic. The evening ended with pálinka, a surprisingly potent fruit brandy dating back to the Middle Ages.

Tuesday's class was cut short by a visit from Joe Biden, who was Vice President at the time. The Secret Service locked down the embassy and the ring road surrounding it before I completed my presentation. The vetted driver scheduled to take me to the conference in Transylvania was nowhere to be found, so the Legal Attaché made a suggestion.

"OK, how about this? Grab your luggage and walk outside, beyond the Secret Service perimeter. There's a roundabout maybe two or three blocks toward town. Just wait there and I'll have somebody from SRI [Romania's Intelligence Service] pick you up."

Without the benefit of a cell phone, GPS, or Google Translate, I dubiously repeated the plan. "So you want me to drag my luggage down the road in that general direction and wait somewhere on the street for an unmarked car full of Romanians to pick me up and drive off into the Carpathians? I don't speak Romanian and have no idea where we're going."

He paused for a moment and admitted, "Yeah, that's not the best idea when you say it out loud. I'll have one of our drivers arrange something better for you. Just wait outside Post One."

Post One is the first security checkpoint within an embassy, manned by square-jawed Marine Security Guards. Within minutes, a blue van pulled around and the driver, a vetted local, tossed my bags in the back. "I am Avram. We will meet others at airport then go to Bran."

Once inside the airport, Avram motioned me to a low faux leather sofa in the bar and walked away. Already seated were two Polish bomb techs and a woman who stood and extended her hand.

"I am Natasha with multi-lateral unit. Sit, we wait for Bruno from France."

For about an hour, we sat there as comfortably as four complete strangers with no common language could. Avram and Bruno soon joined the group and we all climbed into the van for a two-and-a-half-hour ride to the medieval town of Bran, home of Count Dracula.

About halfway there, Natasha handed each of us an envelope sealed with a sticker of our respective nation's flag. It contained helpful information in our native languages about the conference and our accommodations. Our quarters and classroom would be in a SRI facility which had been built by the Communists in 1969. We were free to move about the camp as long as we displayed our photo ID, though some areas were strictly off limits.

Taped to the door of my austere concrete room was a map with a note that read, "As it grows dark, do not wander by forest because of bears. They are not afraid of humans. Meet in dining hall at 1900."

Making a point to avoid the tree line, I followed the map to find several conference attendees already bonding over pálinka and moonshine they'd brought from Hungary, Poland, and Bulgaria. Most were young cops and soldiers who were enjoying the time away from their units. Bruno (the Frenchman) and an Israeli EOD commander were closer to my age, so we sat by the fire and got acquainted.

The conference was designed to discuss lessons learned and best practices related to VBIEDs and countermeasures. David, the Israeli commander, and I were first to present. Because of all the nationalities present, we used "consecutive interpreters." Unlike simultaneous interpretation, this requires a speaker to frequently pause and allow the interpreter time to process and translate the first language into the second. It can break the flow of a regular conversation, and some of the younger soldiers were reluctant to participate. But as the days passed there was robust discussion among all the attendees, especially on the explosives range.

An important part of these conferences is networking and building personal relationships that foster trust and information sharing down the road. With that in mind, SRI graciously planned outings each evening. The first excursion was to Dracula's Castle, looming nearly 200 feet above a strategic mountain pass. Built in 1382, it housed suits of armor, bearskin rugs, and a secret staircase hidden behind a fireplace. Another evening saw a banquet in the Saxon town of Brasov, founded by Teutonic knights in the 13th century. Inside the thick city walls stood the massive Black Church. Completed in 1477, it was the largest Gothic church between Vienna and Istanbul. The conference concluded Thursday evening with drinks and a pig roast high in the snowcapped Carpathian Mountains. By 5:30 a.m., I was on a flight back to Paris.

Summer passed quickly with a couple of presentations at Quantico and some scenario-based training for the Army at Fort Sill. One FTX incorporated roleplaying "terrorists" that smuggled my IEDs onto the post. As the situation played out, I noticed some MPs arresting a man who wasn't part of the scenario.

"Excuse me, sergeant, but he's not part of the FTX."

"Oh no, sir, this is real world. He's a civilian contractor that failed to clear the cordon before the FTX began. Instead of letting us know, he just sat in his car, rolled a huge joint, and was watching the show. He's really under arrest."

South Africa was on the agenda again for September. Sitting in Atlanta's departure lounge, I noticed the *USA Today* headline, "Can Russia be stopped?" referring to Putin's recent invasion of Crimea in Ukraine. Another paper featured ISIS's barbaric rampage in the Middle East, and CNN pundits covered a lethal Ebola outbreak in West Africa. The world was a dangerous place.

I was pleased to see Bret waiting at the boarding gate in Amsterdam. I hadn't seen him since the last trip to Cape Town, and the four-hour layover gave us time to relive our near-death experience at that Trinidadian gyro shop. We finally boarded, but sat on the tarmac for an hour until the captain eventually advised us there was an engine problem. Three more hours passed before we took off on the 12-hour, 4,400-mile flight to Cape Town; it was 3:30 a.m. local time when we landed. An older man named Africa was waiting just outside Customs to take us to the hotel. The fact that we were seven hours late didn't dampen his smile.

However, the delay was going to deprive me of sleep, as I'd booked a 5:00 a.m. shark dive for Saturday in Gansbaai, the Great White Shark capital of the world. Fortunately, the desk clerk relayed a message from the dive master which read, "All dives are postponed until Sunday due to high winds along the Western Cape. We'll see you then."

As scheduled, a driver arrived Sunday morning. He took the Whale Coast Route to Hermanus, where we stopped to watch a pod of southern right whales play in Walker Bay, then finished the drive to Gansbaai to board *Apex Predator*. The captain pushed the custom catamaran through heavy waves and dropped anchor between Dyer Island and Geyser Rock. The crew immediately lowered a cage on the starboard side and began chumming the water as I donned a wetsuit and climbed into the 60°F Atlantic. Once the top of the cage was secured, a deckhand threw a heavy line baited with half a tuna over the cage and dragged it toward us through the murky water. In no time, a huge shadowy figure emerged from the deep and slammed into the cage. I thought we were lucky to see one great white, but they just kept coming. It's no wonder this place is known around the world as "Shark Alley."

Class began Monday and was a repeat of the Major Case Management and ICS course Bret and I taught previously. Just as last time, South African Police Service officers attended from across the country and their hospitality extended into off-duty hours. One evening we joined some counterterrorism officers from Special Task Force at Ferryman's Tavern for pork knuckles and sauerkraut. Reminiscent of the O.J. Simpson trial, they were glued to the TV coverage of Oscar Pistorius, the Blade Runner. A national sensation, he was the first amputee to compete in an Olympic track event and was now on trial for murdering his girlfriend in Pretoria.

The next night a general from Special Task Force took us to a rather sketchy carryout stand for a locally famous Gatsby, a baguette stuffed with spicy steak, french fries, and onions. That was followed by a raucous evening at Shimmy's Beach Club to watch South Africa's Bafana Bafana play Nigeria's football club to a draw.

As soon as Friday's closing ceremony concluded, I flew to Johannesburg to meet Nigel, my old anti–rhino poaching buddy from the first class. He picked me up at 5:00 a.m. for what became a 1,500-mile odyssey through Mpumalanga, Limpopo, and Kruger National Park. We entered Kruger through the southern Malelane Gate and spent hours in the bush. There was no better safari guide, as this 7,576-square-mile national park was Nigel's office. We toured the Lower Sabie until the sun began to set, then pulled up to an old stone bush camp. There were no fences, so curious giraffes and zebras sauntered by as we unpacked the truck.

Nigel arranged a night safari out of Crocodile Bridge Camp. We departed under an absolutely clear sky; the Milky Way and Southern Cross were prominent, as the moon wouldn't rise for several hours. It finally appeared as a huge, orange ball low on the horizon, lending an eerie glow to the savannah.

After just six hours' sleep, we drove back into the veld to beat the heat. The morning temperature was already 98°F and most of the animals were at watering holes or lingering along the aptly named Crocodile River. Huge crocs lounged on the banks, carefully eyeing the hippos and elephants. Throughout the day, Nigel adeptly pointed out endangered rhinos, lions, buffalo, waterbuck, and an endless supply of impalas, which he called "McDonalds of the bush."

As the day wore on Nigel decided we'd seen the best of Kruger.

"Let's head up to Hoedspruit. My family has a place there along the river in Balule Nature Preserve."

After a long drive on the blacktop, we turned onto a nearly impassable trail bounded on either side by the high electric fences of private game preserves. The sun was getting low as we cleared the final sliding gate with its simple warning sign: BEWARE OF LIONS.

Seven wild elephants lined the road as we entered the Rio dos Elefantes estate, the home of Van Reenen van Vuren. I'm sure Walt Disney modeled Wilderness Lodge after this place; the main house was stone clad with hand-hewn decks overlooking the confluence of the Blyde and Oliphant rivers. A tall, well-weathered man with a distinctive Crocodile Dundee air waited in a clearing with a woman. With a firm handshake he began the conversation in Afrikaans, clearly asking about our trip and motioning to the elephants standing just yards away. As I introduced myself, he effortlessly switched languages, saying, "Ah, then English it is. I'm Van Reenen and this is my wife, Agnes."

A fire was already roaring in a stone pit near the river, so Nigel began the "braai" with wild game steaks and kebabs. As we watched the fire dance and sipped cold Namibian Windhoek, Van Reenen recounted fascinating stories of his youth as a tobacco farmer, game ranger, and hired gun in untamed Africa. Now in their later years, he and Agnes were authors and painters; their home was an eclectic mix of old photos from Van Reenen's adventures and hand-painted scenes of Africa's "Big Five" game animals. Dinner was served outside on the upper deck beneath a brilliant sky as elephants crashed through the bush and baboons screamed in the trees. After a night of intriguing conversation about life in the Lowveld, Nigel drove me to my quarters, a one-room stone cuddy in the remote original camp where a signed copy of Van Reenen's book, *Lebombo Journals*, was waiting on the bunk.

Van Reenen picked me up early the next morning in an antique "safari lorrie" for a morning game drive. As the sun rose we plodded through the bush, challenging the truck's four-wheel-drive to claw its way atop a bald knob overlooking a vast expanse of wilderness. After a few moments of silence, Van Reenen clapped me on the shoulder.

"This is one of my favorite places, but let's get back. Agnes will have coffee on by now."

After saying our goodbyes, Nigel plotted a course to the Moholoholo Rehabilitation Center where injured animals are nurtured until they can be safely released into the wild. Those that can't be released are used as ambassadors to stress the importance of stewardship and habitat preservation. I had the rare opportunity to pet a cheetah and hand-feed an endangered Cape vulture; it was an amazing place.

The day ended with a two-hour drive to Mbombela, where I joined nine other passengers on a bush plane bound for Johannesburg. From there it was a 16-hour flight to Atlanta, then on to Oklahoma City.

Things were going smoothly until the last 20 minutes of the flight, when smoke and an acrid odor filled the cabin; it smelled like an electrical fire. The flight attendants quickly ushered everyone to the front of the plane and began searching the overhead bins as the captain announced, "I am aware of the situation. My instruments show no indication of an onboard fire. We'll be landing shortly." Without further explanation, we touched down in OKC and taxied to the jet bridge. I didn't ask any questions.

Twenty

Edge of the World

In August 2014, ISIS took over an Iraqi town and slaughtered hundreds of innocent people, highlighting the group's barbarism. Later that month they posted a video of the brutal beheading of American journalist James Foley. His murder was followed by the beheading of another American journalist, Steven Sotloff. On September 13, they beheaded British aid worker David Haines. Videos of these gruesome, heinous acts were coupled with calls for ISIS followers to commit independent acts of violence as lone wolves.

So when, on September 24, an Islamic convert entered a business in Moore, Oklahoma, screaming "Allahu Akbar" and beheaded a woman, many naturally assumed it was terrorism. The assailant was shot by an off-duty deputy and an extensive investigation followed. Local authorities did an outstanding job on the murder investigation, and JTTF tried to determine if the killer had any links to terrorist organizations.

Exhaustive reviews of his personal relationships were conducted along with examinations of his electronics and social media, which revealed radical terrorist propaganda and research on beheadings. JTTF interviewed the subject in the hospital; oddly, he was in Room 666. The killer showed no remorse and believed he was simply following Islamic teachings. But despite the recovered digital evidence and the investigators' belief that he intended to kill many more people, it was decided (primarily in Washington) that this beheading was merely "workplace violence" with no terrorism nexus (Jolly 2014).

This wasn't the first time questions had been raised about failing to classify terrorism for what it was. By definition, terrorism constitutes violent, criminal acts committed by individuals or groups to further ideological goals. The motivation of the act must be determined.

Five years before the beheading in Moore, Nidal Hasan entered a military processing center at Fort Hood, Texas. Shouting "Allahu

Akbar," he opened fire, killing 13 people and wounding over 30. Hasan, a major in the U.S. Army, had publicly stated that America's war on terrorism was really a war against Islam. There were concerns that he'd become a radical Islamic extremist. At his court-martial, Hasan told a judge he'd gunned down the soldiers to protect Muslims and Taliban leaders in Afghanistan. Yet the Department of Defense classified the attack as "workplace violence," not terrorism. Members of Congress later demanded the Obama administration reclassify the attack as terrorism and provide full benefits to Hasan's victims (Hilley-Sierzchula 2025).

The atrocity in Moore was soon followed by two Canadian soldiers being run down in Quebec. CNN reported the driver had been "radicalized," and the Public Safety Minister declared that the act was "clearly linked to terrorist ideology." The next day, another "recently radicalized" gunman killed a member of the Honor Guard at the Canadian War Memorial and assaulted the House of Parliament in Ottawa. The following day, a lone man wielding a hatchet attacked a group of police officers in New York City. That same evening, a car covered in satanic graffiti careened across the grounds of the Oklahoma state capitol and crashed into a stone monument of the Ten Commandments. These were indeed strange times.

The day after Thanksgiving I flew to Atlanta, endured a six-hour layover, then boarded a 777 for a 14-hour, 7,600-mile flight to Dubai. From there it was a short hop to the Kingdom of Saudi Arabia. Anti-western attacks had been on the rise since the Gulf Wars and a heightened security posture was currently in place for U.S. personnel due to elevated al-Qaeda and ISIS activity in the region. I landed after midnight and was escorted through Customs by an embassy expediter. Once outside, an armored Suburban pulled to the curb and within 30 minutes we entered the Diplomatic Quarter (DQ). It's a secure enclave covering about three square miles in northwest Riyadh and is home to foreign embassies, diplomat living quarters, government organizations, and support facilities. The DQ was closed to the public in early 2000 due to renewed terrorism concerns. The entire facility is now ringed with high-security fencing and a large, heavily armed security force that maintains static checkpoints and roving patrols.

The driver cleared the final checkpoint at 1:30 a.m. and dropped me at a two-bedroom apartment I would share with a linguist. An outer steel door led to a walled courtyard, then the heavy wooden door of the apartment. I gently knocked for several minutes until the throw of four deadbolt locks could be heard. The door opened to reveal Ahmed, my interpreter. He smiled, pointed to his flannel pajamas and murmured in a distinct Egyptian accent, "Please excuse my informality and make yourself at home." With that, he turned and went back to bed.

As is often the case, I didn't know anyone on this assignment. In fact, I wasn't completely sure what we'd be doing, as the mission parameters had changed several times. However, the agenda became clear in the next morning's brief. "The Kingdom" was a strong ally of the U.S., and high-ranking officials from each of their security directorates had recently completed the Advanced Instructor Development course at Quantico. They now wanted to establish a core group of highly skilled instructors to serve as mentors for domestic training teams that could enhance training throughout the kingdom. This was the pilot program of the Saudi Arabian Advanced Instructor Development Course.

The hand-selected attendees were highly educated, highly motivated officers from various security branches throughout the government. Building on the Advanced Instructor's course at Quantico,

Unnamed Internal Security Directors to my left and right at the King Fahad Security College Advanced Instructor Development Course in Riyadh, Saudi Arabia (2014).

the class was designed to "train the trainer." Upon completion of the three-week school, these men would go on to provide advanced instruction at their respective police academies. The original plan called for each FBI mentor to return within a year to shadow the new instructors and provide any necessary assistance.

Our first week in country was primarily spent on logistics, firming up an official itinerary. In the evenings, conscious of the RSO's security admonitions, we wandered through Deera souk, haggled with merchants, and enjoyed a wide variety of cuisine. Though camel was on the menu in several places, no one would serve it because of a new coronavirus scare. The Middle East Respiratory Syndrome (MERS) was first identified in Saudi Arabia and was directly associated with improperly handled camel meat. I decided to stick with beef, which arrived to the table raw, but sizzling atop an 850°F slab of black granite. MERS wouldn't be an issue.

The Saudi work week was Sunday through Thursday and the agenda kept us busy. By Friday, we were ready to shed the confines of the city and hired a couple of SUVs to take the team about 100 kilometers outside Riyadh to Jebel Fihrayn, the Edge of the World. After an hour, we left the paved road and drove through soft, shifting sand until two towering cliffs of the Tuwaiq escarpment parted to expose a sheer drop of 1,000 feet. Below was a prehistoric ocean floor, now a vast sea of sand running to the horizon. Camels followed wadis that once served as ancient caravan routes. It was an impressive sight.

Saturday morning, while at the DQ's bazaar, a young Marine approached.

"Sir, you have a visitor at the gate."

I was surprised to see an old neighbor from Oklahoma who'd moved to Riyadh as a contractor; my wife had told his wife I was in country. We spent the afternoon discussing hometown news over chicken shawarma and Italian ice at the iconic Kingdom Tower. Later, while roaming the souk, I met a goldsmith named Amin Shalabi and asked if he could create a gift for my wife, an 18-karat gold cartouche engraved with our son's name in Arabic. After some good-natured haggling, Amin asked, "As this is a very special item, may I require payment in advance?"

"Of course, but I'm leaving Thursday morning. Are you sure it will be ready?"

Amin simply replied, "Inshallah."

Wednesday evening Amin texted, "The cartouche is ready, I'll meet you in the gold souk at 11:00 p.m." Unfortunately, the RSO had restricted movements outside the DQ because the Senate Intelligence Committee's report on CIA's enhanced interrogation techniques had just gone public. Some believed the revelation of waterboarding might lead to reprisals against Americans. I explained my situation and the RSO reluctantly allowed me to dash into the souk to pick up the cartouche, which was beautiful.

The Kingdom had suffered suicide bombings, car bombs, assassinations, and firefights with terrorists wielding RPGs, machine guns, and other heavy weapons. But the DQ and King Fahad Security College where our course was taught were relatively secure. We traveled between sites in armored vehicles, but when on foot in the souks or in restaurants it paid to be vigilant. We often spotted ham-handed surveillance in the bazaars and tried to avoid any predictable routines.

However, there was one particularly good shawarma restaurant conveniently located along Route 522. At that time, women couldn't drive in the Kingdom and weren't even allowed inside restaurants. We often parked our Suburbans amid their vehicles and went in for a quick meal. Two weeks after our TDY ended, the Legal Attaché advised the Saudis had disrupted a bomb plot targeting that restaurant because it was frequented by "westerners."

The day after returning from Riyadh, I was humbled to be inducted into the Oklahoma Law Enforcement Hall of Fame and presented with the Bill Tilghman Public Service Award. Bill Tilghman was a legendary lawman from the state's territorial days who had previously served on the Dodge City Peace Commission with the likes of Wyatt Earp and Bat Masterson. Being honored by my state and local law enforcement colleagues was a highlight of my career.

The following Friday my cell phone rang. "Barry, it's Jim Comey." The voice on the other end was the FBI Director; not an aide or secretary, but the Director. He called to personally congratulate me on the award and thank me for my service. I'd met every Director since William Sessions, but this was the first time a Presidential appointee had ever called me directly.

A new year dawned, and January 2015 found me in Brasília, Brazil's capital city. I deplaned at 6:30 a.m. and walked outside into the thick, humid air beneath a mottled, inky black sky. An embassy expediter grabbed my bags and motioned for a driver who pulled up in a black Mercedes. With virtually no traffic, we made it to the hotel in 30 minutes. I checked in and slept until noon, then walked over to the

(From left) An unnamed Fugitive Apprehension Agent, Senator Darrell Weaver, author, Chief Phil Cotton, and District Attorney David Prater at the 2014 Oklahoma Law Enforcement Hall of Fame induction ceremony.

Saturday street market at the base of Torre de TV, the city's focal point. A vendor was selling double-decker tour bus tickets, so I hopped on to see the *Guinness Book*'s largest flagpole and the Engineering Society's most beautiful bridge.

The ATA team arrived that evening and we met for drinks in the lobby bar; I recognized a couple of faces from previous assignments. The week began with security briefings at the embassy, a conference with the ambassador, then meetings with some of the country's specialized counterterrorism units. After a full day of conferences, embassy personnel invited us to a Brazilian steakhouse for a glutinous dinner composed almost entirely of meat. The meal was served with fried plantains, some type of root dish, and a salad bar. But I was forewarned by one of the aides: "The sides are for rookies. This place is for carnivores, so focus on the meat."

The various meats were brought to the table on huge skewers and sliced until you signaled surrender by literally turning over a red card by your plate. I sampled lamb chops, sausage, pork ribs, steak, chicken hearts, and some other cuts I didn't ask about. It was a pretty heavy meal and I flipped my red card before the chicken hearts made their second pass.

At 8:00 a.m., we met Brazil's new Director of Training. He was preparing for the upcoming Olympic Games and wanted training on mass casualty response and ICS. Next we drove to the Federal District to meet with a hybrid specialized group known as the National Force. After a very informative briefing from the Branch Chief, their special units for riot control, hostage rescue, and bomb disposal provided practical demonstrations. Once the smoke had literally cleared, we climbed back into our van for a trip to the airport.

The waiting area was stagnant and humid, so I ducked into a restroom and changed from a suit and tie into shorts and a T-shirt. After passing the final security checkpoint, we still had to wait three hours in the sweltering heat before boarding a LATAM flight to Rio de Janeiro. We arrived at the JW Marriott on Copacabana Beach shortly after midnight. It sounds crazy, but American hotel chains provide enhanced security, are conveniently located, and offer the standard government rate for official travel. I had no complaints.

The remainder of the week was busy, often 10- or 12-hour days. In preparation for the Rio Olympics, my focus was the interoperability of Brazil's various counter–IED units. There was the Federal Police, the Civil Police, the Military Police, and the highly specialized Batalhão de Operações Policiais Especiais, or BOPE. When other units required unconventional tactics and highly specialized equipment, they called BOPE. Their mountaintop headquarters offered beautiful views of the sea and less attractive views of Rio's shantytowns known as favelas. These slums are so crowded that a gondola system was designed to move people from place to place above the fray. Attacks on police and tourists, coupled with ruthless gang violence, rendered these hillside ghettos off limits. Due to the levels of violence, BOPE was often charged with "pacifying" the favelas as they encroached on critical infrastructure. The hazards of that mission were evidenced by the bullet-riddled armored vehicles stored in their secure garages.

After a final briefing at the consulate on Friday, it was time to go home. The embassy booked me on the next available flight, which didn't depart until 10:30 p.m. Saturday, so I hired a guide who picked me up early that morning. The temperature and humidity spiked as we entered the Tijuca rainforest. Monkeys and toucans busied themselves in the thick canopy as I trekked to the base of Christ the Redeemer; intermittent fog shrouded the 124-foot statue which added something to the

Author with an unnamed commander and a member of Brazil's Battalion of Special Operation (BOPE) at their mountaintop headquarters (2014).

experience. Like Angkor Wat and Stonehenge, seeing Cristo Redentor was on my bucket list. From there we drove to Praia Vermelha and took the cable cars to the 1,300-foot summit of iconic Sugarloaf Mountain, then spent the rest of the afternoon strolling the South Zone from Ipanema to Copacabana. A driver met me at the hotel at 8:00 p.m. and after 21 hours in transit, I was home in time to watch the Super Bowl.

April marked the 20th anniversary of the Oklahoma City bombing. I hadn't been to many of the previous remembrance ceremonies; they were too difficult. But somehow I wanted to see this one. Time had taken the edge off some of those memories. President Clinton, Director Comey, and other dignitaries were scheduled to attend, so I'd be working the event anyway. Hundreds of people came for the somber reading of those 168 names; as always it was a moving, emotional ceremony. FBI headquarters wanted to acknowledge the anniversary in Washington with an exhibit in the Director's Portrait Hall. I worked with the bombing memorial to provide some artifacts for that display and, as requested, provided a couple of personal items.

As the exhibit came together, JoAnn from the Public Affairs Office asked me to fly out and give an OKBOMB presentation for headquarters and academy personnel; of course I agreed. As a boy dreaming of a career in the FBI, I never thought I'd be asked to speak at the J. Edgar Hoover Building about such a historic and tragic event. There were about 200 people in attendance, many of whom were just children when the bombing occurred.

After the presentation, JoAnn offered the full tour of the Hoover Building, including "Mahogany Row" on the seventh floor. As we rounded the corner, an elevator opened and out stepped Director Comey with his security detail. JoAnn introduced me and explained I was there to commemorate the Oklahoma City bombing. He slowly repeated my name and paused before saying, "I called you about the Hall of Fame, right?" Unlike some other Directors I'd met, he was very personable and seemed quite genuine. JoAnn then took me to the indoor gun range, where the Range Master produced a rare 1928 Tommy gun and let me burn through a couple of magazines.

Twenty-One

Shangri-La

Once back in Oklahoma, I prepared for the next training iteration in Africa. Medics at Tinker Air Force Base administered the required boosters for typhoid, yellow fever, and pre-rabies and provided a supply of malaria medication. But disease wasn't the biggest concern; parts of Africa were becoming too dangerous for non-operational travel. In fact, much like the assignment to Libya, this training assignment was canceled a week before departure due to the assassination of a prosecutor in an upcoming terrorism case.

June found me in Boston to speak before the Society of Former Special Agents and the FBI Citizens Academy Alumni Association. Since school was out for the summer, my family came along for the weekend. My 13-year-old son got a taste of big city life in Boston's subway when he asked a square-jawed, crew-cut transit cop how to buy a multi-day "CharlieCard." The officer patiently explained the process and then casually asked in a very thick Boston accent, "Yeah, no problem. You haven't seen a naked guy running around here, have you?"

I was scheduled to be in Kathmandu in July, but a 7.8 magnitude earthquake had just devastated the country's infrastructure, killing 9,000 people and destroying 600,000 buildings. Instead of Nepal, I spent the next couple of weeks in the Nevada desert. Upon landing in Reno, I rented a car and dialed in the GPS for Naval Air Station Fallon, the new Navy Fighter Weapons School known as TOPGUN. Two hours later I was sitting in the officers' club sharing a few beers with Chaz, a high-energy Navy EOD technician assigned to Detachment Fallon. His group would coordinate our range time and provide the necessary explosives.

Due to the size of the shots, Chaz put us on a remote demolition range about 50 miles out in the Great Basin Desert. An unpaved road traversed the barren remains of an Ice Age lake where endless salt

Author with an unnamed U.S. Navy EOD technician preparing for large vehicle-borne IED post-blast training in Yuma's Great Basin Desert (2014).

deposits looked like snow that eventually vanished into a mirage. Students' vehicles littered the desert with flat tires; one even broke a tie rod. Once everyone safely arrived, we got started.

The class was made up of Navy EOD, various police bomb techs, and FBI ERT members from as far as San Juan. As always, the goal of the course was to integrate these total strangers into cohesive post-blast teams. After a few days of lectures and case studies, we revealed the practical problem in an early morning briefing. The scenario stated that three VBIEDs had simultaneously detonated at police stations in Reno, Las Vegas, and Carson City. The 44-member group had to break into smaller teams and simultaneously process their respective crime scenes. As always, instructors played roles and periodically provided clues or bits of crucial information known as "intelligence injects" throughout the multi-day exercise.

Prior to the students' arrival we detonated three large IEDs concealed in SUVs, which scattered debris across the desert. Each location was out of sight of the others, so a major component of the exercise tested the exchange of information between each location through a central command group known as the Joint Operations Center, or

JOC. As teams recovered critical bomb components or data identifying the vehicles, notional requests for follow-up information were sent through the JOC to instructors playing the part of FBI chemists or NCIC operators.

By Wednesday night, enough information had been developed for a search warrant of my quarters back at NAS Fallon. Search teams found critical evidence like wire cutters hidden in a drawer, packaging for transistors and burner phone receipts in the trash, even a map of Carson City with cryptic notes detailing the plot. For safety reasons we limited time on the range; the temperature hovered around 104°F and we were a long way from any medical assistance. Class began at sunrise, which put us back at our quarters by late afternoon. Since the sun didn't set until after 8:00 p.m., I had time to explore Highway 50, known as "The Loneliest Road in America."

A short hike at Grimes Point led to prehistoric Lake Lahontan. A faded sign identified a dark horizontal line along the base of the distant mountains as the ancient lake's waterline; a few thousand years ago I would have been 400 feet underwater. Farther down Highway 50 was Sand Mountain, a two-mile long, 600-foot-high dune of pure white sand created by 9,000 years of relentless wind. At its base, a trailhead led to the remnants of the Sand Springs Pony Express Station, which had been lost until its rediscovery in 1975.

The class went well and concluded Friday afternoon with comprehensive briefs provided to a federal prosecutor in moot court. Like me, most students couldn't get flights home until Saturday evening, so we continued our team building in the historic mining town of Virginia City. After some quality time at the Bucket of Blood Saloon, we followed the rickety boardwalk to the haunted Silver Queen. This bizarre saloon and wedding chapel is where Samuel Clemens became Mark Twain in 1862 and is home to the Silver Queen of Ripley's *Believe It or Not!* fame. The 16-foot-tall portrait depicts a woman wearing a gown made of 3,261 silver dollars and a belt comprising 28 twenty-dollar gold pieces. Much of the 210 pounds of silver came from the massive Comstock Lode that made Virginia City famous.

Back at the office, hundreds of secure emails were waiting. The most interesting stated the TDY to Nepal was back on and would begin in three weeks. I arrived in Chicago at sunrise, then boarded an Etihad 777 for a 13-hour flight to Abu Dhabi where another instructor was waiting. We'd worked together in Riyadh and rehashed old times during the long layover. The final four-and-a-half-hour flight landed in Kathmandu at 8:30 p.m. local time, which was 10 hours and 45 minutes ahead of my body clock. Nepal Standard Time is one of only three international time zones offset by 45 minutes, which somehow fit the exotic feel of the place.

An embassy expediter ushered us through Customs and into a van with Shangri-La painted on the side. Traffic moved quickly along the rough roads until a herd of cows blocked the main intersection. While waiting for the drove to amble on, I noticed hundreds of workers precariously scrambling along dimly lit and rickety bamboo scaffolding trying to repair the earthquake-damaged buildings. By 10:30 p.m., we arrived at Shangri-La, a small hotel near the Presidential Palace. The friendly staff greeted us with chilled kagati ko sharbat (Nepalese lemonade) and showed us to our rooms. The multiple time zones and 9,900 miles of flying made sleep come easily.

This was monsoon season, so the sunrise deluge wasn't surprising. I perused the Saturday *Himalayan* over gwaramari pastries and yak milk as the rain continued to pour. By midday the storm abated, so I struck out to see the Swayambhunath Stupa, one of the most ancient shrines in the Kathmandu Valley. Known as the "Monkey Temple," this UNESCO World Heritage Site is perched high on a hill overlooking the crowded city. The setting sun shimmered off the golden shrines as thousands of prayer flags fluttered in the humid breeze; macaques patrolled the grounds while Buddhists and Hindus lit candles, rang bells, and spun prayer wheels.

Work began Sunday morning at the embassy. After a series of conferences, we were taken to the National Police Academy for tea with administrators, who advised that emerging events necessitated some schedule changes. The two-week course was initially designed for 25 officers from the national Nepal Police (NP) and their paramilitary branch, the Armed Police Force of Nepal (APF), which is responsible for counterinsurgency operations.

APF was created in 2001 by King Gyanendra to combat armed radicals of the Maoist Communist Party who were waging the "People's War." After a decade of conflict, the 240-year-old monarchy was abolished. In 2008, a newly elected Constituent Assembly declared Nepal to be a Federal Democratic Republic. But attempts to draft a new democratic constitution only led to more violence. Numerous NP officers had recently been beaten, burned, and even hanged in southern parts of the country, so several officers selected to attend this training had been reassigned to address the deadly new security concerns.

Additional schedule changes were requested to accommodate national events, religious observances, and other cultural mores such as daily tea. Itinerary discussions continued over dinner in Durbar Square, which had been the kingdom's hub since the third century. The earthquake had devastated the area and conservation work was underway to save some of the ancient structures. Orange-robed monks stood stoically before the rubble, silently soliciting donations for their cause.

On Tuesday we were told Teej, one of many religious holidays, would be observed the following day, so class should end before lunch. With an entire afternoon suddenly free, the instructors toured Thamel Bazar, a labyrinth of narrow streets and alleys full of shops and street vendors, overrun with the Brownian movement of tuk-tuks and rickshaws.

From there we drove to Pashupatinath Temple, one of the oldest and most sacred Hindu temples in Kathmandu. Set on the banks of the Bagmati River, this World Heritage Site is dedicated to Shiva, the Hindu god of destruction. Hundreds of elderly pilgrims arrive each year to die and be cremated on the riverbank. As our guide explained the ritual animal sacrifices, a solemn group of mourners passed us carrying a stretcher with a body wrapped in white and orange cloth. Following the Hindu antyeshti ritual, the deceased was placed atop a funeral pyre on a platform protruding into the river. After a brief ceremony, the fire was lit and, once the body was consumed, the ashes were washed into the Bagmati which carried them to the Ganges, the Hindu's sacred river.

It was a strange sight: bodies were burning at the river's edge while hundreds of women dressed in bright red saris anxiously queued around the temple to make offerings to Parvati, the goddess of the Himalayas. On the river's eastern bank, another group of women danced before smaller shrines to Shiva. Scattered among those small stone shrines were sadhus, wandering yogis who live in caves along the river. With painted bodies, long beards, and saffron-colored robes, sadhus spend their days striving for the fourth and final stage of life through meditation. It was a scene straight out of *National Geographic*.

On Friday we were advised Sunday's class would be canceled in recognition of "Constitution Day." In this historic event, President Ram Baran Yadav signed the new constitution guaranteeing the people of Nepal the right to autonomy and self-rule; national festivities were scheduled for three days.

With Sunday now open, Bret (my gyro partner from Trinidad) joined me for the Everest Experience Flight. As instructed by the agent from Yeti Travel, we arrived at the domestic air terminal at 4:30 a.m. only to find it abandoned and under construction. The doors were locked and no lights were on; except for two stray dogs, Bret and I were alone. A solitary guard appeared an hour later, gave us a cursory search, and pointed to a Buddha Air representative who had just arrived. She checked our passports and ushered us through Gate One to join eight other tourists aboard a small Beechcraft waiting on the runway.

By 6:45 we were airborne for a 50-minute flight along the Himalayas; the snowcapped peaks piercing the clouds in the early morning light were breathtaking. As we approached Mount Everest, the flight attendant leaned near my ear and whispered, "Come, the view is better from here," motioning to the cockpit. Amazingly, each passenger was allowed into the tiny cockpit for a spectacular view of Sagarmatha, Nepal's "Peak of Heaven."

That evening we enjoyed momos, water buffalo, and goat mutton at a rooftop restaurant overlooking the Great Boudha Stupa. It was the perfect vantage for the night's independence celebration. Traditional Nepalese music blared over loudspeakers as fireworks burst overhead and throngs lit thousands of candles in the markets and courtyards below; this was their Fourth of July.

Classes concluded Friday with comments from Nepalese officials and embassy representatives. My closing remarks stated the obvious: we were in a dangerous business in a particularly dangerous time. I reminded the class that we arrived in Kathmandu on September 11 and were sadly familiar with loss and tragedy. We could empathize with the recent brutal murders of their officers and were proud to stand with them as a new democratic republic was formed.

My plane to the UAE departed at 9:30 that night. From Abu Dhabi it was 7,500 miles to Chicago, then the final leg to Oklahoma City, which completed 29 hours in transit.

Twenty-Two

I Am Zoltan

Defeating IEDs is a cat and mouse game. As bomb techs learn to beat specific types of devices, terrorists change the design to nullify the corresponding render safe procedure (RSP). The new designs are distributed in underground publications such as *How to Build a Bomb in the Kitchen of Your Mom.* Adopting a new pipe bomb design, the Boston Marathon bombers and the San Bernardino terrorists configured their IEDs to thwart the standard pipe bomb RSP; obviously a new procedure was required.

I had the opportunity to collaborate with an exceptional scientist at the FBI's Research and Development Unit in order to overcome the latest bomb design. After months of extensive preparation and theoretical modeling, it was time to test the new render safe tool on live IEDs. This is a hazardous undertaking, as dynamic testing could result in detonations, so Tom, a good friend and SABT in Dallas, arranged for the use of a remote demolition range near Mesquite, Texas.

Ian, the lead physicist, and other FBI PhDs, high-speed videographers, medics, heavy equipment operators, and bomb techs from Mesquite and Dallas joined researchers from the Naval Surface Warfare Center on the scruffy prairie to characterize the new tool. Due to heavy rains, ATVs were required to ferry an array of sensitive scientific equipment to the site. Tents were erected so bomb techs could build dozens of live pipe bombs and hand grenades.

Despite ominous forecasts of floods and tornadoes, we constructed and destroyed as many as 32 IEDs each day for a week. The devices were built in their most sensitive configurations to prove the tool's capabilities in a worst case scenario. Every test was meticulously documented and recorded for subsequent in-depth analysis. The tool proved to be remarkably successful, and we received a U.S. patent which was later given to the FBI. Within a year, the new tool was available to police and military bomb squads across the country.

New tools and technology were constantly required to address the unrelenting threat of terrorism. On Halloween 2015, an ISIS bomb destroyed Kogalymavia Flight 9268 over the Sinai Peninsula. Nine days later, two U.S. contractors were killed at a specialized training site in Jordan. Friday the 13th saw coordinated attacks in Paris followed by an attack in Mali eight days later. The world was a very dangerous place and viable threats couldn't be ignored, regardless of how improbable they seemed.

Late one night in December, I received a text from an OHP Trooper in rural Oklahoma. It read, "Hate to bother you, but there's something I think you need to see. Can you call me?"

The Trooper answered on the first ring. "Yeah, I got a call from Garvin County around midnight. A deputy asked me to meet him out at the Walmart distribution center. One of the forklift drivers was off-loading pallets of Fig Newtons, but at the back of the trailer he saw racks of rockets. They called me and I got the truck pulled over out here on I-40, but the driver only speaks Russian. His logs and manifest are all forgeries. But here's the thing: I made him open up the trailer, and sure enough, there're big racks of rockets in there. I asked where they came from and he just kept saying 'Cuba.' What do you think?"

This could become a political issue very quickly. President Obama had just removed Cuba from the list of state sponsors of terror and a trailer full of rockets is never good.

"Hang on to him. I'll have JTTF run him through our databases, find a Russian interpreter, and call the Army to meet us there. Sit tight."

Military ordnance is the sole purview of the military. If these were actually rockets, Army EOD would need to assess them. During the 80-mile trip to that lonely stretch of I-40, I imagined this had to be some sort of mistake; perhaps they were empty, discarded rocket tubes that collectors often keep as souvenirs. That theory was dashed when the Trooper sent two images from his cell phone clearly depicting 11 steel pallets marked ROCKET LAUNCHER. Each pallet had nine rocket pods in pristine shipping configuration. I forwarded the images to Captain Gates at Fort Sill, who immediately dispatched an EOD team. Within a couple of hours, we converged at Exit 70 near the Chickasaw Jet Stream Casino in rural Oklahoma.

Climbing into the trailer with the EOD tech, our flashlights illuminated 99 rocket pods in steel shipping racks; each pod held seven rockets. The sergeant feverishly consulted ordnance manuals and traced the stenciled serial numbers through the Army's Criminal Investigation Division. They hadn't been reported stolen and appeared to be legitimate ordnance. We attempted to contact the points of origin and terminus listed on the fake shipping documents, but it was 3:00 a.m. One man finally answered the phone, saying, "No, there's no record of that shipment. And whose name is on the bill of lading? No, we don't have anybody here by that name, something's wrong."

The Global War on Terror was just that, a global war. But unlike conflicts of the past, it didn't always involve uniformed armies following historically accepted rules of engagement. So a Russian with a truckload of Cuban rockets had to be taken seriously.

EOD X-rayed the pods with limited success. The sergeant shrugged. "I'm not getting a very good image due to the limited space and these dense shipping containers. There's definitely electronics and wiring, but I don't see any warheads." At least that was good news.

More information became available as the sun rose and people reported to work. We confirmed these were military rockets that had all the internal components and firing circuitry, but no motors or warheads. We also learned they had actually originated in Cuba; not the communist island nation, but a contractor in Cuba, Missouri, who was hired to paint them.

This driver's small trucking company won the bid to transport the pallets from Missouri to an Army depot in southeastern Oklahoma. The truck originally authorized to haul the load had broken down along the highway. Not wanting to lose the contract, our Russian friend simply transferred his pallets of Fig Newtons into the trailer containing the rockets and intended to complete both deliveries. Somewhere near the Oklahoma state line he realized the other driver had failed to provide the required shipping documents, so he fabricated the paperwork using a laptop in his truck. There are strict regulations against forging shipping documents and mixing rockets with Fig Newtons, but those were questions for other people. Since no explosive hazards were present, the Army and I made our way to the casino for some coffee.

No threat could be ignored. Large, well-organized groups, small splinter cells, or even lone wolves could now be expected to target civilians in shopping malls, luxury hotels, and theaters using military precision, automatic weapons, and explosives. That was the nature of terrorism. The lines between criminal activity usually handled by law enforcement and actions best left to the military were continually blurring.

Biometric, financial, and digital data were often needed to track the head of the snake and dismantle an entire terrorist organization. That's the kind of thing the FBI does quite well: gathering and analyzing vast amounts of data for the long game. The military's mission is often more focused on an immediate, short-term resolution. In the murky world of counterterrorism, the relationship between law enforcement and military operations had, by necessity, grown much closer. FBI Agents were routinely embedded with elite military teams abroad to capitalize on ephemeral opportunities to gather intelligence and physical evidence that could unravel a terror network. Once those dots were connected, resolution could come domestically through the FBI or internationally through SEAL Team Six.

In 2003, the FBI created the Terrorist Explosives Devices Analytical Center (TEDAC) to provide comprehensive forensic examinations of IEDs encountered in Iraq and Afghanistan. Its mission grew to include exploiting any IED that had a bearing on U.S. interests, regardless of the source. TEDAC uses cutting-edge scientific and forensic techniques to analyze devices in order to identify a specific bomb maker, intercompare IEDs from around the world, and draw connections between apparently disparate events. One of many success stories centered on a human hair recovered from tape inside an IED. DNA extracted from the hair was linked to a known bomb maker associated with a specific terrorist group. The intelligence value was remarkable; it provided the first indication that this terrorist organization was now operating in a new part of Africa.

In order to facilitate that type of complete forensic exploitation, devices and device components must first be collected, then preserved and transported in certain ways. That's one reason military personnel attend FBI post-blast training. Teaching war fighters to think like cops as they enter a terrorist's lair can provide comprehensive advantages. Extremely useful information may be easily overlooked in the heat of battle, so highlighting its value in mission briefings is essential. During Operation Neptune Spear, Navy SEALs spent additional very dangerous minutes in bin Laden's compound in order to recover documents, five computers, 10 hard drives, and over 100 flash drives which provided invaluable intelligence about al-Qaeda's operations. The effort to gather critical intelligence in high-value locations is known as Sensitive Site Exploitation (SSE). It's not designed for every battlefield engagement, but is limited to areas of special diplomatic or military significance; bin Laden's compound in Abbottabad was obviously a sensitive site.

NATO's SSE training is known as the Weapons Intelligence Course. It teaches unconventional warfighters the long-term benefits of spending a little extra time on target in order to exploit items of value during special operations. Killing the person who deployed a roadside bomb is an immediate, strategic resolution. But forensically identifying the person designing the bombs provides a far-reaching, tactical resolution.

I was pleased to serve as a Weapons Intelligence instructor for NATO's Center of Excellence (COE) in Budapest. COEs are international military facilities that train and educate NATO leaders and specialists. Expertise offered at these institutions influences doctrine and improves interoperability with partner nations around the globe.

As is often the case, my assignment notification arrived as a brief email at 4:30 a.m.; the three-week course would begin in seven days. In addition to the highest U.S. security clearances, I already had a NATO "COSMIC TOP SECRET" clearance which was needed for this course. No visa was required for Hungary, so the short notice posed no problems. I landed at Ferenc Liszt International, about 25 miles outside of Budapest. Unlike other assignments, there was no embassy expediter, just that tersely worded email that read, "Upon arrival rent vehicle. Meet team at Aquaworld Conference Centre 20 km north of Inner City."

After clearing Customs, I found an open rental car service that had a six-speed left-hand drive VW Golf available. There was no GPS, but a small map in the glovebox guided me across the Danube, onto the M0, then toward Dunakeszi. I arrived late that evening and was handed a note upon check-in that read, "Welcome, Mr. Black. There is a meeting in the lobby bar at 9:00 pm."

The original email read "meet team," but failed to say if it was an FBI team or a group of Hungarians. I got to the bar about 8:45 and immediately caught the attention of a group of casually dressed men seated at a table in the back. An affable older man with a thick Irish accent stood to greet me.

"And you must be Barry. I'm Liam, with the Irish Ordnance Corps."

We shook hands as he introduced the other soldiers: a Spaniard, a Romanian, a Dutchman, and our Hungarian host. The Hungarian stood and made some unusual hand gesture as he announced, "I am Zoltan.... Like movie, *Dude, Where's My Car?*"

It took a moment for the "Z" hand sign from the movie to register, "Of course! It's a pleasure to meet you, Zoltan."

This was the team: NATO military officers, each an expert in his field, who'd traveled together as a cohesive training unit for years. I was definitely the odd man out and wasn't sure how well things would go, especially when the steely Romanian paratrooper spoke up.

"You are FBI? We have had this class many times without FBI. This is … good."

I was happy to hear it. Group dynamics are important and we became fast friends over drinks, even though I was the only civilian American accountant in the room. Discussion soon turned to the next three weeks' itinerary; classes Monday through Friday with team-building events each evening. Aldert, the Dutchman, was a history buff. "There is a lot to see here. I can show you if you'd like."

An olive-drab bus picked us up at 8:00 a.m. for a 30-minute ride to a Hungarian Defense Force facility. In a large classroom, the students introduced themselves: forensic lab scientists, EOD techs, military police, and Special Forces operators from Hungary, Ireland, Germany, Brussels, Spain, France, the Netherlands, Romania, and the Czech Republic. The course objective was SSE: how to identify, collect, and exploit intelligence at a "hot" terrorist location. Lectures highlighted the value of digital data, fingerprints, DNA, and detailed photographic techniques to capture actionable intelligence.

Lectures were augmented with explosives and IED demonstrations. We constructed and detonated improvised anti-personnel mines, improvised explosively formed projectiles (EFPs), and demonstrated the effects of buried charges ranging from eight pounds of HME to 53 pounds of TNT. Students could see the components necessary to construct these devices, their destructive potential, and the telltale post-blast signature each would leave behind.

On the weekends, Aldert gave me historic tours around Budapest. We saw the Citadella, a strategic Austrian fortress built overlooking the Danube during the Hungarian Revolution, and later occupied by Nazi and Soviet troops. We toured the nearby ruins of the Roman capital Aquincum, which predated the Citadella by about 1,700 years, then the medieval town of Bratislava, Slovakia; a sovereign nation that had recently separated from Czechoslovakia. We saw a ninth-century fortress atop Castle Hill, the 500-year-old St. Martin's Cathedral, then Devín Castle, which was built in the Dark Ages. Perched precariously on a cliff about 700 feet above the Danube and Morava rivers, the site had been inhabited since prehistoric times. The most poignant site was the bullet-riddled Gate of Freedom Memorial at the base of the crag.

The monument's stark white stone was pocked with bullet holes and served as a tribute to the 400 Czechoslovakians shot by the Soviets as they attempted to flee the Iron Curtain by swimming across the river.

Being multilingual, Aldert was translating the monument's inscription when a large group of exhausted runners plodded by. As one stopped to tie his shoe, Aldert struck up a brief conversation in perfect Slovak. He returned shaking his head, saying, "This man has been running for 21 hours. He's part of the Štefánik Trail race, a 145K [90-mile] ultra-marathon through the mountains. We'll be back in Budapest before his race is over."

Our last stop was the medieval fortress of Visegrád. Other than being hexed by an old Gypsy lady outside the ruins, it was a great weekend.

The training pace quickened over the next few days. Small-scale practical problems became more complicated as instructors provided complex storylines to create a realistic training environment. One team was dispatched to exploit the scene of an armored limousine we'd destroyed with an EFP. Another was sent to a remote training village to conduct SSE on a suspected terrorist bomb factory. Shortly after entering the compound, the team leader's radio crackled; overwatch snipers advised enemy insurgents were regrouping for a counterattack. The

Author with an unnamed Irish Special Forces operator and an unnamed Romanian Special Forces operator at a training site on the outskirts of Budapest, Hungary (2016).

team had to quickly decide which evidence should be removed and which should be destroyed.

The final week culminated with large post-blast exercises followed by an informal dinner at Teddy Beers in Szentendre. During happy hour, Zoltan took great pleasure in announcing to the class that he was born the year I joined the FBI. That stung a little.

It was officially summer, so my family joined me in Budapest. We attended a Picasso exhibit at the National Gallery, strolled the promenade toward the Parliament Building, and took a dinner cruise on the Danube. The next few days were spent in Vienna, Berchtesgaden, and Obersalzberg before taking the Romantic Road to Füssen to see the fairytale Neuschwanstein Castle. Surrounded by Alpine lakes and waterfalls, it's easy to see why Walt Disney chose this castle's design as his park's centerpiece.

The rest of the summer was full of outrageous acts of violence that were sadly becoming the norm. A terrorist drove a truck through a crowd of 30,000 people during a Bastille Day celebration in Nice, killing 86. Passengers aboard trains in Paris, Würzburg, and Sennwald were stabbed; a coup d'état by terrorists in Turkey killed hundreds. Munich suffered a "politically motivated" mass shooting, and ISIS continued its terror campaign throughout the Middle East and North Africa.

Domestically, an ISIS-inspired terrorist detonated multiple IEDs in New Jersey and New York before a shootout with police. Officers were ambushed and killed in St. Louis, Des Moines, Baton Rouge, San Antonio, and Dallas, and a homegrown terror cell was planning mass murder just over the Kansas state line.

Three radical members of a larger militia group known as the Kansas Security Forces formed a splinter cell called the Crusaders. Two of the men lived in Kansas and the third resided in rural Beaver County in Oklahoma's Panhandle. Driven by a deep-seated hatred of immigrants, the group was galvanized into action after the terror attack at Orlando's Pulse nightclub. That shooter, Omar Mir Seddique Mateen, identified himself as an Islamic soldier and pledged allegiance to ISIS.

Disturbed by the Crusaders' growing radicalization, an informant associated with the group approached the FBI's office in Garden City, Kansas, which is home to a large Somali population. The informant agreed to secretly record conversations with the Crusaders, who met in open wheat fields to avoid conventional surveillance. The group discussed acquiring chemicals to make HME, targeting public officials, immigrant housing complexes, and even churches that provided assistance to refugees. With references to Timothy McVeigh and the Unabomber, the informant reported, "They want this to be a wake-up call."

As the threat became more viable, an FBI undercover agent (UCA) was introduced to the group as someone who could build the IEDs they wanted. One Crusader agreed to deliver 300 pounds of ammonium nitrate so the UCA could make ANFO, the explosive used by McVeigh.

The attack was set for November 9, 2016, one day after the U.S. presidential election, in hopes of inspiring like-minded extremists. After several surveillance runs, the Crusaders decided to target an apartment complex predominantly occupied by Somali immigrants; it also happened to house a mosque. Their plan was to deploy four VBIEDs around the complex during prayer time to maximize casualties.

A break in the case came when one of the Crusaders' girlfriends contacted local police claiming she'd been beaten. Angered by the mistreatment, she revealed her boyfriend and his buddies were in a militia, making bombs and stockpiling weapons and chemicals. Based on the domestic abuse allegation, local police arrested the boyfriend, who had an AK-47 magazine and ammunition with him. Once he was in custody, the girlfriend provided additional information about a white powder being made and "cooled in an ice bath" at one of the Crusaders' businesses. That description was consistent with the manufacture of TATP or its chemical cousin, HMTD.

With the attack date looming and this new information, the timetable for intervention was moved up. We planned to simultaneously arrest the Crusaders and execute several search warrants in Kansas and the Beaver County farmhouse. Coordination and logistics would be an issue due to the subject's propensity for violence, the existence of highly unstable HME, and the remote, rural nature of the sites.

The Oklahoma team decided to rendezvous in a small town about an hour away from the farm to avoid raising suspicion. HRT flew in from Quantico and trickled into the small farming community throughout the day along with our SWAT team and ERT, I arrived about 10:30 that night. An identical plan was unfolding across the state line in Liberal, Kansas. After simultaneous briefings at 5:30 a.m., teams in each state executed their warrants.

HRT and SWAT arrested the Crusaders, then secured the search locations as bomb technicians cleared each site. The searches discovered weapons, documents related to IEDs, bags of ammonium nitrate, and an improvised blasting cap filled with HMTD. Once I secured the energetic materials from the Beaver County farm, ERT began their search for additional evidence. Thirteen hours later I began the four-hour drive back to Oklahoma City.

The 10-month investigation resulted in the three men being indicted for hate crimes and conspiracy to use a WMD. Their trial lasted four weeks, but the jury only needed a day to return guilty verdicts on all counts. The men were sentenced to lengthy prison sentences of 25, 26, and 30 years respectively (Southern Poverty Law Center 2024).

Twenty-Three

North Africa

The 2016 presidential election unfolded with unprecedented drama. Social issues boiled into riots; there were concerns about Hillary Clinton's emails and unsecure server, and allegations that Russia was tampering with the election. The media also widely reported nonspecific chatter that terrorists were planning attacks in order to disrupt polling places across the country. In the interest of public safety, the FBI initiated a nationwide canvass asking the public to report any suspicious activity.

One tip received by Oklahoma City's JTTF pertained to a pair of brothers who had recently arrived from the war-torn Middle East. Initial investigation revealed they were naturalized citizens who had already been convicted of numerous felonies. As the investigation continued, several associates reported the brothers were stockpiling weapons. It's illegal for convicted felons to possess firearms, whether they're terrorists or not. So out of an abundance of caution, JTTF spent days prior to the election surveilling the brothers and trying to connect the dots. Thirty-six hours before the polls opened, we executed two search warrants and recovered a significant amount of cash, a loaded handgun, a magazine fed shotgun, and a scoped semiautomatic rifle with high-capacity magazines. Both men were arrested and charged as felons in possession of firearms, but there were no ties to terrorism. The 2016 election concluded amid "mostly peaceful" protests, but no terror attacks occurred.

Political violence continued to be a concern well into the future. Thirty days before the 2024 election, an FBI undercover operation in Oklahoma City disrupted an alleged ISIS-K inspired attack. During the investigation, an Afghan man and his teenage accomplice acquired AK-47 assault rifles, 10 magazines, and 500 rounds of ammunition. In a post-arrest interview, the suspect confirmed the suicide attack would target public gatherings on Election Day.

As the weather cooled, another VBIED post-blast school was scheduled in the deserts of Utah, the 141st iteration. I arrived in St. George late Saturday night and met the instructors at the Dixie Rock classroom Sunday morning. We offloaded three truckloads of gear, then drove into Arizona to inspect an old pit mine that would serve as the explosives range. As usual, the week's class included lectures, explosives demonstrations, and practical exercises. The final scenario began with the detonation of three vans full of explosives in separate areas of the mine; the explosions were heard miles away at Dixie Rock.

Once the students arrived, they were presented with the scenario: simultaneous VBIED attacks in three different cities. They broke into teams and independently processed each site, sharing critical findings through the JOC. At night they executed mock search warrants and at week's end presented case summaries to a federal prosecutor.

The final shot was Friday afternoon. As the class watched from a ridge high above the pit mine, we detonated 650 pounds of high explosives. A huge column of rock and sand shot skyward as the shock wave visibly rolled along the canyon walls. The sound and pressure changes the students experienced were impressive, even from that distance.

Back home, things settled into what passed for routine. During dinner one evening, the JTTF airport liaison officer called. "I hate to bother you, but we may have a problem. We got a very specific telephonic threat saying there's a bomb aboard an inbound plane. It's too close to divert, so they're landing at Will Rogers."

Of course there are plans for this kind of thing.

"OK, coordinate with airport operations and airport police; they'll loop in fire and EMS. Have the plane taxi to the back pad; I'll have a local bomb squad and K9s meet me there. TSA can meet at the CP once JTTF gets it established. Anything else I need to know?"

"Yeah, it's an NBA charter coming in to play the Thunder."

"All right. We have a good relationship with their people; I'll contact them as well."

The plane was a 737 with the number 666 ominously painted on the nose gear. Once the passengers and crew were removed and taken to a safe location, bomb techs and K9s swept the plane, baggage, and cargo; nothing suspicious was found.

However, a bomb threat itself is a federal felony. So JTTF began tracing the plane's history and the call's origin. As it turned out, this call was just one in a series of similar threats impacting air traffic across the country, so our incident was folded into the larger national investigation. Preexisting interagency relationships are key to quickly resolving these types of events.

I enjoyed a long, close working relationship with Army assets at Fort Sill. We trained together on post-blast protocols, imprinted their dogs on TATP and HMTD, and acclimated K9 teams to combat flight operations. So when the new commanding officer of the EOD unit asked for SSE training, I was happy to oblige. He realized that resources responding to an attack on a domestic installation like Fort Sill would differ from assets responding to an attack on a FOB or in an active combat zone. He wanted his soldiers to learn the best techniques to exploit either situation.

An overview of NATO's Weapons Intelligence course, coupled with lessons learned from major domestic events like OKBOMB, PENTTBOM, and the Boston Marathon bombing, provided an academic background. We then moved to the demolition range for practical, scenario-based training. Upon arrival, soldiers dismounted and got to work: one group established a security perimeter, another began conducting "witness" interviews, and a third assessed and collected evidence from the post-blast scenes. After each FTX, the team prepared a storyboard which was presented to the new commander. Every iteration highlighted the value of collecting forensic evidence, as long as the operational environment allowed it. When the training concluded, the commander commented that the volume of evidence collected using this methodology was four times what he'd seen in actual combat deployments.

Three weeks later I departed for North Africa. While changing planes in Frankfurt, a pair of German Federal Police officers, complete with submachine guns, appeared behind the baggage screener examining my carry-on. After a brief discussion with the screener, the senior officer looked in my direction.

"Come with us, please."

The odds of missing my connecting flight just went up. The younger officer extended his hand. "ID please. Can you explain why explosives residue was detected throughout your bag?"

"Oh, yes, sir. I believe I can."

I produced my red "Official" passport and FBI credentials. "I'm a bomb technician with the FBI. I imagine the bag may have some residue from previous deployments."

They examined my IDs and conferred with each other in German before nodding and saying, "Very well, you may go. Enjoy your trip."

"Thank you. Sorry for the trouble."

After giving each of them an FBI lapel pin and bomb tech challenge coin, I sprinted to Gate 28 and arrived just as the boarding doors were closing. This final two-hour flight to Tunis would complete 21 hours in transit.

An embassy expediter was waiting at the jet bridge and escorted me through Customs. Once outside, a driver loaded the bags into an armored Suburban and took me directly to the U.S. embassy, which had been overrun by hundreds of protesters in the wake of the Benghazi attack of September 11, 2012. Once over the walls, protesters tore down and burned the American flag, replacing it with the black flag of al-Qaeda.

Attacks on Tunisian security forces were now common, especially in the mountains along the Algerian border. Thousands of hardline Tunisians who fought with ISIS in Syria had begun filtering back into the country. They wanted to derail a national shift to democracy that began with the "Jasmine Revolution." Despite violent opposition, the 28-day revolution ousted longtime dictator Zine El Abidine Ben Ali and served as the impetus for the pro-democracy "Arab Spring" that swept across the region.

Once inside the embassy's upgraded security, I was greeted by the Legal Attaché. "Welcome to Tunisia, glad you're with us. Here's your satellite phone, a local cell phone, and car keys. We have a house for you on the outskirts of town. Jamal, your interpreter, will meet you there. He's fluent in French and Arabic, so you're in good hands. You'll be working at the National Police Academy in Salammbô. The students were selected from the National Guard's EOD unit, the counterterrorism Special Unit, and the National Police Anti-Terrorism Brigade called BAT. Some of these guys responded to the most recent terror attacks; we'll get you out to those sites. Oh, some U.S. Navy folks from SOCOM [Special Operations Command] will also be in the class. Let me know if you need anything."

I wasn't sure which embassy vehicle I had been assigned, but the keys were on a Hello Kitty keychain. I wandered the secure parking lot clicking the car alarm button until Hello Kitty's lights blinked. It was an armored Land Cruiser equipped with run-flat tires, racing brakes, dual starting systems, and infrared headlights. After winding my way through the streets of Tunis, I eventually found Jamal waiting at the outer security gate of the safe house.

"I'm sure you're hungry. There is a good place not far from here, but you must drive. Traffic is crazy."

Training began early the next morning with a couple of objectives: evaluate the nation's existing counter–IED capabilities, and support the new democracy with counterterrorism training. Each evening at the safe house, I constructed firing circuits for IEDs to be used the following day. They were tailored to resemble devices encountered in recent urban attacks and in the rugged Atlas Mountains along the Algerian border. My devices were deployed along simulated patrol routes, placed on bridges, telecommunications towers, and buses in the Salammbô training village. Based on each unique scenario, teams had to develop render safe procedures that maximized the recovery of forensic evidence. Techniques to disrupt and safely recover devices were encouraged as an alternative to destroying the IEDs with countercharges.

The hosts were congenial and eager to share their country's long history. The Salammbô facility itself was adjacent to the ancient Punic port and archaeological ruins of Carthage. One evening, we toured the North Africa American Cemetery and Memorial dedicated to U.S. forces lost in Africa during World War II. We also visited the Roman aqueducts and villas built by Hadrian in 146 AD. The BAT commander also took us to the sites of Tunisia's most recent terror attacks.

The Bardo National Museum is Tunisia's Louvre, a 19th-century palace housing artifacts including a prehistoric altar, Carthaginian jewelry, and the world's largest collection of ancient Roman mosaics. On March

Author with unnamed operators from the National Police Anti-Terrorism Brigade (BAT) in Salammbô, Tunisia (2017).

18, 2015, terrorists killed 19 people, mostly tourists, and wounded dozens of others as buses arrived from a cruise port. BAT commandos eventually freed the hostages and killed the gunmen; bullet holes still scar the museum's marble walls. ISIS claimed responsibility for the attack, ominously saying it was just the beginning.

Attacks on government security forces became routine; four officers had been killed at a checkpoint just weeks before. But the Bardo Museum assault was the first time tourism was targeted; it's an important component of the Tunisian economy.

The next attack occurred in the seaside tourist town of Sousse, just three months after Bardo. Thirty-eight people were massacred along the beach at a resort hotel, most of them tourists. ISIS claimed responsibility and a subsequent investigation indicated the shooter was trained in the same Libyan ISIS camp as one of the Bardo terrorists (Issitt 2021).

Despite the real threat of terrorism, Tunisia is a beautiful country. Jamal had been there several times and knew the best places to see. We spent many evenings in the clifftop village of Sidi Bou Said. Its cobblestone streets meandered through iconic whitewashed Grecian buildings with bright blue roofs and provided spectacular views of the Mediterranean. The medina, or city center, was also amazing. The ancient city gate of Bab El-Bha led to the souk, a warren of narrow streets and alleys where vendors sold everything from spices and perfume to fezzes and gold.

Sitting in the crowded souk, Jamal shook his head and said, "The city is good. But on our next day off I'll show you the east coast. It's very different."

We followed Trans-African Highway 1 to the coastal town of Hammamet. Jamal parked along the beach beneath some palm trees and said, "Come, we'll have coffee in the kasbah."

Located in the medina, the 900-year-old fortress offered commanding views of the Gulf of Hammamet and the deep blue Mediterranean Sea. We were enjoying the vista, sipping strong coffee with dates and couscous, when Jamal asked, "Want to see the colosseum?"

About two hours south was the desert town of El Jem which was built around a colossal amphitheater. Parking in the main square, Jamal motioned to a huge stone structure.

"This the largest Roman colosseum in North Africa. It was built about 238 AD and could hold up to 35,000 people. They'd come here to see Christians executed and gladiators fight to the death."

Unlike the Coliseum in Rome, this structure was completely accessible, even the holding areas for wild animals beneath the floor. During the games, beasts would appear as if by magic using hidden ramps underneath the arena. As we passed the outer stone arches, a man leading a camel approached. After a brief conversation in Arabic, Jamal smiled.

"He'll give you a tour of the ruins on his camel for five dinars. You must do it."

I did; when in Rome…

When we weren't on the demo range, we had conferences with various entities engaged in Tunisia's counterterrorism and counter–IED missions. Monday's conference was in Bouchoucha with the National Police bomb squad commander. Tuesday was spent in Bizerte at SOCOM's Joint Special Operations Exploitation Analysis Center. Wednesday was dedicated to the national crime lab, and Thursday we met with the commanding general of the Unité Spéciale de la Garde Nationale, the National Guard's Special Unit. The week ended with IED awareness training for the Marine Security Guards back at the embassy. With all the training concluded, I walked upstairs and left the keys to Hello Kitty with the Legal Attaché.

A driver arrived at midnight to take me to the airport for a 2:20 a.m. flight to Germany. Awakened by a rough landing in Frankfurt, I shuffled down the jetway only to realize I'd grabbed the wrong black backpack. I wasn't allowed back on the plane, but was directed to Lost and Found. After a long bus ride to the remote terminal, a Lufthansa rep gave me the news.

"I'm happy to report your pack was already turned in. Regrettably, it's been routed to the Lost and Found office at the main terminal. I'll place a hold on it and you may claim it there. A bus will take you."

I successfully recovered the bag at Lost and Found and stepped through the exit only to find myself outside the security zone. Not wanting to miss my connection, I ran out into the rain and up one level to catch a train back to Terminal 2. Once at Immigration, an attentive inspector scrutinized my passport stamps.

"So you entered Germany just today. But now you are leaving?"

After patiently hearing the tale, he pointed to Concourse D. I was almost through the final security check when Franz randomly selected me for a very thorough and personal search. He chose not to wear gloves as he ran his huge cold fingers through my hair, gave each pocket a lingering squeeze, and lightly raked the bottoms of my sock feet with his fingertips. Once Franz was satisfied, I was finally allowed to board.

The long transatlantic flight would be welcomed, as I'd been awake for 21 hours.

I had settled back into my office routine when someone yelled over the cubicle walls, "The President fired Comey." We gathered around a TV in the squad bay to watch the live coverage. This was a complete surprise; it was even reported that the Director learned of his dismissal on the news.

Factually, every FBI Director serves at the pleasure of the President for a 10-year term. Despite the media's dismay, this wasn't completely unprecedented. Judge William Sessions was dismissed by President Clinton after less than six years as FBI Director. Director Freeh resigned after less than eight years, and Director Muller's service was extended to 12 years after the 9/11 attacks. Director Comey had been on the job less than four years.

But turmoil in Washington didn't impact work in the field. Through the hot summer months, I hosted explosives and narcotics training for police and military K9s and an advanced IED electronics course for Oklahoma's bomb technicians.

Logistics are usually the hardest part of hosting any training event, and the three-day electronics class was no different. Four huge cases of specialized equipment and supplies were to be delivered a week in advance, but didn't arrive until the day before class. The primary instructors, PhDs in physics and electronics, arrived that Sunday afternoon.

After unloading the gear and prepping the classroom, I got home about 7:00 p.m. which should have given me 12 hours before returning to the classroom. But at 10:52 p.m., the Tulsa bomb squad commander called; he was physically in Oklahoma City for the electronics course.

"My dispatch just advised the Air Force recruiting station in Bixby has been bombed. I have a couple of techs heading that way and I'm leaving the hotel now. We'll meet you there."

Military recruiting centers are federal facilities, which fall under the FBI's jurisdiction. Like military bases, they made attractive targets as evidenced by attacks in Chattanooga, Washington, D.C., Little Rock, and New York City.

Bixby, a suburb of Tulsa, is about 112 miles from Oklahoma City. Ironically, the FBI bomb tech assigned to Tulsa was in OKC for the electronics class, along with most of the Tulsa Police and OHP bomb technicians that covered that area. I called Tulsa's JTTF and ERT supervisors to get a CP established as soon as possible.

I arrived at 1:30 a.m. to find the Bixby police efficiently manning a perimeter, a functioning JTTF CP, and ERT setting up the post-blast gear. However, there were people from another three-letter agency milling around inside the scene. I'd had professional differences about crime scene protocols with ATF before in various scenes across the country. So I found the JTTF supervisor in the CP and asked, "Have you already opened an FBI case, bombing of a federal facility?"

"Yes, I have."

"Are all those folks inside the scene assigned to an FBI Task Force?"

"Well, no," came the tentative answer.

"Then why are they in our crime scene? It looks like they're collecting evidence and interviewing witnesses, right?"

"Well, yes. But I like to try and work with our partners."

"That's great, but bombing investigations are unique and fast breaking. It's been my experience that these guys will start doing their own thing and we won't have a full picture of what's happening. If they're not on your Task Force and not reporting to you, how will we know who they've interviewed? Who'll establish a chain of custody? How will evidence get packaged and properly submitted to *our* Lab? These are all discovery issues that can bite us down the road."

"Well, yeah. But I don't really think I can cut them out, you know?"

"Being nice is fine, but this has caused real issues in the past. Beyond ensuring we have a complete operational picture, there can only be one voice in an FBI investigation and it has to be ours. I've seen this before; sensitive investigative details or inaccurate information will be released and we're left to clean it all up. This is going to be a problem."

My phone rang as those words left my lips. It was SIOC (Strategic Information Operations Center) at FBI HQ. "Hey, I know you're busy. But the White House Situation Room is on the other line and they have some questions."

I listened and shook my head as SIOC explained what the White House wanted to know. Looking at the JTTF supervisor I said, "I'm in the CP now, let me put you on speaker. OK, repeat that please."

"Sure. The White House wants to know why ATF in Dallas issued a press release stating this bombing was domestic terrorism. They want to know how you know it's terrorism and why they didn't hear it from the FBI first."

"That press release is premature. We don't know if it's DT or not. I'm with the JTTF supervisor now. We've opened a case and are interviewing witnesses; ERT is just now collecting evidence. It's too soon to know anything for certain so no press release has been authorized. I'll let you know as we learn more."

"Roger, keep us advised."

The supervisor nodded sheepishly. "OK, I get it now. I'll tell them to pack up."

Unfortunately, bombings and shootings happen with some frequency, but not every occurrence is terrorism. To meet the definition of terrorism, the act must have been perpetrated to further an ideological goal driven by political, religious, social, racial, or environmental beliefs. The motive has to be examined, and misidentifying a crime as terrorism has complex ramifications. Agencies must be certain before making blanket assumptions, and in my experience, this other agency desperately wants to be the media darling, first with information, even if it's inaccurate.

The post-blast scene was not particularly large, but the explosion had significantly damaged the recruiting station. As JTTF scoured the area for witnesses, critical physical evidence was recovered on scene. That evidence led to an initial assessment of the device: a steel pipe bomb, concealed in a military ammo can, detonated at the front doors of the office. The crucial piece of evidence was a small, shattered piece of printed circuit board (PCB) with custom integrated circuitry serving as the firing system.

I sent an image of the fragmented PCB to the FBI PhDs already in town for the electronics course. After examining the image, they believed we were dealing with a digital time bomb. Unlike the huge mechanical clock hands of a Wile E. Coyote time bomb, a digital device counts down invisibly. Devices like this have been encountered overseas, but were unusual in the U.S.

Just before 6:00 a.m., we released the scene to local authorities. I drove back to Oklahoma City as a fresh shift of JTTF investigators began reviewing images from surrounding surveillance cameras and following up on witness statements. I'd been asleep for two hours when the phone rang; a suspect had been identified and JTTF wanted help drafting a search warrant affidavit.

Overnight, analysts had combed through police reports and learned that the recruiting station's vehicles had been vandalized just days before the bombing. A review of all the witness statements revealed several reports of a red racing motorcycle driving erratically in the area just before and after the blast, and several airmen identified a disgruntled former coworker who warranted further investigation. With those few threads of information, the FBI's massive analytical machine sprang into action.

Using Air Force records, the disgruntled airman was fully identified. A DMV check showed only one vehicle registered to him, a red racing motorcycle. His social media referenced the vandalized Air Force vehicles, and posts touted his proficiency in building sophisticated electronic alarm systems. Property records provided a couple of probable addresses, a house in his parents' name and an apartment on the outskirts of town. We dispatched surveillance teams to both addresses and waited.

Our surveillance aircraft quickly spotted the red Ducati heading toward the apartment. As the subject dismounted, perimeter security teams arrested him just 17 hours after the blast. While he was being processed and interviewed, a judge signed the search warrant.

A backpack was strapped to the back of the motorcycle; X-rays revealed it contained a loaded pistol but no IED. We then used a robot to gain entry through the apartment's sliding glass door. Its cameras revealed no furniture, just a workbench covered with various electrical components, soldering irons, steel pipes, chemicals, and chemical recipes. The most interesting item was a large black gym bag secured with a padlock located in the bedroom closet. X-rays revealed it contained two sealed ammo cans, each containing an IED.

The X-ray images confirmed our assessment of the first IED's design: galvanized steel pipe bombs with multiple power sources and integrated circuitry, locked inside metal ammo cans. There was no way to know if they'd already been programmed with a time to detonate, and the subject wasn't talking. We could address the devices where they were, but even the best render safe procedure can result in detonation. We had to consider possible damage to the apartment complex and the number of residents we'd already evacuated. We also had to consider the team's level of fatigue; most of us hadn't slept much in the last 36 hours.

Given all the parameters, we decided to remotely move the bag into a specialized total containment vessel (TCV), a large, trailer-mounted sphere designed to contain and withstand a blast. We could then safely transport the IEDs to a remote range where we'd have more control and plenty of time. I followed the TCV to the range as other techs completed searching the apartment. They recovered two more firing circuits, schematics, a hand-drawn map of USAF officers' housing, a scoped assault rifle, ammunition, thousands of dollars in cash, and a new passport.

It was 10:00 p.m. when we arrived at the rural demolition range. The night was still, steamy, and pitch black as the moon hadn't risen yet. A collective decision was made to get some sleep and address the devices in the daylight. If the time bombs detonated in the interim, all the components would be captured within the TCV. Even though the facility was secure, with three concentric fences topped with razor wire and encrypted entry keypads, we posted an officer to watch the trailer from a safe distance overnight.

I arrived in the small town of Owasso at midnight, but every hotel was booked for a big rodeo. An old motel at the edge of town had one room left, so I got a few hours' sleep and was back on the range at sunrise.

We constructed protective barricades around the work area to contain any fragmentation, then remotely placed the gym bag in the center. This render safe solution was unique. A soft-sided bag containing a pair of latched steel ammo cans, each with a pipe bomb inside that could detonate at any second.

Following the old adage, "How do you eat an elephant? One bite at a time," we decided to turn the single big problem into three smaller problems. The first explosive tool, designed to tear the gym bag apart, successfully separated the two ammo cans. They came to rest in opposing corners of the protective works. One problem solved.

The force of the tool also tore away the metal latch from one of the ammo cans, allowing the robot to carefully expose the intact IED inside. It was identical to the first time bomb; multiple batteries and a unique firing circuit were duct-taped to the body of the pipe on opposing sides. In an effort to preserve as much forensic evidence as possible, we used a laser designator to target a specific part of the IED that would render it safe without destroying the custom electronics. The shot successfully disrupted the pipe bomb, completely removed the electric detonator, and preserved the circuitry. Problem two solved.

The second ammo can had been padlocked closed, so we changed tools and remotely removed the can's lid with a special projectile. With the IED now exposed, we applied the same render safe logic, which produced the same results: successful disruption and preservation of the firing circuitry.

The energetic material within each IED was an unusual HME, consistent with some of the chemicals recovered in the apartment. We used a portable mass spectrometer and old-fashioned flame tests to presumptively classify the powder. Samples were sent to the FBI lab for full analysis along with all the electronics, maps, notes, and chemicals recovered in the apartment.

The lab's engineers determined the firing systems were sophisticated, functional firing circuits that incorporated a series of time and anti-disturbance features. The schematics and notes recovered in the apartment confirmed that assessment. Chemists tested all the powder samples and reviewed the chemical recipes to identify the HME within the bombs. The lab's conclusion was that both devices were fully functional and identical to the bomb used at the recruiting station.

The subject was indicted on seven federal felonies, but defense attorneys claimed he was mentally incompetent to stand trial. That assertion prompted months of psychiatric evaluations which resulted in a bench trial, a trial with no jury. The defense didn't dispute what happened or who was responsible but, citing the psychiatrist's report, they successfully argued their client was not guilty by reason of insanity. The judge agreed and remanded the defendant to a mental facility for continued observation. About two years later he was released on the condition that he continue psychiatric treatment.

Twenty-Four

Fight Club

My 29th Bureau anniversary was just weeks away. I could've retired four years earlier, but still loved the job and was reminded just how much when a couple of JTTF Agents stopped by to talk. "Do you remember a guy named Ellis? You convicted him a few years ago for threatening to bomb the police station in Norman."

"Sure, I remember him. What's up?" I asked.

"Well, he was sentenced to 30 months on your case, then was supposed to be on supervised release. But when he violated probation, the judge issued an arrest warrant for him. He was a fugitive for a while but got arrested and went back to jail. He must have grown a conscience, because now he has a pretty wild story about some guy he met while on the lam."

They went on to say that while Ellis was a fugitive, he had become acquainted with a man named Jerry Drake Varnell. It seems Varnell was enamored with the movie *Fight Club* and wanted to reset everyone's debt clock by blowing up the Eccles Building in Washington, D.C., home of the Federal Reserve Board.

Every threat is taken seriously. But due to the number of threats received, the first step is a viability assessment to gauge the capabilities and resolve of the suspect. Ellis agreed to continue meeting with Varnell and gathered more information. Through a series of conversations, we learned Varnell wanted to build a McVeigh style VBIED. He was very specific about the type of bomb: 1,000 pounds of ANFO that could be detonated using a cell phone. He claimed to have experience with electronics, had experimented with explosives, and lived in a rural farming community with easy access to ammonium nitrate fertilizer and diesel fuel, the ingredients for ANFO like McVeigh had used. Through encrypted messages and face-to-face meetings with Ellis, his plan unfolded. Varnell wasn't just talking; he had the means and motivation to carry out the attack. There's always a concern that someone like this will proceed on their own. It was time to introduce an undercover agent to ensure we had a window into what was happening.

If you're the terrorist, making an IED with HME has some risks like a misfire or "low order" detonation. So as we prepped the background story for our UCA, I made a few suggestions. "Tell him you're an apprentice to a commercial blaster in West Virginia and that guy also hates the government. Say he's been stealing commercial explosives from quarry jobs but is too afraid to do anything and you think you can talk him into giving you what he's stolen?"

Varnell liked the idea of using foolproof commercial explosives, and the planning phase continued. Realizing it would be difficult to transport a half-ton IED 1,300 miles from Oklahoma City to Washington, D.C., a second target was discussed, the IRS building in Dallas. But that was still a three-hour drive, so a local target was selected. While under surveillance, Varnell and the UCA performed reconnaissance on one of the largest banks in Oklahoma, BancFirst.

BancFirst headquarters was in the heart of downtown Oklahoma City, about four blocks from where the Murrah Building stood. There was an alley behind the building with a loading ramp leading beneath the structure, an ideal place for the bomb. With the target selected it was time to build the device, which posed another issue. Unlike Hosam Smadi in 2009, Varnell wanted to build the bomb himself.

Smadi was a Jordanian citizen in the U.S. on an expired visa. His social media espoused loyalty to Osama bin Laden, and those online rants led him to an al-Qaeda sleeper cell in Texas. Over time his plan took shape: to use a VBIED to bring down Dallas's Fountain Place skyscraper as the next 9/11. Smadi was explicit in the type of bomb he wanted his cohorts to obtain and discussed the plan in detail. He didn't know his fellow terrorists were all Arabic-speaking UCAs. As soon as Smadi attempted to detonate the device, he was arrested in the culmination of a 10-month undercover operation (FBI 2010).

Varnell's desire to be "hands on" in constructing the IED posed unique challenges because of his professed knowledge of explosives and electronics. The first logistical hurdle was where to construct a 1,000-pound VBIED without getting caught. I gave another suggestion to the UCA. "Tell him the reason you're here from West Virginia is to visit your girlfriend whose grandmother just died. Say grandma had a storage unit out in El Reno somewhere and you can get the key to it. That way it's not tied to you or Varnell."

The FBI rented a storage unit in the small town of El Reno and filled it with garage sale furniture, old clothes, and high-tech CCTV. At the designated time, the UCA rolled up in a big Ford dually, complete with West Virginia plates. Beneath a tarp in the bed were twenty 50-pound bags of commercial ANFO, varying lengths of detonating cord, and a mixed bag of dynamite and explosive cast boosters. Finally, wrapped in a paper sack from a fish house in Wheeling, West Virginia, were two blasting caps.

"OK, here's all the stuff. My guy also made the firing system you wanted, with a cell phone. Here are instructions on how it works."

Varnell began pouring the ANFO prills into plastic trash cans, which were then placed in the back of a van. As he opened one bag he said, "I love the smell of diesel." ANFO does have that odor. Picking up a stick of dynamite he blurted, "This is the good stuff."

All the audio and video from the storage unit were being recorded and tended to show that Varnell knew what he was doing. The Special Agent in Charge, Assistant U.S. Attorney, police chief, and other stakeholders were with me in the Emergency Operations Center as we listened and watched Varnell build the bomb in real time via CCTV. I really hoped he wasn't going to go through with it, but as the WMD took shape, his intent became apparent. It was time for me to go to a CP I'd established at the Skirvin.

The Skirvin Hotel had been an Oklahoma City landmark since 1911 and was located across the street from BancFirst. The previous day I'd rented Room 1104, a corner room that covered every approach to BancFirst and the alley behind it. Electronics technicians established secure communications links and joined me in the CP with elements of the SWAT team and ERT.

I still hoped Varnell might change his mind, but soon our aerial surveillance called over the radio, "The van is on the move from El Reno."

The plane and vehicle-borne surveillance discreetly followed Varnell along I-40 for 32 miles until the van appeared below the Skirvin's windows. As it turned onto Broadway toward the bank, a random private security vehicle pulled to the side of the street and blocked the alley. Varnell kept driving; I-35 to Dallas was just blocks away and I worried he might change targets back to the IRS. We'd already coordinated with our Dallas office and Texas Department of Public Safety in case that happened.

But the plane called every turn as the van made the block for a second pass. By then, the security guard had left and the entrance to the alley was clear. At 12:39 a.m., Varnell pulled down the loading ramp. Thermal imagery and static cameras caught him calmly walking down the street to meet the UCA in his pickup truck. Varnell planned to dial in the firing code from a bus station several blocks away so he could see the blast.

The written instructions for arming and firing the device were intentionally complex and ended with a call to a West Virginia cell phone wired into the bomb; I know because I wrote the instructions. The complicated sequence afforded Varnell the opportunity to omit any single step if he really didn't want the bomb to detonate. He'd have to work to make it explode.

The AUSA called as Varnell pulled away in the pickup. "I don't think he was in the alley long enough to arm the thing … go check."

Surveillance assured me Varnell was en route to the bus station, so I walked across the street and down the ramp. It was a chilling sight: there was the white van, lights on and the windows blacked out. I tried to open the doors to check the firing system, but they were locked. Fortunately, I'd made a duplicate key once we knew which vehicle Varnell was going to use. I unlocked the passenger door and there, sitting on the front seat beneath a sweatshirt was the fully armed firing system. All he had to do now was dial the phone number.

I lost cell signal in the Skirvin's elevator on the way back up to the CP. But as the doors opened, my phone rang; it was the firing code. What Varnell didn't know was the West Virginia number in the firing instructions didn't dial the bomb. It rang to my cell phone and all the explosives in the van were chemically inert. I stuck my head into Room 1104 and gave a thumbs-up to the SWAT communications guy, who keyed his mic and gave the order: "Execute, execute, execute."

With that, a SWAT team that had been covertly waiting in and around the bus station took Varnell into custody. The operation had been a success, but we now had to prepare for trial.

Often claims of entrapment are made when undercover operations are revealed. So the UCA had given Varnell every opportunity to back out. Alone in the van, he could have abandoned the bomb or omitted any single step in the firing sequence, but he didn't. His intentions were clear.

The trial would eventually be held in the Oklahoma City federal courthouse across the street from the National Bombing Memorial.

With McVeigh's 5,000-pound IED as a reference, I envisioned a defense attorney making the argument that this was nothing like McVeigh's bomb; this was a mere 1,000 pounds of ANFO. To preemptively thwart that argument, I felt a demonstration was warranted.

The SABT in Kansas City was a good friend and enlisted the assistance of the 774th EOD unit at Fort Riley, Kansas. En route to the post, my partner and I stopped at Geary Lake, where McVeigh and Nichols had mixed their bomb in 1995; they'd been stationed at Fort Riley together.

Within three weeks of Varnell's arrest, a team of state, local, and Army bomb technicians met me at Demo Range 42 to recreate his VBIED. Using ERT photos from the back of the van, we replicated the device with the same booster configuration, number of trash cans, and ANFO weight Varnell had used. As we constructed the bomb, videographers from the FBI's Forensic Imaging Unit readied their remote equipment to record the blast at 6,000 frames per second.

With cameras rolling, we retreated to a safe area 1.5 miles away and remotely detonated the bomb. After the ensuing range fires were doused, we plotted what was left of the van on a map, but stopped searching 1,000 feet from the crater. The high-speed slow-motion video was amazing. It was so amazing that the judge ultimately decided it was too prejudicial and wouldn't allow the jury to see it. Various pretrial motions and hearings were scheduled, which postponed the trial for 18 months and afforded me time for the next TDY.

There were several units with a hand in the Bureau's counter–IED and counterterrorism missions: CIRG, CIEDU, OIO, ITOS, and TEDAC, not to mention State Department's ATA unit. One fall afternoon TEDAC called. "Hey, I know you're supposed to be back in Tunisia Friday, but could you meet some folks in Nairobi instead? Someone from OIO will make the arrangements."

Nairobi, the capital of Kenya, had seen its share of terrorism. In 1980, the Palestine Liberation Organization killed 15 people in a hotel attack. In 1998, al-Qaeda bombed the U.S. embassy, killing 213 people and injuring over 4,000. Al-Shabaab attacked the affluent Westgate Mall in 2013, resulting in a four-day siege that killed 67 and injured 150. In the months leading up to this assignment, there'd been a significant increase in bombings and armed ambushes with suspected links to ISIS.

Within an hour, Danielle from OIO called. "I have some flights for you, but they're a little tight. You'll only have an hour in Houston to get to the international terminal. Then it's nine hours to Frankfurt and another nine to Nairobi. Someone will meet you at the airport."

Of course things started off poorly. My flight from OKC was delayed by 30 minutes, which meant I'd miss every connection. I explained the situation, but the United rep had no encouraging news.

"Well, we can get you on the next flight to Houston, but then you'd have to go to Newark before flying to Frankfurt. With that connection, you'd be in Nairobi around midnight the next day. Or you can cross your fingers and hope the captain makes up some time in flight. Maybe your original itinerary will still work."

There were no good options, so I boarded the little commuter jet and crossed my fingers. Tailwinds were favorable and it looked as if I might make it to Houston's international gate on time. But when I arrived at Gate 12, the boarding area was empty. A blinking screen announced a gate change. I raced to the next gate and was pleased to see a crowd. But then the gate agent made an announcement.

"I'm sorry, this fight has been delayed. We're waiting on a different aircraft and it'll be about an hour."

The plane that finally arrived was a new double-decker Airbus A380–800. I eventually queued up with my group of fellow travelers relegated to rows 75 through 99 and settled in for the transatlantic flight. After 27 hours in transit, we touched down at Jomo Kenyatta International at 8:30 p.m. local time. Once through Customs, I walked out into the cool, humid air to see a man holding a sign with my name on it.

"Mr. Black, I'm Radhi. How was your trip?" His English was flawless. Most Kenyans speak three languages: one of 44 tribal languages, English, and Swahili. "I'll take your bag and we'll be off."

We drove for about an hour into Nairobi's suburbs. At the end of a dead-end road on a wooded hilltop, a security guard opened the outer gates to reveal a large house surrounded by high walls topped with barbed wire.

Radhi said, "There are several other Agents already here working on other matters. Your first meeting with the Legal Attaché is at 0700. Please let me know if you need anything."

I met my new roommates and went straight to bed. At the embassy the next morning, I was escorted to a large conference room to meet the Legal Attaché and RSO.

"Thanks for coming. As you may know, Kenya is a strong counterterrorism partner for the U.S. Their counterterrorism assets are divided among three branches of the National Police Service: the

Administration Police, a paramilitary group called the General Service Unit, and the Directorate of Criminal Investigations, which includes the Anti-Terrorism Police, the bomb squad, and cyber investigations. I'd like you to work with the bomb squad and take a look at the lab's forensics capabilities. There're about to be some upgrades and we want to have a hand in that. Here's a local cell phone and your keys."

Unlike Hello Kitty, this armored Land Cruiser was a right-hand drive and it took a minute to reacclimate to driving from the right seat in the left lane while negotiating roundabouts. The week was pretty routine until the Legal Attaché called Wednesday evening. "There's been a little change of plan. We need you in Mogadishu for a day or two. Wheels up around dawn."

Al-Shabaab's prolonged terror campaign was wreaking havoc in Mogadishu; 32 VBIEDs had detonated already that year and suicide bombings were becoming routine. TEDAC was interested in specific details of the devices encountered by the camp's team of international EOD techs. They'd have a wealth of information on current trends and TTPs, which would help our analysts connect the global dots and our scientists design effective countermeasures.

A chartered Bombardier Dash 8 left the runway in the dark. But once above the low, black cloud layer, a brilliant orange sunrise was revealed. Two hours later we landed at a heavily protected facility situated along the Somali coast. The Indian Ocean served as a natural barrier to the east; frothing white waves slammed into the jagged, rocky coastline which was prominently posted with shark warnings and guard towers. Rough sand roads wound through a maze of concrete barricades and Hesco barriers, all topped with miles of razor wire. MRAPs and other heavy vehicles dwarfed the armored SUV that shuttled me to the far end of the camp. As we entered each new security zone, my driver pointed out the nearest shelter in case of rocket or mortar attack.

Meetings with the international EOD teams were successful and I was back in the Nairobi safe house Friday night. Over dinner, one of the agents from New York asked if I had plans for the weekend.

"Weekend plans? Uh … no; haven't really thought that far ahead."

"Why don't you come with me and my partner? We've booked a two-day safari along the Tanzanian border."

He didn't have to ask twice. The twin-engine Otter had 18 folding seats and the forward emergency exits were literally accessed through the open cockpit. After a bumpy 90 minutes, we landed on a dirt airstrip at Kichwa Tembo. Gazelles scattered off the narrow runway as elephants and giraffes grazed on either side. A young man met us planeside.

"Good afternoon, I'm Carver. I'll be taking you to the camp. Here are some standard liability waivers. We're located deep in the bush; there are no fences to keep the wild animals out."

We arrived well after dark and were met by a tall Maasai tribesman dressed in the traditional red shuka. There were no lights, just lanterns and a couple of campfires.

"Dinner will be served at 9:00 p.m. Your safari departs for Maasai-Mara at 8:00 a.m."

Guards were assigned to escort us along dark footpaths leading to each of the 12 tents that comprised the camp. But armed only with sticks and flashlights, they offered little comfort.

After an early breakfast we climbed aboard a modified Land Rover and struck out; it was amazing. The annual migration was underway with vast herds of wildebeest, zebras, and gazelles stretching to the horizon. We watched as a cheetah pulled down an impala, and lion cubs tumbled and played in the tall grass. At one point, a *National Geographic* crew joined us to film a bloat of hippos at a watering hole.

After 10 hours in the bush, we'd seen four of the "Big Five," lions, rhinos, elephants, and buffalo, but we were missing the most elusive. As the sunlight waned, our guide stopped the Land Rover and whispered, "There ... in the tamboti tree; a leopard." That was number five.

We left camp at 6:00 a.m. Sunday and crossed into Tanzania's Serengeti; lions were much more active in the cool morning air. One lioness brought down a wildebeest before retreating into the bush when a big male moved in to finish the kill. The day ended at sunset when a single-engine Caravan landed on a short dirt strip to return us to Nairobi.

The following week went quickly with meetings at the Directorate of Criminal Investigations and the Anti-Terrorism Unit. The goal was to assess current training and forensic capabilities, then determine what could be done to bring the lab up to international standards. Over the next seven years, four billion Kenyan shillings ($30,000,000) was invested to provide the lab with the latest forensics technology.

After a final meeting with the Legal Attaché, we toured August 7 Memorial Park, a small green space in the center of Nairobi that marks the site of the American embassy that was bombed by al-Qaeda in 1998. The names of those killed are engraved on a wall alongside a sculpture created from salvaged pieces of the building. It brought back memories of Oklahoma City and 9/11. Survivors' stories recorded in the museum were so similar to those I knew too well, many expressing guilt that they'd survived or were unable to help others. A black granite obelisk stands on the grounds of the new embassy in memory of those who lost their lives there.

The journey home began at midnight with an eight-hour flight to Amsterdam, then nine hours to Atlanta and a two-hour hop to Oklahoma City. It might have made more sense to stay in Africa, as I was only home for two weeks before returning to Tunisia, but I didn't make the travel plans.

On Friday the 13th, I flew to Tunis via Huston and Munich. An expediter walked me through Customs and into a waiting armored SUV. The route was familiar, as I'd stay in the same safe house as last time. When the outer gates opened, Jamal was standing next to Hello Kitty in the driveway. He tossed me the keys and said, "Welcome back."

Sunday began with regional briefings from the RSO. After lunch at Sidi Bou, we were recalled to the embassy and told there'd been a pair of attacks in Mogadishu. A massive VBIED had detonated at the central K5 Junction, about a mile from where I'd been working just three weeks before. A second blast devastated the Medina district about two hours later; hundreds were wounded and more than 500 killed in the deadliest attacks in Somalia's history. Within three months, an al-Shabaab leader responsible for the carnage was convicted and sentenced to death by firing squad.

The remaining time in Tunis was spent building on intelligence and training successes established in the first TDY. The goal this time was to codify a mutually beneficial system of sharing physical evidence and technical IED information gleaned from devices encountered throughout North Africa. TEDAC could assist in identifying terrorists operating in the region while broadening its global database of IED characteristics. With tentative agreements in place, the week ended with briefings for the ambassador and generals overseeing the National Guard and National Police special counterterrorism units. I departed Tunis that night. This time a series of flight cancellations gave me an unexpected long weekend in Paris. I got to stay home for 11 days before departing for Eurasia's Western Steppe.

Twenty-Five

Wolves and Smugglers

By the second century BC, present-day Uzbekistan was the heart of the Great Silk Road connecting China to the Middle East and Rome. The region was eventually conquered by Arabs, Persians, Mongols, Russians, and the Soviet Union. Uzbeks gained independence from the USSR in 1991, but remained under control of the authoritarian Uzbek Communist Party. With high levels of corruption and its proximity to Afghanistan, Pakistan, Iran, and Syria, Uzbekistan was fertile ground for international criminals and terror organizations.

In the 1990s, the Islamic Movement of Uzbekistan (IMU) formed to overthrow the government and establish a radical caliphate. A few years later, the Islamic Jihad Union broke away from the IMU and began its own terror campaign. Both groups were based in Pakistan's Federally Administered Tribal Areas and conducted transnational terrorist operations throughout the region. ISIS later became a threat as terrorism spilled over from Afghanistan and Uzbek fighters returned from jihad in Iraq and Syria.

I landed in Tashkent at 9:00 p.m. after 25 hours in transit. An expediter ushered me through Customs, then to a hotel in the city center. The nation's government was changing and efforts were in place to ferret out corruption and effectively combat terrorism. In 2016, President Shavkat Mirziyoyev succeeded the former repressive president and attempted to rehabilitate Uzbekistan's dark history. Just one month before my arrival, he created a new state security service known as O'zbekiston Respublikasi Davlat Xavfsizlik Xizmati (DXX) to replace the National Security Service, a clone of Stalin's feared NKVD. Under the new structure, DXX, the National Guard, and the Ministry of Interior would build and maintain dedicated counterterrorism units. We were there to help.

After a few hours' sleep, the team convened at a secure facility near the embassy and began building the week's IED circuitry. Though it was Saturday, we had a meeting scheduled with DXX and the National Guard early that afternoon. We quickly completed the TPUs and asked Abdullah, the driver, where we could get something to eat before the DXX conference.

"Of course, we will go to Plov Center."

Located outdoors, beneath Tashkent's iconic 355-meter TV tower, cooks toiled over enormous propane-fired kazans, basically 10-foot-diameter woks. With paddles they stirred rice, chickpeas, quail eggs, beef, lamb, and horse into the national dish called plov. After a generous serving of plov and black tea, Abdullah ushered us to the van.

"Come, we should leave for DXX. It is a long way and commanders will be waiting."

We were met by the post's commander, who gave us a tour of the remote facility and the demo ranges. A captain then took us to the explosives magazines and provided cases of Russian TNT to be used in our IEDs.

There was no schedule for Sunday, so we set out early to see the city. The somber Museum of Victims of Political Repression was built on the banks of the Bozsu Canal where academics, poets, and writers were executed by Stalin during the Great Terror; mass graves were discovered during its 2001 construction. One of the more chilling exhibits inside was the Black Raven, a black sedan used by the NKVD to "disappear" political dissenters.

Class convened Monday morning with students from DXX, National Guard counterterrorism units, and military EOD. We quickly moved to the range and detonated a series of progressively larger IEDs, each preceded by the wail of a Soviet era air raid siren.

Lunch was served each day on the range beneath a field tent. One afternoon we were gathered around a cauldron of steaming plov and nibbling on sheep tail fat when a soldier mentioned his social media was blowing up. Nearby villagers were speculating with wild theories about the sirens and large explosions emanating from the compound.

An important part of these assignments is developing rapport with commanders and operators of the host country's counterterrorism units. So naturally we accepted when DXX commanders invited us to dinner. Abdullah followed the staff car through small villages and into the jagged, snowcapped Piskom Mountains along the Kyrgyzstan border. As chilled bottles of Royal Elite vodka arrived, linguists translated

Uzbek military officers and field cooks preparing plov on a bomb range outside Tashkent (2018).

a series of heartfelt toasts. Over platters of horse, tongue, and pickled herring, the older officers recounted stories of their time under Soviet rule.

The two-week class was successful and my return journey began with a 5:30 a.m. flight to Istanbul. I was suffering with an intestinal issue blamed on some tainted horse, so the morning didn't start well. It could have gotten much worse when a Turkish screener stopped my carry-on in the fluoroscope and said, "We have problem."

I glanced at the X-ray screen and saw one of my EOD multi-tools, which I'm sure was covered in explosives residue. It's like a giant Swiss Army knife with multiple folding blades, wire strippers, fuse-wire cutters, a C4 punch, and blasting cap crimper; how it passed security in Tashkent was a mystery. I was pretty sick when I packed the night before and must have inadvertently thrown the tool in my backpack instead of the checked bag.

Still choking down the horse, I mustered a smile.

"No problem. Can you just keep that and we're all good?"

She looked at me with disdain, tossed the tool in a bin, and pointed to the departure gate. The plane to Frankfurt hadn't left, so I fell into my seat and tried to sleep until arriving in D.C.; it was not a pleasant flight.

Within 10 days I was back in the deserts of Purgatory for another VBIED post-blast school. This was the 143rd iteration and would probably be my last. Retirement was beginning to sound good, but a week of blowing things up in the desert was reinvigorating.

The next TDY sent me back to the former Soviet Union. In 2013, unrest had erupted in Ukraine's capital of Kyiv. Known as the Maidan Revolution, protesters demanded President Viktor Yanukovych and Prime Minister Azarov move away from Russia's influence and closer to the European Union. Yanukovych was eventually overthrown, but a counterrevolution of pro–Russian separatists grew in Ukraine's eastern Donbas region along the Russian border. In what some called a "hybrid war," pro–Russian forces backed by specialized Russian military units began fighting Ukraine's military. In March 2014, the Russian Federation annexed Ukraine's Crimean Peninsula.

Years of fighting and worldwide condemnation followed. Since Russia's annexation, the U.S. had provided Ukraine over $1 billion in aid; another $200 million in "security assistance" was released days after President Trump's 2018 Helsinki summit with Putin. Six weeks after the summit, I was on a plane to Kyiv. There was no expediter, so I found the officially regulated taxi kiosk and waited patiently for the next car. Without looking up, the uniformed attendant barked, "Out door, first car, silver Skoda."

A note from the Legal Attaché was waiting at the hotel. It read, "Walk down the hill toward Independence Square, you'll see an Irish pub on the right. Meet me for dinner at seven."

Over goulash and schnitzel, we made plans for the next few weeks. "You're going to be pretty busy. The first week you'll be at a SBU camp near here, then out to Khmelnytskyi to work with the Ukrainian special forces. Tomorrow may be your only day off. There's a group from the embassy going out to Chornobyl [Ukrainian spelling] if you'd like to join us."

I met eight other Americans outside the embassy about sunrise. Soon a van from an extreme tourism company arrived for a three-hour trip to Chornobyl's Exclusion Zone. Checkpoint Dytiatky was the final stop before entering the 1,000-square-mile restricted area. Armed guards checked our entry permits and lifted a security gate that led to an eerie, postapocalyptic world.

The town of Pripyat was built as a socialist utopia for the nuclear power plant's employees. But it was evacuated so hastily after the nuclear disaster, everything was left in place. Books were still open on school desks, dolls and toys lay on rusty bed frames, and the bumper cars and Ferris wheel of Pripyat's amusement park sat eerily silent. The area is still radioactive. Our Geiger counters beeped and chirped as we walked through dilapidated buildings and homes.

The first "sarcophagus" designed to contain radiation leaking from the damaged reactor was already failing, so a new one was being constructed. For lunch, we joined construction workers at Canteen 19 for bread and borscht; it was the first time I had to pass through a radiation portal monitor for a meal.

Our visit to the Exclusion Zone was quickly coming to an end, as too much time in a radioactive area isn't good for your health. As we left the reactor site, our driver warned, "We will enter Red Forest. Radiation detectors will alarm, but I will speed through to limit time."

The Red Forest is a two-square-mile woodland adjacent to the reactor. When the reactor exploded, the forest received tons of radioactive contamination that killed much of the vegetation instantly, leaving it a rusty red color. It remains one of the most contaminated places on earth, so to limit our time in the high radiation zone, the van raced down the abandoned road toward Checkpoint Leliv, the first of three security stations where the van and each passenger were screened for radiation before being allowed to pass. Out of curiosity, I checked the cumulative figure on my dosimeter. It registered 0.003 millisieverts; a chest X-ray is about 0.2 millisieverts.

Jetlag and the 14-hour Chornobyl adventure allowed me to sleep soundly until class began Monday morning. At exactly 8:00 a.m., a gray van arrived at the hotel and a young lady emerged.

"I am Alexandra from SBU. I will accompany you to training center."

The other instructor joined me and two translators for an hour's drive across the Dnieper River. The van eventually slowed and turned down an unmarked road that wound through a thick pine forest and terminated at a checkpoint. Armed guards matched our passports to their clipboards, then raised the gate and waved us through.

SBU (Sluzhba Bezpeky Ukrayiny) is Ukraine's state security service responsible for "special law enforcement functions." Alpha Group, SBU's top tier counterterrorism unit, would be our students for the week. Automatic weapons fire rang through the trees as we lectured in the classrooms. The secluded facility was completely self-contained with lunch served in the officers' mess. It was standard Ukrainian fare of cabbage, borscht, chicken, and salo, thick slices of cured fatback. Each evening we returned to Kyiv.

I hadn't seen the demo range, which is often the source of significant logistical issues; it needed to be prepped by Wednesday and I was getting a little anxious. But Alexandra assured me a suitable location had been secured, saying, "We will meet at hotel at 0500 and go to site 140 kilometers from here. It will be fine."

In the early morning hours, we cleared a checkpoint that looked a lot like Checkpoint Dytiatky. Guards escorted us to an abandoned, heavily wooded village with crumbling buildings that were being reclaimed by the forest. I left the van to talk with a camouflaged SBU operator who was standing there alone. He had a Beretta, an AK-47, and a dosimeter; I had none.

"Good morning, we're here for the explosives training. Is this the combat village?"

"Yes, is village."

"I see you're pretty well armed; is that for wildlife?"

"In winter we have wolves, but now just smugglers. From Belarus, a few kilometers away. They use roads and buildings here to avoid checkpoints. We must take precaution."

"I see. So the dosimeter … are we in the Exclusion Zone?"

"No. Exclusion Zone ends at other side of street."

The initial plan was to detonate IEDs inside these buildings, but interior blasts shake loose a lot of material in uncontaminated areas. I wasn't about to detonate anything inside structures that still had radioactive alpha and beta particles lying around.

I told the team, "OK, change of plan. We'll use the roads and trails for today's exercises; no interior blasts."

Four explosions echoed through the ghost town as Alpha Group arrived. Team leaders immediately set up a secure perimeter and used linguists to interview instructors serving as witnesses. Each team then processed their post-blast scene and prepared a report to present to the commanders on Friday.

That evening we joined our hosts for a farewell dinner at a Georgian restaurant near the golden domes of St. Sofia. After appetizers of bone marrow and spicy pig snouts, a choice of special entrées was offered: veal cheeks, lamb tongues, or stroganoff. The stroganoff sounded most appealing, but I wanted a little clarification. "Is it beef stroganoff?" I asked.

The waiter replied, "No, no. It is the horse stroganoff." Still reeling from the horse in Tashkent, I ordered pâté and rabbit dolma from the standard menu.

The next available train to the special forces camp in Khmelnytskyi wouldn't depart until Sunday, so on Saturday morning, I toured the Pechersk Lavra Cave Monastery, a UNESCO World Heritage site. The caves were inhabited in the early 11th century by monks pursuing a life of solitude. For 200 hryvnias (about seven U.S. dollars), a guide gave me a candle and led me into the labyrinth 50 feet underground.

The low, narrow tunnels were lit only by flickering sconces and the candles of pilgrims there to view the relics of 73 monks interred in niches along the walls. The first monk was laid to rest in 1073, and cave burials continued for 700 years. The naturally mummified bodies were covered in elaborate tapestries and visible through glass-topped coffins. In the dim candlelight, some of the desiccated remains could be seen protruding from the fabric.

That afternoon we went to the enormous EpiCenter Mall to purchase components needed for next week's class. We bought pressure cookers, galvanized pipes and end caps, cell phones, micro switches, transistors, wiring, batteries … and no one batted an eye. We built the devices, except for the explosives, at the hotel and loaded them into Pelican cases for the four-hour train ride to Khmelnytskyi.

Upon arrival, a cab took us to the designated hotel which was more like an aging Alpine village, single-room cottages nestled in woodlands around a central swan pond. It was rather modest; the light in my tepid mini-fridge was brighter than the single bare bulb hanging from the ceiling. Our schedule indicated we were to meet some U.S. Green Berets in the restaurant at 8:00 p.m. They'd been working with Ukraine's new Special Operations Forces (SOF) and would turn that group over to us for additional training. After gaining independence in 1991, Ukraine moved away from the Soviet–style Spetsnaz and formed SOF in 2018 as an independent military branch specializing in irregular warfare.

Since Russia's invasion of Crimea, the conflict with pro–Russian separatists in Donetsk and Luhansk had been called an Anti-Terrorist Operation (ATO). However, the battlespace changed when the Russian military openly engaged Ukrainian forces. To signal a shift from a counterterrorism operation to an actual military campaign, the ATO became known as a Joint Forces Operation (JFO).

I've had the honor to work with America's elite warriors on several occasions, and the men we met that evening were straight out of central casting. Over dinner they briefed us on the local political situation and combat in the eastern regions and detailed the training they'd provided so far. As the evening concluded, one of the sergeants offered to take us to the SOF site the next morning.

After brief introductions, it was obvious the SOF soldiers didn't need any rudimentary training. We spent a few hours in the classroom, then boarded buses for a trip to a remote wooded training area. Once on site, we loaded the devices, post-blast kits, and a sufficient quantity of Soviet TNT onto M-RZRs which easily handled the rough terrain. Working with the Green Berets, we designed three JOF-based scenarios that included command-detonated roadside bombs and drones. The SOF major spoke some English, so as the day progressed I asked, "Is this training what you wanted?"

He smiled and nodded. "Yes, we are terrorists. Training is good."

I looked at the translator curiously. "I'm not sure he understood the question. Will you ask him again?"

After an exchange in their native language the translator laughed and explained, "Yes, this is good. He said they operate behind Russian lines and are seen as terrorists there, by the Russians. You're teaching them what clues are left behind; things they should avoid in order not to be caught themselves."

The week in Khmelnytskyi ended Friday evening with farewell toasts of homemade chacha followed by dinner of pork shashlik and varenyky. I was sad to later learn many of these soldiers didn't survive the war that followed; both training bases had been targeted by Russian missiles.

The final week back in Kyiv was spent in conferences at the embassy and providing IED and X-ray interpretation training for the local security force and Marine Security Guard. By 4:00 a.m. Saturday, I was en route home. The long flights provided ample time to think.

A full career for most FBI Agents is 20 years; I was approaching 30 and had been considering retirement for some time. As if reading my mind, an email from FBI HQ's Special Projects Unit was waiting in my inbox. It read, "Would you be interested in coming back to headquarters and recording an interview about your career for the FBI Experience?"

The FBI had been promoting its work through public tours of FBI HQ since 1937. Originally in the Department of Justice building, headquarters had moved into the J. Edgar Hoover Building in 1975, and the tours hadn't changed much since then. In the aftermath of 9/11, public tours were suspended for 16 years, which provided an opportunity to modernize the Bureau's public face. Working with the Smithsonian

Institution, the FBI Experience was designed with interactive multimedia exhibits, recorded interviews of Agents discussing major cases, and artifacts and evidence spanning the Bureau's history. Curators were still preparing the galleries when I was interviewed about my experiences at Waco, Oklahoma City, and 9/11. After the interviews, my family and I were given a personalized tour of headquarters and the Academy at Quantico. Things had changed a great deal since 1988.

Twenty-Six

Wrapping Up

About 3:00 p.m. one Wednesday afternoon, the watch commander from Lawton PD called with a chilling statement.

"I think we may have an HME lab just off post."

The city of Lawton supports Fort Sill, home of the U.S. Army Field Artillery School and one of only four posts in the country that provides Army Basic Combat Training. Military bases remained attractive terrorist targets, so a bomb factory that close to the installation was concerning.

"Can you tell me what happened?"

"Yeah, we got a 911 call early this morning from a frantic woman saying she was being held at gunpoint, then the line went dead. The call traced to an apartment, so we sent an officer over. No one was there when he arrived, but he saw beakers, chemicals, jars of powders and liquids, even a centrifuge. We thought it was a meth lab so we called in a DEA team. They suited up in Level A and started inventorying everything, but backed out when they found explosives and guns. We're holding the scene now."

"All right, lieutenant. I'll have OHP's bomb squad meet me there. JTTF will look into the tenant's background and draft a search warrant affidavit."

When I arrived with OHP, the clandestine lab team provided photos from their search and confirmed the air in the apartment was safe to breathe without our SCBA, the self-contained breathing apparatus used by firefighters. I gained entry with two OHP bomb techs and what we saw was disturbing. The apartment had been converted to a laboratory and rigged with surveillance cameras inside and out. The kitchen and living area were stacked with unlabeled powders and liquids, beakers, pipettes, electrical components, fuels, oxidizers, commercial explosives, and firearms. However, the bedroom was like something from *Silence of the Lambs*; there were mirrors on the ceiling, handcuffs, masks, cattle prods, a disco ball, a stripper pole, and high-tech recording equipment.

It was nightfall by the time we completed our initial assessment. The volume of unknown substances was too extensive for the sampling equipment on our bomb response trucks. We needed a full mobile laboratory, and of course we have a plan in place for that. The National Guard maintains highly specialized units called Civil Support Teams (CST). I'd worked with the local commander and was fully aware of their robust capabilities, so I gave him a call. As I briefed the colonel, Troopers called up their chain of command because, as a state asset, CST must be deployed by the governor. Trusting our close working relationship, Colonel Flurry already had his CST rolling by the time the official call came from the governor's office.

CST arrived about midnight with its full complement of equipment: a state-of-the-art mobile lab manned by PhDs in chemistry and biology, sophisticated sampling technology, air monitoring equipment, mass decontamination capability, and secure satellite communications. As we'd practiced in training, Flurry's soldiers immediately set up decon and began testing all the unknown materials.

The first liquid was identified as sulfuric acid, the second was nitromethane; both can be used to make explosives. But things got more interesting about 1:10 a.m. when the first sergeant approached. "Sir, Colonel Flurry would like to see you."

He escorted me to the command trailer where Flurry and his Science Officer, Lt. Thompson, were huddled around a monitor. Flurry nodded at the lieutenant. "Tell him."

"Sir, we tested the unknown substance in that pressurized beaker. FTIR came back as CX."

That wasn't good. Fourier-transform infrared spectroscopy (FTIR) is an analytical technique that uses infrared light to scan a sample and observe its unique chemical properties. The lieutenant's FTIR results showed the presence of phosgene oxime (CX), a chemical warfare agent. Impure CX is a yellowish-brown liquid, like the one in the beaker. It can also be found in a solid crystalline form, like many of the substances in the unlabeled jars. FTIR is an excellent technology, but it can't provide exact molecular structure. The gold standard in an instance like this is gas chromatography–mass spectrometry (GC–MS).

"What's your degree of confidence in the FTIR results?" I asked.

"Fifty percent. We discussed the FTIR limitations before notifying you. I've already begun GC–MS, but that'll take a while. What's troubling is some of the other chemicals we tested are precursors for CX production."

As the FBI's WMD Coordinator, I was familiar with the national protocol for situations like this, but never thought I'd need to initiate it. The first step is a secure conference call enabling scientists from all relevant agencies to provide an expert assessment. Lt. Thompson, a PhD in chemistry, was intimately familiar with FTIR and GC–MS, so I asked him to relay his findings firsthand. At 1:19 a.m., I established a secure link for the conference call with the FBI's Lab, WMD Operations Unit, Counterterrorism Division, and chemical weapons experts from the whole of government.

We discussed the FTIR results, the presence of CX precursors, explosives, and other dual-use chemicals. I added, "JTTF identified the suspect and are searching for him now. He's a convicted felon with a criminal history of weapons and IED–related charges. A review of his social media profile found a recent post that read, 'I'm just one lab accident away from being a super villain.'"

The lead scientist sighed. "Given the circumstances, I think we need to send a team out."

With that, 11 scientists boarded a Bureau G6 in Virginia and a Hazardous Evidence Response Team was dispatched from Dallas. The Bureau's footprint grew as assets arrived throughout the morning and continued the search. We recovered commercial pyrotechnics, explosives, numerous weapons, over 1,400 rounds of ammunition, and illegal narcotics.

Samples of all the unknown chemicals were flown back to the FBI Lab, where exhaustive analysis concluded there was no CX; the FTIR had provided a false positive. Many presumptive tests are designed to err on the side of caution. It's better to plan for the worst-case scenario as opposed to misidentifying a WMD.

The 911 caller was later identified as a woman personally involved with the subject. She cooperated fully and believed the lab was an attempt to create hallucinogens, not HME. The Lab's chemical analysis supported that theory. The subject was eventually located, arrested, and indicted for illegal possession of firearms and explosives. In a plea agreement, he was sentenced to eight years in federal prison.

Meanwhile, eighteen months had passed since Varnell tried to destroy BancFirst with a VBIED. His defense team initially claimed he was mentally incompetent to stand trial, but after extensive examinations medical experts determined he was competent. Trial was set for February 2019.

The original informant testified and set the stage for the plot. His testimony was followed by the UCA who was on the stand for two days. I was the third witness called to provide expert testimony on the construction of the IED and its destructive potential.

Although the judge ruled the high-speed slow-motion video from the Fort Riley recreation was too prejudicial, he allowed the jury to see still images clipped from it. I explained the effects of the huge fireball and the shockwave that appeared as a wavy bubble emanating from the blast at supersonic speeds, then explained the exponential power created when that pressure is contained and reflected within the confines of a concrete alley and subterranean loading dock.

As expected, the defense's only argument was to say Varnell had been entrapped. To refute that assertion, the jury saw encrypted texts and emails where Varnell laid out his plot and motives long before the government was ever involved. Those written messages were augmented by recorded conversations and overt physical acts which made Varnell's intent clear. After a nine-day trial, the jury deliberated for four hours before returning a guilty verdict on both counts: attempting to use a WMD and attempting to destroy property used in interstate commerce. The conviction was front-page news in Oklahoma City, a city that had suffered enough from domestic terrorism. All that remained was the sentencing phase, but they'd have to call me out of retirement for that.

I was 24 years old when I joined the FBI in 1988. At that time, the mandatory retirement age for federal law enforcement was 55. It was later extended to age 57, which I would celebrate on my next birthday. I was offered a special exemption to work beyond 57, but my mind was made up. I'd participated in some of the nation's most historic events, arrested my share of criminals, traveled the world, survived cancer, and done things I'd seen in movies as a kid. Practically speaking, the accountant in me couldn't ignore a surprising estimate provided by the Payroll and Benefits Section. Given my age, time in service, and all the payroll withholdings that would stop in retirement, my take-home pay would actually *increase* when I retired. I was losing money by coming to work, so I decided to retire at the end of the year. But that was several months away, and there was still work to do.

The situation in the Middle East continued to deteriorate. Iran had become particularly belligerent with their support of the Houthis in Yemen, and other terrorist networks throughout the region were emboldened. In the summer of 2019, six oil tankers were attacked off the coast of the UAE. That September, drones attacked a refinery in Riyadh, setting it ablaze and fueling international panic over Iran's growing regional influence. Within a week of the Saudi attack, I was en route to the Emirates to teach a post-blast evidence collection course. Being able to forensically tie post-blast evidence to its country of origin can strongly affect international condemnation.

My departure from Heathrow was delayed by five hours due to a labor strike; the 777 finally landed in Dubai at 3:30 a.m. Saturday. After meeting the other instructors at the airport, we dialed in the GPS for a route to a secure base in the Arabian Desert where we unloaded the gear, prepped the classroom, and built the week's IEDs.

Training began at 7:00 a.m. Sunday with lectures for specialized police and military units and scientists from the government's forensics laboratories. We quickly transferred to the range in a vain attempt to avoid the 111°F heat. Before the students arrived, we set up practical problems and detonated a series of IEDs. One scenario involved a drone attack on a VIP convoy; that device destroyed an armored limousine. Another problem dealt with an IED located in the bowels of a disused refinery. Each team had to assess the situation, locate and properly record and collect evidence, then prepare a comprehensive report for their commanders.

Our hosts were gracious with their time and made a point to meet us each evening for dinner and polite conversation. We visited the top of Burj Khalifa, the world's tallest building, and saw an amazing performance of La Perle in Al Habtoor City, a stunning Cirque du Soleil–style spectacle with acrobats, lasers, motocross, and waterfalls cascading from the ceiling.

As the second week ended, a graduation ceremony was held at Dubai's state-of-the-art forensics lab with the Directorate's major general officiating. The general kindly mentioned that this was my last FBI deployment, which generated some humbling applause and a post-retirement job offer which I politely declined.

Since this was my final assignment, I decided to spend the weekend at Palm Jumeirah, one of three artificial archipelagos constructed in the Persian Gulf. A friend at the consulate made the reservations with one condition: "You have to go to the Empty Quarter while you're here. I'll arrange a guide with Arabian Nights."

The Empty Quarter, or Rub' al-Khali, is the largest area of continuous sand in the world, spanning 250,000 square miles of the Arabian Desert. Ramzan, my driver, transported me through an endless rolling sea of red sand. There were no roads, so he lowered the tire pressure for traction and said, "Now we go dune bashing!"

It was like driving on ice; fishtailing and sliding up and over the massive dunes, sand flying in every direction. We finally came to rest beneath a particularly large dune and Ramzan motioned to the top. "Climb up for sunset."

It was still about 100°F, and the hot wind carved mesmerizing designs into the sand. Its fine, powdery consistency made it virtually impossible to scale the slope. But once on top, the astonishing magnitude of the desert was revealed. Once the sun slowly sank as a huge orange ball, Ramzan called from the Land Cruiser: "Come, we will go to camp for dinner."

Large tents soon appeared among the dunes, their sand floors covered with Persian carpets and large pillows. As I sat down, Ramzan clapped his hands and traditional musicians began playing, belly dancers performed, and servers delivered platters of shawarma, kibbeh, and hummus. I felt like a Nabataean king. By midnight I was back at Palm Jumeirah with just a few hours to pack before departing. The trip to Oklahoma took 30 hours and as soon as the plane touched down, I received a text from the airline that read, "Congratulations and thank you for flying over one million miles with us."

I retired on December 31, 2019. It was a little daunting to leave a job I still loved and had been doing for most of my adult life, especially since they would have let me stay even longer. But 31 years was enough. It was time for a new chapter. Friends planned a fantastic dinner celebration at the Oklahoma City Petroleum Club, which ironically overlooked BancFirst and the Murrah Bombing Memorial.

It was humbling for me and my family to be joined by FBI personnel from across Oklahoma and FBI HQ; state, local, federal, and military partners; and even high school and college buddies. Friends and colleagues presented the coveted bronze G-man statue, a replica Tommy gun, and mementos from various headquarters units and police departments.

One good friend and mentor who made his mark by solving the three-million-dollar extortion and bombing of Harvey's Casino in 1980 presented a highly unique gift. True to his cowboy roots, Bill had retired years before to a sprawling ranch in the Sierra Nevada

My final visit to Quantico following a counterterrorism presentation at FBIHQ (2019).

mountains with horses and a blacksmith's shop. For my retirement, he hand-wrought an "FBI" branding iron and mounted it with a copy of the cowboy poem "Ride for the Brand." Extolling the virtues of honor, loyalty, and dedication, Bill's note that I "rode for the brand" was a high tribute coming from someone I respected so much. The evening was a wonderful ending to an exciting career.

As the sun rose on New Year's Day, I was officially retired. The credentials and badge I'd carried since the age of 24 were now mounted on a plaque. It was strange to have no demands on my time; I could finally turn off my cell phone.

Even though I was retired, there were some loose ends to tie up. I was served with a subpoena to testify as an expert at the sentencing hearing for Jerry Varnell, the man who tried to destroy BancFirst. The hearing would be held in the federal courthouse across the street from the Murrah Building, one month before the 25th anniversary of McVeigh's attack, which Varnell had wanted to imitate. My testimony, coupled with statistics and data from academic studies and actual bombings, gave the judge a sense of the horrific destructive potential Varnell's device possessed. When the hearing concluded, the 26-year-old was sentenced to 25 years in prison and a lifetime of supervised release (NBCNews.com 2020).

A group of highly respected FBI scientists and specialists had gathered after their retirements at the University of Central Oklahoma's

Forensic Science Institute. Recognized as the nation's leading school of its kind, I was honored to be invited to join their ranks and educate the next generation of FBI Agents, police officers, and forensic scientists. In addition to teaching, I was occasionally asked for comment by various networks and newspapers, participated in several documentaries and podcasts, and accepted a few speaking engagements. I was always happy to get calls from the Bureau to discuss "purely hypothetical" questions related to bombing cases or just tell war stories over a beer.

In September 2023, the FBI held a 9/11 Honor Ceremony in New York City. I was privileged to be among other FBI first responders and their families to remember those lost that dreadful day, and those who have died from medical issues related to deployments at the World Trade Center, Shanksville, and the Pentagon. After the ceremony with Director Wray, my wife and I were given a tour of the solemn 9/11 Memorial, which brought back memories of my time at Ground Zero and all the other tragedies.

The following year an unexpected call came from a congressional aide with the U.S. House Subcommittee on Oversight. "We'd like you to testify as an expert on how bombing investigations are conducted. Specifically, the January 6 investigation exploring the bombs found outside the RNC and DNC."

On January 6, 2021, throngs of people massed at the U.S. Capitol as a joint session of Congress convened to certify the results of the presidential election. What was lost in all the coverage was an incident that occurred the night before. Between 7:30 and 8:30 p.m., someone placed two pipe bombs in the Capitol Hill neighborhood of Washington, D.C. One was left in an alley behind the Republican National Committee headquarters and the other by the Democratic National Committee headquarters.

The devices weren't discovered until about 1:00 p.m. on January 6, just as the Capitol was being overrun two blocks away. Vice President-elect Kamala Harris was evacuated from the DNC within minutes of the discovery. In the chaos of that moment, Capitol Police arrived and addressed the devices. Neither bomb detonated and, once rendered safe, the components were hand-delivered to the FBI lab for forensic analysis. A massive investigation was launched; thousands of man-hours were spent following hundreds of tips, conducting 900 interviews, and performing exhaustive forensic examinations. Over time, a $100,000 reward grew to $500,000, but the culprit couldn't be identified.

I told the aide, "I was retired by then and had nothing to do with that investigation."

"We know, that's why we want you. You're not a government employee anymore and have a wealth of experience in major events. We've seen your analysis of other cases on various networks and believe you could answer some questions for the Committee. Some members feel the FBI isn't doing enough, that after three years, the bomber should've been caught. But in interviews about the Nashville Christmas bombing, you said these things take time; that's what people need to understand. The FBI Director and other high-level officials have already testified, but some still think the Bureau is dragging its feet."

"Well, if you think it would be helpful, I'll be glad to. When is the hearing?"

"That's the thing: it's next Tuesday."

I arrived on Capitol Hill and was ushered into the hearing room. The chairman spelled out concerns of some who felt the FBI's inability to identify the bomber was indicative of complacency or even a cover-up. After being sworn in, I reminded the committee that cases like this aren't always solved as seen on TV. The "CSI effect" has people believing every crime can be solved in 60 minutes using facial recognition, DNA, and fingerprints. In the real world, trace evidence simply may not be recoverable.

Video images captured the bomber on foot wearing a hoodie, facemask, glasses, and gloves, completely covered from head to toe. It was impossible to even determine the bomber's race or gender. Additionally, the IEDs themselves offered few clues. They were constructed from very common household materials which are nearly impossible to trace, and the explosive filler material was homemade.

I went on to say investigators need something, a single bit of information or thread to pull. The right piece of physical evidence or one solid tip can bring a case into focus. I reminded the Committee it took three years to link Eric Rudolph to the Olympic bombing, and it was an eyewitness tip that had finally led to him, not forensic evidence. Another example was the Unabomber. Even after exhaustive forensic examination of multiple devices, it took 17 years to identify Ted Kaczynski. In that investigation, again, it took a tip, not forensic evidence to crack the case.

If the perpetrator was a true lone wolf and this was their first and only crime, it will be difficult to make an identification. But most people can't resist the temptation to talk. A $500,000 reward is ample incentive for someone to come forward if and when the bomber slips up. The men and women of the FBI, and America's law enforcement professionals, have very long memories. Cases may go cold, but they're not forgotten. New leads, advanced forensic procedures, and investigative techniques may eventually lead to an arrest (Congress.gov 2024). When Kash Patel became FBI Director, he placed an emphasis on solving this case, and I believe the culprit will eventually be identified.

It's been a long time since black-and-white episodes of *The FBI* and Efrem Zimbalist, Jr., captured my imagination. I appreciate my parents, teachers, and a Little League baseball coach for encouraging me to pursue my dream of joining the Bureau, despite the long odds. As with most endeavors, perseverance and hard work paid off. Of course my career wouldn't have been possible without the support and understanding of my family. The long hours and time away were hard, but they always urged me on.

It was an honor to serve the country for more than 31 years, doing things and going places I couldn't have dreamed of as a child. But most remarkable were the amazing people I met: stoic victims of heinous crimes, courageous witnesses, bomb technicians, K9 handlers, police officers, firefighters, spec ops soldiers, pilots and divers, nuclear weapons designers, and scientists. Their integrity, selflessness, and servant's hearts are hallmarks that make America great.

Further Reading

Australian Federal Police. 2024. "2002 Bali Bombings." Australian Federal Police, June 6. https://www.afp.gov.au/about-us/history/unique-stories/2002-bali-bombings.

Baldwin, Diana, and Judy Kuhlman. 1998. "Jury Shown Missile From Bomb Site Weapon Triggered Post-Explosion Bomb Scare." *The Oklahoman*, March 25.

BBC News. 2007. "UK | Tourists Hurt in Maldives Blast." BBC News, September 29. http://news.bbc.co.uk/2/hi/uk_news/7019929.stm.

Centers for Disease Control and Prevention. 2025. "Program Statistics—World Trade Center Health Program." May 1. https://www.cdc.gov/wtc/ataglance.html. 23.

CNN. 2022. "Mumbai Terror Attacks Fast Facts." CNN, November 11. https://www.cnn.com/2013/09/18/world/asia/mumbai-terror-attacks.

Congress.gov. 2024. "'Three Years Later: Assessing the Law Enforcement Response to Multiple Pipe Bombs on January 6, 2021.'" Congress.gov, March 12. https://www.congress.gov/event/118th-congress/house-event/116959.

Danforth, John C. 2000. PURSUANT TO ORDER NO. 2256–99 OF THE ATTORNEY GENERAL. SPECIAL COUNSEL John C. Danforth Interim Report JULY 21$ (n.d.).

Department of Justice. 2015. "David Coleman Headley Sentenced to 35 Years in Prison for Role in India and Denmark Terror Plots." Northern District of United States Department of Justice, July 23. https://www.justice.gov/usao-ndil/pr/david-coleman-headley-sentenced-35-years-prison-role-india-and-denmark-terror-plots.

Department of Justice. 2018. "Evaluation of the Handling of the Branch Davidian Stand-off in Waco, Texas February 28 to April 19, 1993." https://www.justice.gov/archives/publications/waco/evaluation-handling-branch-davidian-stand-waco-texas-february-28-april-19-1993.

Department of Justice. 2022. "Ruby Ridge, Idaho—Special Report—Department of Justice." Special report, November 15. https://oig.justice.gov/sites/default/files/archive/special/0211/chapter5.htm.

ESPN.com. 2011. "Ice Falls on People at Cowboys Stadium." ESPN, February 4. https://www.espn.com/dallas/nfl/news/story?id=6089688.

FBI. 2010. "Terror Plot Foiled." FBI, November 5, 2010. https://archives.fbi.gov/archives/news/stories/2010/november/terror-plot-foiled.

FBI. 2016a. "Amerithrax or Anthrax Investigation." FBI, May 17. https://www.fbi.gov/history/famous-cases/amerithrax-or-anthrax-investigation.

FBI. 2016b. "9/11 Investigation." FBI, May 17. https://www.fbi.gov/history/famous-cases/911-investigation.

FBI. 2016c. "Oklahoma City Bombing." FBI, May 18. https://www.fbi.gov/history/famous-cases/oklahoma-city-bombing.

FBI. 2016d. "Eric Rudolph." FBI. May 18. https://www.fbi.gov/history/famous-cases/eric-rudolph.

FBI. 2020. "Richard Reid's Shoes." FBI, December 1. https://www.fbi.gov/history/artifacts/richard-reids-shoes.

FBI. 2023. "Boston Marathon Bombing." FBI, April 13. https://www.fbi.gov/

history/famous-cases/boston-marathon-bombing.

Harding, Able. 2010. "FBI, SEC Say McLeod Masterminded $34 Million Ponzi Scheme." *The Florida Times-Union*, June 25.

Hilley-Sierzchula, Emily. 2025. "U.S. Supreme Court Denies Petition Filed by Nidal Hasan, Infamous Fort Hood Mass Murderer." *The Killeen Daily Herald*, April 7. https://kdhnews.com/military/u-s-supreme-court-denies-petition-filed-by-nidal-hasan-infamous-fort-hood-mass-murderer/article_7913088b-71d9-4d52-bc66-381d49240ea4.html.

Issitt, Micah. 2021. "Port El Kantaoui Attack (2015): EBSCO." EBSCO Information Services. https://www.ebsco.com/research-starters/political-science/port-el-kantaoui-attack-2015.

Jolly, Joanna. 2014. "Alton Nolen: A Jihadist Beheading in Oklahoma?" BBC News, September 29. https://www.bbc.com/news/magazine-29408139.

Kean, Thomas H. 2024. "National Commission on Terrorist Attacks Upon the United States." National Commission on Terrorist Attacks Upon the United States, January 24. https://govinfo.library.unt.edu/911/archive/hearing7/9-11Commission_Hearing_2004-01-26.htm.

Killackey, Jim. 1996. "Left Leg Belongs to Identified Bombing Victim." *The Oklahoman*, February 24.

Malone, Jim. 2009. "9/11 Conspirator Moussaoui Sentenced to Life in Prison." Voice of America, October 31. https://www.voanews.com/a/a-13-2006-05-04-voa34/315258.html

Mireles, Edmundo, and Elizabeth Mireles. 2017. *FBI Miami Firefight: Five Minutes That Changed the Bureau*. Stafford, VA: Edmundo Mireles.

NBCNews.com. 2020. "Man Who Tried to Blow Up Oklahoma City Bank in Anti-Government Plot Sentenced to 25 Years." NBCNews.com, March 23. https://www.nbcnews.com/news/us-news/man-who-tried-blow-oklahoma-city-bank-anti-government-plot-n1167156.

The New York Times. 1995. "Unidentified Leg Found in Bomb Rubble." August 8. https://www.nytimes.com/1995/08/08/us/unidentified-leg-found-in-bomb-rubble.html.

Office of Inspector General. 2006. "A Review of the FBI's Handling of Intelligence Information Related to the September 11 Attacks." Special report: A review of the FBI's handling of intelligence information related to the September 11 attacks (full report), June. https://oig.justice.gov/sites/default/files/archive/special/s0606/chapter1.htm.

Office of Justice Programs. 1993. "NCJRS Virtual Library." Report to the Deputy Attorney General on the Events at Waco, Texas: February 28 to April 19. https://www.ojp.gov/ncjrs/virtual-library/abstracts/report-deputy-attorney-general-events-waco-texas-february-28-april.

Oklahoma Department of Civil Emergency Management After Action Report. 2005. "The Oklahoma Department of Civil Emergency Management After Action Report Alfred P. Murrah Federal Building Bombing 19 April 1995 in Oklahoma City, Oklahoma, March 1, 2005."

Shelby, Karen. 2025. "20 Years Later: The Lingering Health Effects of 9/11." Mesothelioma Center—Vital Services for Cancer Patients & Families, May 6. https://www.asbestos.com/featured-stories/9-11-lingering-health-effects/.

Southern Poverty Law Center. 2024. "3 Members of a Kansas Militia Once Plotted to Bomb a Mosque, Now Are Going to Prison." Southern Poverty Law Center, December 3. https://www.splcenter.org/resources/hatewatch/3-members-kansas-militia-once-plotted-bomb-mosque-now-are-going-prison/.

UMKC Law School. 2003. "Substitution for the Testimony of—Khalid Sheikh Mohammed, 2003." http://law2.umkc.edu/faculty/projects/ftrials/moussaoui/sheikhstmt.pdf. 3.

Voice of America. 2009. "Triple Bombing in Athens Raises Concerns About Olympic Security—2004–05–05." Voice of America, October 27, 2009. https://www.voanews.com/a/a-13-a-2004-05-05-10-1-66347817/545462.html.

Ziezulewicz, Geoff. 2024. "Inside the Navy's Marine Mammal Program." *Navy Times*, April 16. https://www.navytimes.com/news/your-navy/2024/04/15/inside-the-navys-marine-mammal-program/.

Index

www.ingramcontent.com/pod-product-compliance
Ingram Content Group UK Ltd.
Pitfield, Milton Keynes, MK11 3LW, UK
UKHW040044200726
7281IPUK00013B/167

9 781476 699929